AF412665

Global Governance, Conflict and Resistance

Global Governance, Conflict and Resistance

Edited by

Feargal Cochrane
Lecturer in Politics and International Relations,
Lancaster University, UK

Rosaleen Duffy
Lecturer in Politics and International Relations,
Lancaster University, UK

and

Jan Selby
Lecturer in International Politics,
University of Wales Aberystwyth, UK

First published 2003 by
PALGRAVE MACMILLAN
Houndmills, Basingstoke, Hampshire RG21 6XS and
175 Fifth Avenue, New York, N.Y. 10010
Companies and representatives throughout the world

PALGRAVE MACMILLAN is the global academic imprint of the Palgrave
Macmillan division of St. Martin's Press, LLC and of Palgrave Macmillan Ltd.
Macmillan® is a registered trademark in the United States, United Kingdom
and other countries. Palgrave is a registered trademark in the European
Union and other countries.

ISBN 1–4039–1637–3

This book is printed on paper suitable for recycling and made from fully
managed and sustained forest sources.

A catalogue record for this book is available from the British Library.

Library of Congress Cataloging-in-Publication Data
        Global governance, conflict and resistance / edited by Feargal Cochrane,
    Rosaleen Duffy, and Jan Selby.
            p. cm.
        Includes bibliographical references and index.
        ISBN 1–4039–1637–3
        1. Globalisation. 2. International relations. 3. Conflict management.
    I. Cochrane, Feargal. II. Duffy, Rosaleen. III. Selby, Jan, 1972–

JZ1318.G5568 2003
327.1—dc21   2003046921

10 9 8 7 6 5 4 3 2
12 11 10 09 08 07 06 05 04

Printed and bound in Great Britain by
Antony Rowe Ltd, Chippenham and Eastbourne

Contents

Part III   Resistance to Global Regimes   153

Notes on Contributors

John Christensen is an applied economist who was employed for 11 years as an economic adviser to the States of Jersey. During that period he made a detailed study of the industrial structure of that island's economy, covering in particular the growth of the off-shore finance centre and the structural decline of the tourism and agriculture sectors. In 1998 he left Jersey to take up a post as a Director of Menas Associates, a political and economic research group in the United Kingdom.

Christopher Clapham was Professor of Politics and International Relations at Lancaster University until the end of 2002, and is currently an associate of the Centre of African Studies, Cambridge University. He has written extensively on African politics, including *Africa and the International System: the politics of state survival* (1996), and *African Guerrillas* (ed., 1998).

Feargal Cochrane is a Lecturer within the Department of Politics and International Relations at Lancaster University. His research focuses on Northern Ireland, the Irish Diaspora, NGOs and civil society, and emerging peace processes within divided societies. His latest book is *People Power? The role of the voluntary and community sector in the Northern Ireland conflict*, 2002.

Michael Dillon is Professor of Politics at Lancaster University and Associate Fellow of The Royal Institute for International Affairs. He is the author of several books on politics, defence and security, and is currently completing *The Liberal Way of War*. He publishes in political and cultural theory as well as international relations and security. International editor of *Taking on the Political* (a political theory book series), he also co-edits *The Journal for Cultural Research* and is currently directing a two-year research project, *Knowledge Resourcing for Civil Contingencies*, funded by the ESRC's Domestic Responses to Terrorism initiative.

Rosaleen Duffy is a Lecturer within the Department of Politics and International Relations at Lancaster University. Her research interests include global environmental politics, tourism and global governance. She is author of *Killing for Conservation* (2000) and *A Trip Too Far* (2002), as well as co-author of *Tourism and Ethics* (2003). Recently, she was Principal Investigator of an ESRC funded project centred on the politics of trans-frontier conservation in Southern Africa and Central America.

Mark P. Hampton is a Lecturer in the School of Management at the University of Surrey and has published in academic journals including *World Development, Third World Quarterly, Environment and Planning A, Crime, Law and Social Change, Geographische Zeitschrift, Human Relations,* and *Annals of Tourism Research*. He is also author of *The Offshore Interface: Tax Havens in the Global Economy*, 1996. He has also edited (with Jason Abbott) *Offshore Finance Centres and Tax Havens* (1999).

Judith Large is a consultant/practitioner working in conflict research, analysis, policy, education and training. Her particular interests are the prevention and reduction of violent conflict, and participative design for the involvement of broad-based representation in peace-building. She is an Honorary Research Fellow at the Richardson Institute of Peace Studies, Lancaster University.

Hugh Miall is a Reader in Peace and Conflict Research and Director of the Richardson Institute at Lancaster University. He is a specialist in conflict prevention and is the co-author of *Contemporary Conflict Resolution*.

Jan Selby is a Lecturer in the Department of International Politics at the University of Wales Aberystwyth. He is author of *Water, Power and Politics in the Middle East: The Other Israeli–Palestinian Conflict* (2003).

Ngai-Ling Sum is a Lecturer in Politics and International Relations in the University of Lancaster. Her main research interests are globalisation, global economic governance, and informational capitalism. She has published in such journals as *Economy and Society, Capital and Class, Urban Studies, Critical Asian Studies,* and *Das Argument*. She has also co-edited *Globalisation, Regionalisation and Cross-Border Regions* (2002) (IPE Series) with Marcus Perkmann.

Peter Wilkin is a Senior Lecturer the Department of Politics and International Relations at Lancaster University. His publications include: *Noam Chomsky: On Power, Knowledge and Human Nature* (1997); *The Political Economy of Global Communication* (2001); and he is also co-editor of *Globalisation and the South* (1997); *Globalisation, Human Security and the African Experience* (1998). He is currently editing a book, *Global Communication and Social Change: Into the C21* (forthcoming 2004).

Acknowledgements

This book began life as a series of informal conversations between colleagues within the Department of Politics and International Relations at Lancaster University around the theme of global governance, its multiple forms and its various sites of resistance. The final version of this book emerged from a seminar series convened by the editors, which brought together a wide variety of our research interests within the Department. Our aim was to examine various conceptualisations of global governance and specifically to explore what is being governed, how it is governed and what the response is to such governance at the local level.

We are indebted to all the contributors for their commitment to this project over a two-year period, and we hope that the energetic intellectual debate that these discussions engendered, has made its way into the chapters of this edited collection.

We would also like to thank our colleagues within the Department of Politics and International Relations at Lancaster University for their help and support during the course of this project. The following people deserve a particular mention: Gordon Hands, Head of Department in Politics and International Relations at Lancaster University, who provided essential support at the outset of the project and attended book seminars when he had a thousand other things to do; Susan Riches, Trish Demery, Christine Brown and Maureen Worthington, the secretarial team in Politics and International Relations at Lancaster, for their invaluable help during the course of the project and especially while the manuscript was being collated; our colleagues Alan Warburton and Ann McAleer at Lancaster University, for their fortitude and patience in listening to frequent reports on the progress of the project; Professor Robert McKinlay, Dean of the Faculty of Social Sciences, as well as Rachel Price and the *Friends Fund* at Lancaster University, for providing financial assistance that allowed us to hold a half-day workshop for contributors to the collection; and Tracy Sartin and Graham Smith, research students within the Department for their help in proof-reading and collating the final version of the manuscript. We are extremely thankful to them and to the rest of the research student community in the department for their participation and interest in the project. Thanks also to Elaine Lowe of the Department of International Politics,

University of Wales, Aberystwyth, for her help during the completion of the manuscript.

Finally, we would like to express our thanks to the anonymous reviewers who provided some extremely useful suggestions on an early draft of the manuscript and to Beverly Tarquini and Alison Howson from Palgrave Macmillan, for their professional management of the project.

Feargal Cochrane,
Rosaleen Duffy, Jan Selby

Abbreviations

AGM   anti-globalisation movement
AIA   Anglo-Irish Agreement
APEC   Asia Pacific Economic Cooperation Forum
APII   Asia Pacific Information Infrastructure
ASEAN   Association of South East Asian Nations
BiH   Bosnia
BSA   Business Software Alliance
CI   Channel Islands
CITES   Convention on Trade in Endangered Species
CSCE   Conference on Security and Cooperation in Europe
DAN   Direct Action Network
DFID   Department for International Development
EIA   Environmental Investigation Agency
ELF   Earth Liberation Front
EPLF   Eritrean People's Liberation Front
ES   Eastern Slavonia
EU   European Union
EZLN   Ejército Zapatista de Liberación Nacional
FATF   Financial Action Task Force
FBI   Federal Bureau of Investigation
FIU   Financial Intelligence Unit
FRY   Former Republic of Yugoslavia
FSF   Financial Stability Forum (G7)
FYROM   Former Yugoslav Republic of Macedonia
G7   Group of Seven
G8   Group of Eight
GATT   General Agreement on Tariffs and Trade
GDP   Gross Domestic Product
GDR   German Democratic Republic
GFA   Good Friday Agreement
GII   Global Information Infrastructure
GWP   Global Water Partnership
HCNM   High Commissioner for National Minorities
ICT   Information and Communication Technology
IDP   internally displaced person
IFAW   International Fund for Animal Welfare

IFI	International Fund for Ireland
IMF	International Monetary Fund
IPC	Intellectual Property Committee
IPR	intellectual property rights
IUCN	World Conservation Union
IWRA	International Water Resources Association
JIC	Joint Implementation Committee
KLA	Kosovo Liberation Army
NAFTA	North American Free Trade Agreement
NATO	North Atlantic Treaty Organisation
NEPAD	New Partnership for Africa's Development
NGO	non-governmental organisation
NII	National Information Infrastructure
NPFL	National Patriotic Front of Liberia
NSM	new social movement
OAS	Organisation of American States
OAU	Organisation of African Unity
OECD	Organisation for Economic Cooperation and Development
OFC	offshore finance centre
OSCE	Organisation for Security and Cooperation in Europe
PA	Palestinian Authority
PGA	People's Global Action
PLO	Palestine Liberation Organisation
PRIO	Peace Research Institute Oslo
PWA	Palestinian Water Authority
RMA	Revolution in Military Affairs
RPF	Rwandan Patriotic Front
SFOR	Stabilisation Force (Bosnia)
SICDP	Springfield Inter-Community Development Project
SIE	small island economy
TNC	trans-national corporation
TRIPs	Trade Related Intellectual Property Rights
UCAN	Ulster Community Action Network
UNDP	UN Development Programme
UNESCO	UN Educational, Scientific and Cultural Organisation
UNHCR	UN High Commission for Refugees
UNICEF	UN Children's Fund
UNITA	Uniâo Nacional para a Independência Total de Angola
UNREDEP	UN Preventive Deployment Force (Macedonia)
UNTAES	UN Transitional Administration for Eastern Slavonia
USAID	US Agency for International Development

USTR	US Trade Representative
WB	World Bank
WHO	World Health Organisation
WIPO	World Intellectual Property Organisation
WMD	weapons of mass destruction
WTO	World Trade Organisation
WWC	World Water Council
WWF	World Wide Fund for Nature
ZNA	Zimbabwe National Army

1
Introduction

Jan Selby

Since the turn of the millennium the question of resistances to the liberal project of global governance has come to occupy centre stage in global and international politics. From the mass demonstrations at the Seattle WTO summit in November and December 1999, to the attacks on the World Trade Centre and Pentagon in September 2001, to the Bush administrations' ambivalent, if not downright hostile, attitude towards multilateralism – all of these can be thought of especially conspicuous instances of resistance to global governance. If the 1990s were dominated by the collapse of Communism and the consequent resurgence of liberal hopes and political agendas – these encapsulated in the notions of 'globalisation', 'global governance' and the 'new world order' – the period since has been dominated by challenges to and conflicts within this triumphalist liberal project.

This book provides a wide-ranging series of analyses of challenges and resistances to global governance. It concentrates primarily on actors at the 'receiving end' of global governance – that is, on those who are governed, and on those who evade, adapt to or oppose projects and policies of global governance. It does this by examining governance and resistance in a variety of sites and at a variety of scales: in the norms and discourses of state, intergovernmental and civil society actors; in post-conflict zones where local authorities, international organisations and NGOs come together to reconstruct societies after years of conflict; in international regimes where resistance is carried out by a diversity of state and non-state actors. It seeks neither to romanticise resistance, nor to normatively privilege the global governance agenda. Instead it seeks to present a descriptively rich set of accounts of global governance and resistance in action, and, by inflecting the latter back onto the former, to shed fresh light on the limits and the nature of the global governance project.

This introductory chapter makes a case for why this should be considered a worthwhile ambition. It does this first by considering current debates on global governance – by exploring the roots and implications of the notion of 'global governance', and by surveying the various ways in which global governance as a phenomenon has been explained. We then examine some of the ways in which conflict and resistance have been depicted thus far within global governance discourse, and end by briefly outlining the structure of the book and the chapters to follow.

'Governance' and 'global governance': a genealogy

The term 'governance' has not traditionally occupied an important place within the lexicon of the social sciences. Rarely used, and still less often contested, it has during the last 15 years, however, become increasingly central to discussions across a wide range of fields, from political economy and social policy to development studies and international relations. Equally, talk of governance has become central to the discourse of a wide range of both public and private actors, from local authorities and international organisations to multinational organisations and NGOs. 'Governance' has become one of the leading buzzwords of the late twentieth and early twenty-first centuries.

Generally denoting forms of control, ordering and management that are distinct from, or that encompass more than, hierarchical state-centric 'government' (Reinicke, 1989; Rosenau and Czempiel, 1992), the notion of 'governance' has its roots, etymologically speaking, in Latin and Ancient Greek words for the 'steering' of boats (Jessop, 1998). The recent proliferation in use of the term, though, is perhaps a function of three developments. On the one hand, its rise has been born from a pervasive dissatisfaction with existing analytical terms and categories, and with simplistic binary oppositions in particular. Where once the distinctions between 'public' and 'private' sectors, between 'state', 'market' and 'civil society', between 'governmental' and 'non-governmental' spheres and responsibilities, and between domestic 'order' and international 'anarchy' were the largely taken-for-granted starting points for analysis, such dichotomies have often been attacked as essentialist, misrepresentative and conceptually inadequate. The broad and inclusive notion of 'governance' has often been used in response to characterise forms of management and rule that criss-cross such binary oppositions, involving complex patterns of coordination between state and non-state actors on a variety of scales. On the other hand, and no doubt in large part constitutive of this widespread intellectual dissatisfaction, the spread of governance discourse has been symptomatic of profound social shifts in the structure of developed capitalist societies, and in the international system as a whole. Amongst others, these shifts have included the privatisation of hitherto state-run enterprises and the emergence of correspondingly novel forms of regulation; the growth of 'partnerships' and other forms of coordination involving both public and private sector actors; the continuing development of more and more refined monitoring, surveillance and disciplinary practices – what are often, following Foucault, referred to as techniques of 'governmentality' (Foucault, 1979; Burchell *et al.*, 1991; Dean, 1999); and the mushrooming of both non-governmental and inter-governmental organisations. Taken together, these various developments would seem to testify to a pluralisation of the sites and mechanisms of social steering and control, as well as to the increasing importance of non-governmental civil society actors in exercising – to adapt Rosenau and Czempiel's well-known formulation – 'governance beyond government'. Governance discourse is in large measure an attempt to capture and articulate these fundamental changes in state–society relations.

Beyond this, though, the emergence and dissemination of the language of governance also owes something to its rhetorical functions in legitimating and promoting various political agendas, above all those associated with neo-liberalism (Pagden, 1998: 7–8). This can be seen most clearly in the case of the World Bank, which initially introduced the word into international policy discourse (World Bank, 1989). Keen to preserve what one Bank Vice-President referred to as the 'delicate balance' between on the one hand its increasingly commonplace interventions in matters of government – its promotion of accountable, transparent and limited state structures through policy-based lending – and on the other hand the problem of having to be seen to be respecting its Articles of Agreement – which formally prohibit it from intervening in political issues – the Bank thus started emphasising the importance of 'governance' within development policy (Shihata, 1991: 53). Defined unthreateningly by the Bank simply as 'the manner in which power is exercised in the management of a country's economic and social resources for development' (World Bank, 1992; see also 1994), governance was thus presented as a neutral, technical matter of social ordering. The 'good governance' agenda that is now so central to international development policy has, in turn, become presented as a technical and apolitical project for promoting high quality management, participation and fairness across the developing world (Woods, 1999). For critics, the language of good governance is but a refurbished means of 'blaming the victims' of the current global order, creating the impression that internal mismanagement rather than global economic structures are the root cause of their plight (George and Sabelli, 1994: 160). Whether this is a fair assessment or not, it is clear that the discourse of governance presents both a liberal and pluralistic model of social power relations – 'governance', as the Commission on Global Governance puts it, 'is the sum of the many ways individuals and institutions, public and private, manage their own affairs' (1995: 2) – and an apolitical model of social order, within which governing is reduced to technical expertise, and in which fundamental ideological and value conflicts have been all but resolved. Governance, it might be said, is a notion that lies, rhetorically if not actually, at the very 'end of history' (Fukuyama, 1989, 1992).

The notion of 'global governance' bears the discursive traces of each of these three developments – a sense of dissatisfaction with long-established ways of thinking, a recognition that fundamental changes are occurring in international (or, better, global) politics, and, less often commented upon, the post-Cold War ideological hegemony of liberal democratic and expert-led conceptions of social order. But the idea of global governance is at the same time a function of a growing concern, amongst scholars and practitioners alike, with the political dimensions of globalisation and global change. 'Globalisation' has since the early 1990s become the master signifier of the immense changes taking place in worldwide social relations, and has also become, in the view of many writers, 'the central thematic for social theory' (Featherstone and Lash, 1995: 1) and 'key idea by which we understand the transition of human society into the third millennium' (Waters, 1995: 1; see Rosenberg, 2000: 2). 'Global governance', equally, has become a conceptual centrepiece of the new language of global politics, and a crucial site for analytical and normative discussions of multilateralism and the newly proclaimed 'post-Westphalian' world order (Linklater, 1998; Buzan and Little, 1999).

The prefix 'global', here, tends to mean one of two things. In one of these sets of meanings, it refers to governance as conducted by global institutions such as the United Nations, International Monetary Fund and World Trade Organisation, or else to governance that is practised through regimes and policy networks that likewise span the globe and operate at a global level. Here the notion of global governance functions either as a neologism for multilateralism, denoting forms of organisation which may be proliferating, but which are not backed by any centralised, sovereign authority and thus do not yet constitute anything like a world 'government' (here global governance institutions are those that were hitherto most commonly referred to as 'international organisations' – see e.g. Young, 1997; Paolini *et al.*, 1998; Diehl, 2001; Wilkinson and Hughes, 2002); or alternatively, global governance refers both to these public international organisations as well as to those transnational private and public–private regulatory bodies that increasingly characterise world affairs. Included in this latter understanding of global governance would be private credit-rating agencies such as Moody's and Standard and Poor's; coordinated global activity between state, interstate and NGO actors such as that found within conflict resolution and civil reconstruction zones (Weiss and Gordenker, 1996); and 'epistemic communities' (Haas, 1992) of consultants, academics, government policy makers and other assorted experts. Yet either way – whether global governance is understood narrowly as a synonym for formal multilateralism, or more capaciously as also including private, public–private and networked forms of regulation, or even as denoting a set of globally accepted 'norms' (Vayrynen, 1999) – the focus here is on forms of steering activity that bring together a range of actors from a wealth of different states, that operate globally, and that have decidedly global effects.

In a second sense, by contrast, the prefix 'global' is suggestive not merely of institutions, networks or norms located at a 'global level', but instead of the multiple scales and levels at which governance is now practised across the globe. Global governance, in this broadest of senses, is governance that is practised within rather than by the global. Global governance, here, is no longer a descriptive term denoting a range of political realities, but a conceptual analytic or problematic for studying world politics in a post-Westphalian age. At a time when nation-states and their societies are so evidently losing their economic, political and cultural autonomy, it no longer makes sense, so the argument goes, to assume the nation-state as the most appropriate unit of analysis. Instead both analyses of contemporary change and ethical reflections on questions of freedom, democracy, inequality and so on, need to 'scale up' and take the world as a whole as a single integrated unit of analysis. Within such a 'global governance analytic' (Latham, 1999: 32), global governance is not simply 'all-encompassing … embracing every region, country, international relationship, social movement, and private organisation that engages in activities across national boundaries' (Rosenau, 1992: 12). Not only this; it also represents no less than a new 'common sense' for the post-Cold War order, an emergent 'intersubjective ontology for understanding world affairs' (Rosenau, 1999: 290, 296).

Given all these different layers of meaning, and given also the essential slipperiness of the concepts of 'governance' and 'globalisation', it is hardly surprising that the idea of 'global governance' has received so much criticism, even scorn. Latham has portrayed global governance discourse as indicative of a 'dialectic of the overwhelmed', of a sense of helplessness when faced with the limitless, boundless totality of the globe (Latham, 1999: 23); others have labelled it 'a theme in need of a focus' (Groom and Powell, 1994), and claimed that global governance appears to include 'virtually anything' that we may want (Finkelstein, 1995: 368). Yet notwithstanding these criticisms, there is at least some unity to the various different understandings of global governance. In the first place, global governance is about the thickening social density of international relations (or world politics), and about transformations in the locations and scales at which politics is conducted. And second, global governance is – like 'governance' – a definitively liberal idea, conveying a pluralistic and post-ideological conception of the world. The global governance project, if we may call it that, is normatively about dispersing power away from hegemonic centres of power, especially states, about extending and overcoming resistance to liberal democratic values and procedures, and about ordering people and things through recourse to reason, knowledge and expertise. Global governance is no less than a project for rationalising global social relations.

Explaining global governance

Yet while global governance is to this extent a liberal idea and project, and one moreover that is a clear symptom of the current post-Cold War and post-historical conjuncture, it has nonetheless been explained in numerous different ways. For liberal internationalists, it has variously been understood as the result of states endeavouring to satisfy their own objective functional interests (Keohane and Nye, 1977; Keohane, 1984); as a corollary of the liberalisation and democratisation of the domestic structures of developed capitalist states, especially those of the hegemonic US (Ikenberry, 2001); and, implicitly if not explicitly, as the product of a multi-causal 'virtuous circle' of reason and recognition, in which the expansion of free trade, of liberal democratic governance, and of international law, norms and institutions have all supported one another (see for instance McGrew, 2002). From such explanatory perspectives, global governance is not simply an avowedly liberal project, but is also the outcome of fundamentally liberalising structures, processes and dynamics.

From other perspectives, by contrast, the liberal project of global governance tends to be depicted as resultant from, or as a mask for, structures and relations of power that are far from being tamed. From a realist (or neo-realist) perspective, thinkers such as Robert Gilpin and Kenneth Waltz have continued to maintain that 'global or world politics has not taken over from national politics' (Waltz, 1999), and that 'the territorial state continues to be the primary actor in both domestic and international affairs' (Gilpin, 2002: 238; see also Gilpin, 2001). For realists, the international system is by definition anarchic, lacking a unified sovereign authority, and it thus follows that 'international governance' is in the final analysis either circumscribed by the absence of legitimate enforcement mechanisms, or else is no longer an 'international' form of governance at all, since the foundational distinction between international and domestic spheres would have disappeared. Thus as Gilpin neatly puts it, the 'idea of a realist theory of international governance is a contradiction in terms' (2002: 237). Irrespective of the rise in the number and density of international institutions, NGOs and trans-national networks, states continue to dominate the international political arena. States, state power and the dictates of anarchy are what shape international institutions and global governance (Waltz, 1999).

Marxists, quite differently, have sought to explain global governance as the product of (or at least in relation to) the developing structures and dynamics of contemporary capitalism – these being variously defined in terms of the general expansion of the capitalist world economy, in terms of the relations between capitalist classes and powers, or in terms of the ideological and institutional dictates of neo-liberalism. For Kees van der Pijl (1984, 1998), global governance institutions and ideals are the products of a trans-national Atlantic ruling class which is still evolving and deepening, but which has long transcended state boundaries. Peter Gowan (1999), by contrast, depicts the newfound scope and power of neo-liberal multilateral institutions in almost realist fashion, as following from the breakdown of the Bretton Woods system in the early 1970s and from Washington's consequent 'Faustian bid for world dominance'. Somewhat more pluralistically, Robert Cox (1981, 1983) and other neo-Gramscians (e.g. Gill, 1990; Murphy, 1994; Rupert, 1995) portray the contemporary 'internationalisation of the state' as resulting from the internationalisation of production and the attendant emergence of a trans-national managerial class, and as also performing a vital ideological role in legitimating and enabling the development of particular conceptions of world order. Each of these accounts differs in its assessment of the precise roots of global governance. What they share in common, though, is a belief that it needs to be explained within the context of developments in late-twentieth-century capitalism, and as the products not of liberal reason and recognition, but of ongoing and developing social conflicts, struggles and forces.

Others – strongly influenced by Foucault's work (1977, 1978, 1980) on the relations between knowledge, institutions, and techniques of social discipline and control – have argued that global governance procedures, institutions and norms represent newly reconfigured means of monitoring and regulating social conduct. Focusing on humanitarian interventions in those 'new wars' that are seemingly proliferating in the global South (Kaldor, 1999), Mark Duffield (2001) has argued that these follow from a reproblematisation of the idea of 'security', and a merging of 'security' and 'development' discourse. Stephen Gill (1995) has emphasised the extent to which global governance has been made possible through the extended power of worldwide surveillance systems. Meanwhile Michael Hardt and Antonio Negri have argued of the new global system that they label 'Empire' that, while it is 'a *decentred* and *deterritorialised* apparatus of power', it is nonetheless premised on the extension of 'biopolitical' mechanisms for controlling and disciplining social conduct (2000: xii, 22). While global governance is from such perspectives a quintessentially liberal project, this liberalism does nonetheless involve the development of often insidious new ways of defining, invigilating, managing and indeed governing social relations.[1]

There have been other critical voices too. Feminist scholars have sought to draw attention to 'the gendered nature of the institutions, practices and discourses of global governance', as well as to 'the ways in which women have sought to change them' (Meyer and Prugl, 1999: 4; see also Steans, 2002). Moreover, a range of thinkers and institutions have developed proposals for the reform of contemporary global governance systems, these ranging from liberal reformist calls for the fuller empowerment of 'distorted' international institutions (Murphy, 2000; see also Commission on Global Governance, 1995; Simai, 1994), to calls for the proper democratisation of these institutions (e.g. Held, 1995; Camilleri *et al.*, 2000), to arguments for the complete structural overhaul of the politics and political economy of the contemporary world (dis-)order (e.g. Falk, 1995; Arrighi and Silver, 1999; Thomas, 2001). It is evident that while there is clear consensus as to the liberal character of the project of global governance, there is equally clear disagreement as to where its roots lie, who benefits from it, and whether and how it should be restructured or reformed.

Global governance and resistance

There are significant differences between these various explanatory and normative approaches to global governance, as briefly summarised earlier. Nonetheless, these no doubt divergent approaches all share at least a minimally common aim, that of analysing and reflecting upon global governance as an *explanandum*. Irrespective of how it has been characterised and explained, it has been the object or concept of global governance that has remained the central focus of analysis.

In marked contrast to this, very little systematic attention has been paid to examining the relations between on the one hand global governance, and on the other hand those actors, structures, practices and states of affairs which are subject to global governance, which evade, oppose or have to adapt to it, or which lie outside its orbit. There has been a great deal of discussion of resistance to globalisation (Pile and Keith, 1997; Scott, 1997; Smart, 1999; Gills, 2000; Mittelman, 2000). The same cannot be said, however, of responses and resistance to global governance. It is our aim in this volume to go some way to rectifying this situation, by presenting a series of analyses of the relations between global governance, conflict and resistance.

The approach we adopt can perhaps be most readily articulated by contrasting it with a couple of existing works on global governance. In an excellent recent volume entitled *Contesting Global Governance*, Robert O'Brien *et al.* (2000) consider the relations between four multilateral economic institutions and three global social movements, specifically those concerned with the environment, labour and women's rights. On the strength of these cases, O' Brien *et al.* conclude that in response to the criticisms of multilateral economic institutions made by global social movements, there has been 'a transformation in the nature of governance' to a situation of 'complex multilateralism', involving the growing incorporation of NGO actors into policy making and implementation (2000: 206). We do not disagree with this conclusion. However, in this volume we consider a far broader range of sites of governance–resistance interactions, and operate with a much broader understanding of global governance. We explore encounters with global governance not just at a global level, but at a range of scales; and we examine these encounters in a variety of different fields, from environmental regimes, to war making, to conflict resolution zones. Our purpose is to provide a diverse series of analyses of the challenges and responses to global governance.

Our approach can also be usefully contrasted with that of the best-known theorist of global governance, James Rosenau. In Rosenau's hands, as already noted, the term 'global governance' denotes not simply an emerging set of global-level norms, rules or institutions, but also a conceptual analytic, an 'emergent ontology' for understanding world affairs (1999: 296). Resistance, opposition and obstruction do play an important role within this global governance analytic. However, they are always conceptualised therein as problems to be overcome through the extension of – and development of new forms and mechanisms of – global governance. In common with so much of the liberal 'problem-solving' (Cox, 1981) literature on global governance, resistant actors and states of affairs are studied as problems to be resolved, overcome and done away with. Moreover, resistance is always depicted within Rosenau's work as the absolute antithesis of governance. 'Governance' is equated with 'order', 'stability', 'authority' and 'control', while on the other side of the equation sit a myriad 'disruptions', 'instabilities', 'uncertainties', and forces of 'fragmentation' and 'chaos'. Those outside or resistant towards global governance tend – and note the collocation here – to 'defy steerage and resort to violence' (Rosenau, 1995: 16). This is a Manichean world where – as in Jack Straw's or Tony Blair's post-9/11 speeches – all opposition to liberal global governance is by definition disorderly and potentially violent. In Rosenau's work, the move away from a sharp realist distinction between the domestic and the international leads but to its replacement by another binary opposition, albeit this time between forces of order and forces of chaos.

More generally it is worth noting that the global governance analytic systematically downplays conflict and resistance. As Robert Latham argues in an excellent critique of Rosenau and others, global governance discourse – or at least that part of it which conceives of global governance as an analytic – has a strongly structural functionalist quality, prioritising co-ordination, integration and value consensus, rather than power, domination, conflict and contradiction. This involves both an explanatory and a normative commitment to governance, in which governance, order and effectiveness become ends in themselves, and in which questions of who wins and who loses, and for what ethical and political purposes, get largely elided. Moreover, just as Parsonian structural-functionalism (see especially Parsons, 1951) was roundly criticised for its elision of power and domination (e.g. Mills, 1959), and for its inability to explain social deviance and social pathologies (e.g. Habermas, 1987: 284–5), so an analogous critique applies to Rosenau *et al.* As an analytic or field of problems, global governance discourse simultaneously ontologises resistances as an undifferentiated 'other', and deeply underplays their social and political importance.

In this volume, by contrast, we seek to study 'governance' and 'resistance' as a differentiated and conflict-riddled arena of enquiry. We emphasise the numerous contrasting types, styles and practices of both governance and resistance, and stress that the relations between governance and resistance are complex, multi-faceted and often not merely oppositional. Our aim is neither simply to critique global governance projects, norms and institutions – though some of the individual contributions clearly do so – nor to develop suggestions as to how conflicts and resistances could be overcome – though, again, some of the chapters are more oriented towards problem-solving than others – but to present a variable series of cases of the many-sided relations between global governance, conflict and resistance.

Each of the contributions focuses on a particular site of liberal global governance and resistance. In doing so, they ask questions such as the following:

- Where are the resistances? Are they external or internal to structures and projects of global governance?
- At what scales or levels do conflicts and resistance occur?
- What do resistant actors aim to achieve? Do they seek to oppose, bypass, subvert or simply ignore global governance? Do they oppose global governance per se, or merely specific forms and instances of it?
- Who is resisting? What sort of actors and structures stand in the way of global governance?
- What practical form do challenges to global governance take?

Moreover, each of the contributions also seeks to enquire what the study of these diverse patterns of conflict and resistance can tell us about the structures, norms and projects of global governance, and about the utility of global governance perspectives. In this regard they ask questions such as:

- How powerful are global governance structures and mechanisms? To what extent do they constrain social, political and economic activity?
- Are governance structures responsive and adaptive to opposition?
- Does global governance create its own sites and forms of subversion?
- To what extent does global governance normatively privilege certain actors, values, ideas and interest groups over others?
- What dangers inhere in the concept of global governance?

Clearly, many of these latter questions have already been the subject of a great deal of debate. Our hope is simply that by focusing more directly on questions of conflict and resistance than has hitherto been the case, we can bring new light to bear on the contested question of global governance.

Organisation of the book

The book is structured into three parts. The first of these considers global governance and resistance in large scale and thematic terms, concentrating especially on the activities of states, the practices of war and the workings of global capitalism in relation to questions of governance and resistance. Part two focuses on global governance in post-conflict zones, on situations where governmental, inter-governmental and non-governmental actors come together in an attempt to stabilise and reconstruct war-torn societies within the context of uncertainly developing 'peace processes'. Then finally we turn to global regimes, examining the complex interactions between on the one hand international regimes in the environmental, informational and financial arenas, and on the other hand those various local, regional and global attempts to resist or subvert these multilateral agendas. A concluding summary chapter identifies some of the common threads and key differences between these individual analyses.

Part I: states, war and capitalism

In the first chapter, Michael Dillon presents an explicitly Foucauldian analysis of the relations between global governance and resistance: 'global governance', as he puts it, 'is a Foucauldian system of power/knowledge that depends upon the strategic orchestration of the self-regulating freedoms of populations'. Following Foucault, Dillon argues that forms of power and forms of resistance are always found together, and necessarily share many common features. Characterising global liberal governance as a quite specific regime of power – whose central features are its pluralism and dynamism, and the predominance within it of networked forms of organisation – he argues that resistances to this networked regime of power necessarily also take on a diverse, dynamic and predominantly networked form. Illustrating this through an analysis of the developing discourse and practices of 'network-centric warfare', Dillon argues that contemporary liberal war-making, as well as the many threats and challenges to the current liberal order, all revolve around the idea and the actual importance of networks. Under the regime of power that is global liberal governance, networks are equally central to the practices of the state and the practices of anti-globalisation or terrorist groups. For Dillon, power and resistance are necessarily analogous and complementary in form.

In the following chapter, Christopher Clapham considers the problem of state collapse for the contemporary project of global governance. Unlike Dillon, Clapham conceives of contemporary global governance as but the latest in a series of global governance projects or 'hegemonic conceptions of world order'. Under the latest and current conception, states are viewed not as absolutely sovereign actors, but instead as the regulatory building blocks of world order. Yet the paradox here, as Clapham emphasises, is that state actors are often incapable of, or unwilling to, perform their necessary regulatory and governance functions. This is especially the case in Africa, where state failure is both a vitally important humanitarian and political concern, and a key reason why, given the regulatory functions of the state, this problem is so difficult to address. Clapham observes that the good governance agenda has received a remarkable degree of backing from a wide range of Western governmental and non-governmental actors, and has also achieved a fair measure of success (in promoting democratic governance, for instance). But he also argues that the capacity of the contemporary project of global governance to address the problem of African state failure is inherently circumscribed by the continent's dependent position within the global economy and the state-subverting actions of regional elites, as well as by the very ambivalence of global governance itself – since global governance programmes and institutions often end up acting as substitutes for decaying state institutions, the very institutions which good governance is meant to empower as regulatory agencies.

Hugh Miall's chapter considers the relationship between global governance and conflict prevention. Miall concentrates especially on what he identifies as two important aspects of the global governance project, those of democratisation and good governance and seeks to ask whether these have aided the prevention of violent conflicts. After considering this question in general terms, he then examines in some depth the role of global governance norms and institutions in preventing the outbreak of conflicts in transitional areas of Eastern Europe, especially Estonia, Macedonia, Albania and Kosovo. He points out that the record of global governance in Eastern Europe has, to say the least, been very mixed, with democratic transitions, for instance, having in some cases triggered ethnic conflicts. Democratisation and the good governance agenda have been resisted both by local and especially ethnic political actors, as well as by major powers such as the United States. Miall points out that democratisation, good governance and conflict prevention have not been sufficiently important priorities of the agencies of global governance, in that they have often been dispensed with when they clashed with other more pressing priorities. And he concludes on the back of this, in classical liberal fashion, that the project of global governance needs extending in the face of local politics and international plays of power.

Peter Wilkin, by contrast, argues that global governance – which he presents as an essentially neo-liberal project – needs to be critiqued, resisted and overcome. Working within a world systems theory framework (Wallerstein, 1974, 1995, 2001), Wilkin portrays global governance as an anti-democratic and elite driven process committed to the Washington consensus agenda of privatisation, liberalisation and deregulation. Empirically, his chapter focuses on the rise of the anti-globalisation movement, which he sees as representing the only progressive and fundamental challenge to global governance currently on offer. He charts the root causes behind its rise (specifically, the end of the Cold War, the post-Cold War hegemony of neo-liberalism and the revolutionary developments in information and communications technologies), offers an account of its decentralised form of organisation and its ethico-political commitments, and gives a qualified defence of the anti-globalisation movement against critics of both left and right. Bringing this introductory section full circle, Wilkin thus portrays global governance in a starkly different light from the previous three contributors: unlike Clapham and especially Miall, he sees the contemporary project of global governance as fundamentally regressive; and unlike Dillon, he views governance and resistance not as sharing an analogously networked form, but as being diametrically opposed in their forms of organisation and their normative and political commitments.

Part II: global governance in post-conflict zones

The second part of the book considers global governance in three particular 'post-conflict zones', the former Yugoslavia, the West Bank and Gaza and Northern Ireland. In her chapter on Eastern Slavonia and Bosnia, Judith Large emphasises that broadly similar cases of intervention can result in quite different outcomes. On the one hand, the UN's 1996 intervention in Eastern Slavonia helped to avoid a potential bloodbath. On the other, in Bosnia a situation of civil war has but been replaced by one of 'uncivil peace', where ethnic cleavages have been consolidated rather than weakened, where the black market trades in guns, drugs, people and stolen cars thrive and where local elites and patronage networks continue to hold sway. Like Clapham, Large does not claim that the ideals and aspirations associated with global governance are misplaced. What she does do, though, is emphasise that there are clear limits to intervention – this even being the case in East Slavonia where, despite a bloodbath having been avoided, ethnic divisions have become entrenched, with widespread and institutionalised discrimination against the Serb minority. Moreover, like Clapham she emphasises the essential ambivalence of global governance, since while the global governance project in Bosnia has placed great stress on democratisation, this project has itself been fundamentally anti-democratic, being premised on unelected and unaccountable international representatives imposing legislation and administering Bosnia as a de facto protectorate. Thus global governance, for Large, is both in conflict with various local political dynamics, and itself riven with internal contradictions.

Yet if Large, like Clapham, stresses the essential ambivalence of global governance, Jan Selby's chapter, on governance and resistance within the context of the Oslo peace process, is far more sceptical about the global governance agenda. Selby charts three distinct types of resistance to global governance: simulated adherence to its norms; confrontational opposition to its practices and institutions; and quiet everyday activity devoted to avoiding and bypassing power. He argues that the Oslo process was premised from the beginning upon a simulated commitment to good governance norms, these norms serving above all as a screen for plays of interest and state power. By this account global governance, far from being well-intentioned if contradictory, is instead a conspiratorial cover for the interests of the Israeli state, the United States and Yasser Arafat's Palestine Liberation Organisation (PLO). Yet global governance is also, Selby emphasises, a material apparatus of institutions and procedures, one that has been powerfully deployed in the West Bank and Gaza. While as a set of norms global governance has been simulated, as an ensemble of institutions and procedures it has met various forms of resistance arising from the continuation of the Israeli occupation, and the institutional weakness of the Palestinians' proto-state institutions. In a theme that resonates throughout this volume, Selby thus emphasises that resistances to global governance commonly develop within the context of fragile regulatory and administrative institutions. What he adds, though, is that such resistances are often not merely 'resistances': they can also be thought of as alternative modes of 'governance', albeit ones that use very different means and that follow very different normative and political agendas.

While Large and Selby examine post-conflict zones which have seen intense involvement from multilateral institutions – and in the case of Bosnia have seen the creation of no less than an international protectorate – Feargal Cochrane focuses on a very different post-conflict arena, Northern Ireland. Here, the British state and the European Union (EU) have played the key roles in promoting conflict resolution and reconstruction, while the input of civil society organisations has also been significant. Cochrane concentrates particularly on the latter. He observes that contemporary global governance discourse places great stress on the importance of developing a functioning civil society, and holds great faith in the power of civil society organisations (NGOs) in helping to promote such changes. But he argues that such organisations are not 'an intrinsic force for peace', with their relationship to peace-building often being deeply ambivalent. On the one hand, many civil society organisations in Northern Ireland developed in defence of the values and interests of one or other sectarian community. NGOs, as a result, often promote their own interests and push forward sectarian agendas. Moreover, liberal discourse, including the language of rights, is often superficially adopted by NGOs in their bid to attract funding. Nonetheless, many of those once involved in violence are now involved in community projects. Thus civil society is simultaneously a positive and a negative force within Northern Ireland. Where Clapham and Large call attention to the contradictions that inhere in the globally led drive for strong state institutions and democracy, Cochrane draws attention to the ambivalence inherent in that other great hope of liberal global governance, civil society.

Part III: resistance to global regimes

The final section of the book considers three different sites of resistance to global regimes. Rosaleen Duffy focuses on resistances to CITES, the Convention on the International Trade in Endangered Species, paying particular attention to its prohibitions on the global ivory trade. Duffy analyses two types of resistance to this regime: public forms of resistance premised upon dissonant views of good practice in wildlife conservation; and those illicit forms of resistance that together constitute the global trade in ivory. With regard to the former, Duffy emphasises that global conservation norms such as CITES are premised upon a normative commitment to the 'precautionary principle', as well as upon often uncertain scientific truths, and that these are often contested by local state actors. Conflicts over wildlife governance, in short, often revolve around conflicting scientific knowledge claims, while the reach of global governance is often dependent on its ability to present itself as the arbiter of scientific truth (as Duffy emphasises, international wildlife NGOs have to this extent played a vital role in bolstering the CITES regime). But Duffy also stresses that, quite apart from the public conflict between pro- and anti-prohibition actors, CITES also meets resistance from the illegal trade in ivory. In southern Africa, this illegal trade brings together local subsistence poachers, global criminal networks, corrupt state officials and military and rebel groups into a fluid yet highly organised business. The complicity of state officials is of particular importance, Duffy argues, since this effectively neutralises the enforcement capabilities of global regimes. The global governance project – as Clapham, Large and Selby all in various ways argue – is undermined by the weakness and criminalisation of the state. But that is not to say that in such sites of 'dysgovernance' (Latham, 1999) there is only chaos. To the contrary, resistance is often, as Selby also emphasises, a form of governance; in the southern African context, 'disorder' can be 'a political instrument' (Chabal and Daloz, 1999).

Like Duffy, Ngai-Ling Sum emphasises that resistance to global governance regimes takes on both public and illicit forms. Working within a neo-Gramscian international political economy framework, Sum analyses the recent development of the Global Information Infrastructure (GII) and expanded intellectual property rights regime, paying particular attention to challenges and accommodations to that regime in East Asia. Sum interprets these regimes, and global governance more broadly, as attempts to legitimate and consolidate the currently dominant neo-liberal form of globalisation, reinforcing 'US economic hegemony through material and discursive powers and resources'. Sum charts the development of the GII and its associated regimes, and then highlights three different types of response to them: counter-hegemonic state challenges to the GII which seek to contest the continuing dominance of Microsoft by promoting an alternative 'open source' software system, Linux; the piracy of software and media products through a mixture of local everyday practices and global criminal networks; and, by contrast with these two forms of resistance, various forms of adaptation to US-led calls for the development and liberalisation of domestic information infrastructures. Sum emphasises that what she calls 'glocal' interactions are not always conflict-ridden, and moreover that actors readily switch between tactics of resistance and adaptation. Like Wilkin, Sum stresses the essentially capitalist context within which both global governance and resistance to it must be understood; unlike him, however, and indeed more clearly than anywhere else in the volume, she emphasises this hegemonic (neo-)liberal project is met with a wide variety of shades of accommodation and resistance.

In the final chapter, Mark Hampton and John Christensen analyse the changing place of small island tax havens within the international financial system. As they spell out in some detail, there have, since the late 1990s, been a series of multilateral initiatives aimed at governing offshore finance centres. Before then, and indeed since the 1960s, many small island economies had been able to take advantage of the boom in international financial flows to establish for themselves an extremely productive and profitable – if nonetheless still dependent – niche within the global economy. Now, however, given the developing trend towards greater global and regional regulation of offshore finance, many of these small island economies are losing their prior advantages, and face the prospect, Hampton and Christensen argue, of serious economic down-turns. These offshore finance centres find themselves, moreover, in a position where non-compliance with new global and regional gover-nance systems would bring with it the threat of economic sanctions, and would thus herald economic demise. Many of the chapters in this collection emphasise the weakness of, or at least the limitations inher-ent in, projects of global governance. This final chapter, by contrast, serves as a useful reminder: global governance may in many arenas be poorly developed – or perhaps even essentially incapable of tackling the problems that it sets itself – but in other arenas global governance structures and institutions are reshaping the world, forcing local actors to conform and accommodate themselves to its dictates. The chapters to follow seek to illustrate and explore just some of this complex dialectical pattern of governance and resistance.

Note

1. While emphasising that these various perspectives follow Foucault in his emphasis on the disciplinary, surveillance and bio-political character of mod-ern governance, we should also note that they owe much, and in some cases more, to the Marxist tradition. This is especially so in the cases of Gill (see 1990, 1993) and Hardt and Negri (2000).

Part I
States, War and Capitalism

2
Global Liberal Governance: Networks, Resistance and War

Michael Dillon

Introduction

There is clarity in simply asking why there is resistance to liberal governance, what forms that resistance takes and how global liberal governance anticipates and responds to resistance. But that clarity may also be misleading if we do not immediately acknowledge also that power and resistance are always found together, correlated in a co-productive and co-evolutionary dynamic. No power, no resistance. No resistance, no power. Behind this proposition is the closely allied one that forms of war and forms of life are also correlated. The dialectic of this complex process of violent differentiation is, of course, a dynamic one. It has no predetermined or certain resolution. From this perspective, then, it would be absurd to think that there would not be resistance to global liberal governance. It would be equally absurd to think that global liberal governance would not be actively involved in anticipating, and making provision for dealing forcefully with, opposition to its currently dominant regime of power. In short, the liberal way of peace is correlated with a liberal way of war. The liberal way of peace is currently characterised by global liberal governance. Its particular correlation of power and resistance has been most evident in the many police actions, wars and operations other than war that liberal regimes have prosecuted since global liberal governance first rose to international prominence after the Cold War (Duffield, 2001). Many transnational social protest movements have also grown up to challenge and contest globalisation and its allied economic institutions of global liberal governance in particular. One thing at least is notable about all of these different if correlated instances of resistance and 'pacification' under global liberal governance. They have varied enormously in their character.

Global liberal governance is a plural and diverse regime of power comprised of many heterogeneous practices and rationalities of governance, continuously engaged also in remedial critique of its own governing practices as well as authoritarian enforcement of them (Dean, 2002). Since the regime of power is plural and dynamic, so also has resistance to it been diverse and varied.

The purpose of this chapter is to explore certain aspects of this correlation of power and resistance particularly in respect of the emphasis that global liberal governance places on the concept of 'networks'. First, it makes a case for how the power of global liberal governance can be understood in network terms, and does so critically by drawing on Foucault. Second, it shows how global liberal governance is as much concerned with network-centric warfare as it is with network-centric peace. Third, it illustrates how some global governors seek to impose a Manichean friend/enemy distinction globally against networks of terror conflating many different manifestations of resistance to global liberal governance.

The advent of networks

The idea of networks is a key term of art in most narratives of the social and political transformations that have led to the advent of governance nationally and internationally. Much has been written, for example, about the fundamental transformations that the Keynesian social-democratic and national-welfare state underwent throughout the last two decades of the twentieth century. Novel forms of governance seem initially to have come to attention as a response to the challenge of governability, posed by the limits of both states and markets that these states experienced in the late 1970s. They made their way into international relations via new regimes of international development and aid that followed the failures of the 1980s. There was evidently a great deal of borrowing across the national/international divide as new organisational systems, ideologies and policy programmes restructured the governing of international relations as much as they did the restructuring of national ones. Key elements in the wider story involved here included: Fordist mass production for mass markets giving way to post-Fordist flexible production for niche markets; the replacement of planning by marketisation, contractualism and state rollback; the undermining of capacities for national economic management by the emergence of a globalised economy; the shift in economic management towards the cultivation of enterprise cultures that would make domestic economies competitive in a globalised market place; the increasingly differentiated character of 'autopoietic' systems and institutions; the transformation of top-down hierarchical 'command and control' organisations into flatter and looser forms of association and organisation; the displacement of centralised national government with its characteristic bureaucratic processes, by polycentric, interactional, borderless networks of socio-political governance operating through the choice and agency of reflexive individuals; the re-engineering of the relation between donor and lending states and institutions with their clients and recipients with the strategic transformations which followed the dissolution of the Cold War. What increasingly emerged, nationally and internationally, was a reliance upon 'governance without government' that sought to work through the liberal subject's powers of freedom rather than against their potentially explosive Hobbesian appetites and desires (Rosenau and Czempiel, 1992).

While governmental networks take many forms (public–private partnerships, community participation, use of volunteering, quasi-markets in public services, and even terrorist networks) they also worked on many different levels (inter-personal, inter-organisational and inter-systemic). They came to be defined as a form of 'heterarchical' regulation distinguishable from the hierarchical regulation of bureaucracy and the anarchical regulation of the market. Thus while Daniel Bell first spoke of post-industrial society (Bell, 1973) and Jean-Francois Lyotard of post-modern society (Lyotard, 1979), more contemporary social analysts began to speak of network society (Castells, 1996; Messner, 1997). This language of network and governance came to dominate many aspects of international relations (Rosenau and Czempiel, 1992) as it did public administration, public and private sector management, national and international economics, as well as political science and public policy generally. It is impossible, then, to describe or account for these developments in exclusively public or private, national or international, terms. They represented, instead, a general mutation in the operation and character of liberal power both nationally and internationally.

It is nonetheless remarkable how incompetent people can be at the exercise of the self-regulating freedom of governance. Some just don't get it, cannot get it or seem wilfully opposed to having it (Cruickshank, 1999; Dean, 2002; Dillon, 2002; Dillon and Valentine, 2002; Hindess, 2002). Self-regulating freedom is a discipline, the talent and the taste for which seem to be unequally distributed within as well as between societies. Recalling Kantian conceptions of enlightenment, global liberal governance relies upon a doctrine of development or maturation.

Bentham's principle of 'less eligibility' informs its project of promoting the self-regulating, self-improving subject. Liberal political philosophy's moral cartography of natural equality is thus necessarily redrawn by liberal governance into a distribution of power, force and correction once it encounters resistance to its norm of self-regulating freedom and begins to identify the recalcitrant, the deviant and the un-safe (Cruickshank, 1999). Responsible autonomy is the hard labour that governance requires of its subjects and some just don't have what it takes. Others just won't learn. For each, liberal governance often prescribes quite despotic and brutal forms of care, punishment and containment (Dean, 1991, 1999; Cruickshank, 1999). Consider, for example, also the detailed political conditionalities that have progressively been attached to global aid and global development assistance policies throughout the last decade. In the process translating its moral cartography into cartography of power, liberal governance effects complex formations of criminalisation up to and including the criminalisation of state regimes. Liberal governance is then regularly resisted and such resistance calls for an account of liberal governance as a regime of power and not simply a process by which self-evident liberal values are applied in practice.

The biopower of networks

There are, of course, various ways in which liberal governance might be construed as a regime of power. If you understand global liberal governance in a Hegelian/Fukuyama way to signal the end of history through the realisation of world spirit in the form of contemporary liberalism and global capitalism, then resistance to this historically guaranteed project might be regarded as the opposition of benighted traditionalists. Traditionalists closely defined as traditionalists, of course, by the modernising ideology and processes of this understanding of global liberal governance itself. Destined to be rolled-over by history, traditionalists become the slag heap of waste that history leaves in its wake. Or, to change metaphors, such global liberal governors are very much inclined to say that you have to break a few eggs to make liberal omelettes.

If, however, you understand global liberal governance in a Kantian cosmopolitan way to be the extension of universal human values commonly recognised worldwide by civic cultures struggling to free themselves from the oppressive domination of many forms of tyranny and misrule, then resistance to governance might be figured differently. Rogue states, political tyrants, militarists, fundamentalists, international law breakers and rapacious soldiers of fortune comprise a diverse rogues' gallery of anti-liberal elements against which global liberal governance has to war in order to advance towards the goal of perpetual peace. Note here that the project of perpetual peace has a distinctly martial face as well.

A third illustration will serve to bracket the political spectrum. If you understand liberal governance to be a vehicle for the extension globally of monopoly capitalism and the geo-strategic power of the United States, you will interpret resistance to it in yet a different way. It may then become a struggle of the global masses, formed by the very practices of global liberal governance and capital, to free themselves from despoilation and exploitation for global corporate profit (Hardt and Negri, 2000). Resistance to imperialism once took the form of wars of national liberation. No such neat term has yet been coined by theorists of empire.

The interpretation of global liberal governance that informs this chapter is instead a Foucauldian one. Amongst its many advantages for this project, including its subtle and plural account of power, is the intimate correlation between resistance and power assumed by Foucault's account of governmental power/knowledge in particular. One further advantage is that Foucault distinguishes liberal forms of governmentality from other forms of governmentality. An excellent secondary literature has further explored and developed this account of liberal governmentality. That literature not only explains how governmentality operates as a regime of self-regulating freedoms (Dean, 1999; Rose, 1999), but also how, simultaneously a regime of correction, it deploys a range of authoritarian practices against those who resist its insistent call to assume the structures and habits of self-regulating freedom (Cruickshank, 1999; Barry, 2001; Dean, 2002; Hindess, 2002). More recently it has begun to address how liberal governmentality has been extended, via a transformation of the project of liberal internationalism, into a global project (Dillon and Reid, 2001; Dillon, 2002).

Liberal internationalism is not simply comprised therefore of the normative political theory and ideals of liberal philosophy, or of its commitment to an international rule of law. Neither is it confined to the sovereign geo-strategic power of the United States. Just as we have been witnessing what Foucault called a governmentalisation of the state, so we have also been witnessing, in part, a governmentalisation of the United States as well. Liberal internationalism is now also comprised of dynamic and heterogeneous ways of governing the conduct of conduct that are directed at the management of populations more than they are at the control of territories. To be precise, global liberal governance is a Foucauldian system of power/knowledge that depends upon the strategic orchestration of the self-regulating freedoms of populations, the relations between whose subjects form complex and dynamic networks of power. These networks operate through the strategic manipulation of different generative principles of formation: profit, scarcity, security and so on. Initiating and orchestrating domains of self-regulating freedom also requires detailed knowledge of populations and the terrains that they inhabit. The object of power here is the exercise of power over life, rather than power over death. Global governance is therefore very much more a domain of 'bio' rather than 'geo' politics.

The discursive conditions of emergence of global liberal governance were, as the previous section indicated, many and complex. Biopolitics has a long tradition of development in the historical development of modern forms of power. Two prominent reasons why governance has become such a feature of global power relations recently were, however, the dissolution of Cold War politics and the failure of the economic structural adjustment programmes for world development in the 1980s. The collapse of the Soviet empire created a vacuum in geopolitics that allowed power over life an opportunity to displace the priority that had been accorded to power over death in the ideological bipolar politics that followed the Second World War. Better means of managing the life processes of the global poor, itself an aspect of the emergence of wider global population management in the extension of the self-regulating freedoms of global capital economics, were also sought in the process of effecting a wide-ranging reform of global development policies throughout the 1990s. It was no coincidence, then, that the World Bank was first responsible for putting the term 'governance' into use at the global level through a series of influential reports issued between 1989 and 1994 (World Bank, 1994: 2; Dillon, 2003).

Power is conceived and deployed here less as a commodity that is possessed by a pre-formed subject, than a force that arises in the context of, serves to form and continuously circulates through, complex networks of relations. Power is:

> ... something which only functions in the form of a chain. It is never localised here or there, never in anybody's hands, never appropriated as a commodity or piece of wealth. Power is employed and exercised through a net like organisation. (Foucault, 1980: 98)

Power thus comes to presence in the context of the freedom of human beings acting in effect as the conductive material for power's very circulation and strategic organising. If we were not free, by which Foucault means radically undetermined creatures governed by no general *telos*, natural law or historical determination, we would not conduct or enact power relations. We would instead be comprised of raw material whose properties and behaviour could be read-off from the *telos*, natural law or historical determination said to govern our existence. For Foucault, then, there are no power relations in human affairs without this key attribute or medium of human freedom. There is dominance, but that is another thing. Similarly, there is no freedom in human affairs without the existence of power relations.

Herein lies the explanation for Foucault's account of correlate resistances to power that informs this chapter. All conductive material exhibits resistance to the force that circulates through it. Suffused by that force, conductive material ought not to be conflated with the power that it enables and enacts. Struggle is thus an involuntary manifestation of the very way in which many other thinkers in addition to Foucault, drawing on the philosophical sources which nourished his work, also understand human freedom (Agamben, 1998; Rancière, 1999; Vatter, 2000). That is to say they conceive of an excess of (human) being over its (powerful) appearance (Heidegger, 1977). Free, in the ways just specified, human conductive material exceeds the force in which it participates while that force circulates strategically through it to fashion human being into historical shape and form. Such freedom, never a 'power-less' condition, and underwritten by no guarantees of emancipation, is a positive and not a negative thing:

> We must cease once and for all to describe the effects of power in negative terms: it 'excludes', it 'represses', it 'censors', it 'abstracts', it 'masks', it 'conceals'. In fact, power produces; it produces reality; it produces domains of objects and rituals of truth. The individual and the knowledge that may be gained from him belong to this production. (Foucault, 1980: 194)

The power of global liberal governance is such a biopower. Here freedom is organised into the self-regulating freedoms of liberal subjectivity. It is concerned more with cultivating life, making it more developed, productive, secure, rather than with threatening death. Power over life is nonetheless also never very far removed from power over death; something we shall note further in a moment. To pursue this project of governing life, the very nature of life processes have themselves to become epistemic objects, known in their details, and known for their dynamics, as topics requiring systematic human scientific investigation. Consider, for example, the volume of reports, statistics, plans and programmes that comprise the terrain of global liberal governance. Its vast labour of epistemic work is not only directed at assembling detailed knowledge about all aspects of life but also with continuously subjecting that knowledge to continuous revision and critique. Thus the term biopower: the strategic organisation of networks of relations among population groups identified according to many different generative principles of formation, regularities and norms of behaviour disclosed by the human sciences of power/knowledge.

From this Foucauldian perspective human beings are, therefore, more than liberal subjects. They are, for example, more than subjects of universal human rights. Their moral compass and ethical sensibilities, their historical store of experience and cultural traditions, their dreams and desires, their amities and enmities, all exceed the political and ethical accounts within which global liberal governance seeks to confine them as subjects of rights. Similarly, human beings are more than self-interested economic subjects exhibiting behaviour characterised by market rationality; and more than mere consumers of goods and services provided by such economies.

It follows that no regime of power can be resistance free. All regimes of power will inevitably encounter resistance from a (human) material that, while peculiarly conductive of power and essential for its circulation, is nonetheless irreducible to power:

> There are no relations of power without resistances; the latter are all the more real and effective because they are formed right at the point where relations of power are exercised; resistance to power does not have to come from elsewhere to be real … it exists all the more by being in the same place as power; hence, like power, resistance is multiple and can be integrated in global strategies. (Foucault, 1980: 142)

Strictly speaking, then, the question to be addressed is not, why resistance? Resistance is to be expected in some form or other. The question is how resistance? The forms of resistance, the manifestation of resistance, the timing of resistance, the ways in which global liberal governance anticipates, construes and responds to resistance, the timing and happenstance of violent responses on some occasions and not others, the characteristic ways in which those responses are organised and deployed. These are historical questions, themselves prompting different and often violent interpretations, forming an integral part of the resistances to, as well as the martial responses of, global liberal governance. Thus, while many commentators have emphasised the reduced power of states affected by the growth of the complex non-governmental as well as quasi-governmental networks of non-state actors so characteristic of governance nationally and internationally, and by implication questions of war and resistance, more have recently acknowledged how the western state has become re-engineered rather than eclipsed by these developments, and how it is in certain ways more powerful and more intrusive into the lives of its citizens and subjects than ever before (Hirst and Thompson, 1996; Jessop, 2002). The face of resistance to liberal power has also changed with this transformation of the organisation of liberal peace, and so has the liberal way of war.

Network-centric warfare and resistance

Given that the very rationale of global liberal governance is the improved self-regulation of whatever processes it addresses, self-improvement (specifically normatively sanctioned self-improvement), cannot simply be left as a desirable goal for governance. It becomes a positive social, indeed moral and political, obligation. It is for these reasons that global liberal governance not only develops as a complex network of improvement, correction and punishment. Ultimately it has also to decide whom it is permitted to kill: that is to say upon whom it will make war as well as impose correctional measures. The network character of global liberal governance is reflected as much in the ways in which it now prepares for network-centric war and network-centric resistance as it has been in the ways in which it organises network-centric peace.

Under the US 1986 Goldwater-Nichols Department of Defense Re-organisation Act, a Roles and Missions Commission must present a report to the Secretary of Defense every three years. The report issued by the commission in 1996 argued that a central mission to guide the US armed services was missing and urgently required to provide overall strategic cohesion and direction for the twenty-first century. The outcome was a document entitled Joint Vision 2010 (1996). This advocated a strategy of network-centric warfare, moving to more lethal military capabilities not simply by adopting the information and communication technology fuelling the so-called Revolution in Military Affairs (RMA) more extensively and more intensively than hitherto, but by systematically utilising information as the generative principle of formation for all aspects of military organisation. A revised Joint Vision 2020, issued in May 2000, extended and embraced network-centric warfare as the principle of formation governing all US national strategy. It also raised the question of how the NATO alliance could be drawn into the evolving strategic web of network-centric thinking (Dillon and Reid, 2001; Dillon, 2002).

Network-centric thinking is consciously modelled on fundamental changes that have taken place in the mutation of the political economy of power referred to earlier and in the capitalistic transformation of the US and global economies throughout the 1980s and 1990s with which these changes have been closely associated. These developments draw their inspiration not simply from the revolution in information and communication technology and the molecular revolution in biology, but also from a confluence of the two that takes place because each shares in the fundamental ontology of code. Here, a convergence of thinking based on the overarching power of code is not only fuelling new forms of governance but new ways also of interpreting threat and of making war. Network organisation and network operations are now claimed, for example, to deliver to the US military the same powerful advantages that they produced for American and global businesses. In network-centric warfare, just as in network economies and governmental processes, information, speed, self-synchronisation and flexibility are said to be at a premium (Alberts and Czerwinski, 1994; Cebrowski and Gartska, 1998; Alberts and Stein, 1999). The new network strategy is officially characterised by four themes.

1. The first is the shift in focus from the weapons platform – the battle tank, the aircraft carrier, the strategic bomber – to the information network, as the key unit of military organisation.
2. The second is a shift of focus from the character and dynamics of individual military actors or units to that of radical relational systems; from viewing actors as independent operators to viewing them as part of autopoietic military systems operating in the constantly changing fitness landscapes of varied 'battlescapes'.
3. The third is a tendency towards interpreting the operations of complex adaptive military systems in biological terms. Like 'natural' organisms, military systems are now said to co-evolve and adapt ecologically through interaction with each other and the battlespace-as-ecosystem that they inhabit.
4. The fourth feature is the conviction that information is the prime mover in military as in every other aspect of human affairs, the basic constituent of all matter. This elevation of information does not

simply open up new enterprises for the military as it does for business (information warfare and digitised battlespaces for the military, e-commerce and so on for businesses). Neither does it mean that information is merely a force multiplier, increasing the firepower and effectiveness of traditional weapon systems. Information is embraced as the new principle of formation for all military systems, initiating a whole-scale re-thinking of the very basis of military organisation, doctrine, force requirements, procurement policies, training and operational concepts. Military formations no longer simply rally around the flag; they form up, mutate and change around information networks (Dillon and Reid, 2001; Dillon, 2002).

Network-centric warfare has also been stimulated by the self-interest of the military as the US defence establishment sought new rationales for itself following the end of the Cold War. It also remains a controversial and contested strategic doctrine within the US strategic community. The platform specialists, the service advocates and the old geopolitical warriors, for whom weapon systems, states and territories remain the single most important elements of international politics, all contest its assumptions and loathe its new jargon. Indeed the vast expansion of the US defence budget recently announced by President Bush testifies to the continuing power of the warfare traditionalists. But it is the warfare revolutionaries who are leading the way in the development of the military doctrine and force deployments of global liberal governance.

Many protagonists in this strategic debate also try to maintain that the revolution in information and communication technology has not caused much of an RMA, or that it has only done so in the United States. In a sense opponents of network-centric warfare and critics of the RMA thesis are correct. There has been no revolution exclusive to military affairs. The RMA is the military face of the revolution in global affairs brought about in particular by the coincidence of the fall of the Soviet Union with the revolutionary digitalisation of information and communication technology globally. Suffice to say then, that the RMA is as much an exclusively American way of making war, as capitalism is an exclusively American way of making a living, or governance an exclusively American way of developing the operational capabilities of power as a network phenomenon. These are not exclusively American affairs. US society is being re-engineered by these processes as much as any other.

To the extent that the digital revolution in information and communications technology has contributed to the processes of global liberal governance, information has become the new metaphysics of power for many of its proponents. This applies especially to those revising its strategic account of war. 'Information,' two of its RAND based strategic thinkers tell us, 'is the prime mover' (Arquilla and Ronfeldt, 1993: 144). However, if the military now network, so do the resisters. Modern life and modern governance, as people in the West know it, has come to depend upon the ever more sophisticated and close-coupled networks of complex techno-structures and organisational systems of biopower that have been extended internationally through global liberal governance. This applies to its organisation for peace as well as war. Whether they are tied to communication, nutrition, energy, transportation, finance, pensions, insurance, housing, medicine, education, consumption, security and so on the ordinary technical artefacts and processes associated with all these afford innumerable assets and opportunities for destructive use by those resistant or existentially hostile to as well as criminalised by global liberal governance. Contra-functioning the everyday applications of the socio-technical processes and systems that comprise the globally linked knowledge intensive networks of liberal governance may create lethal capabilities for those that wish to exploit them in that way. Resourceful resisters have access to the international arms economy that global liberal governance also sustains but where that fails they may create weapons from whatever is available to hand. The internet, finance markets operating 24 hours a day, seven days a week, global airline systems, agricultural fertilisers, rental vehicles and tourist industries may, in addition to the international arms bazaar fuelled by military economies of global liberal governance as much as those of the dire states of the former Soviet bloc, provide the organisation, intelligence, weapons material and targets of opportunity for resistance: from demonstration to terrorist attack. An astonishing symbiotic (a)symmetry obtains, between the vital capillaries of global liberal governance, its emergent ways of making war and the opposition that it encounters. Traditional territorial boundaries matter much less here than the radical relationality of complex systems and the exploitation of network capillaries for the mobilisation of resistance too as much as the spread of global liberal governance.

The integration of telecommunications and computer systems into energy, transportation, human services, telecommunications, finance and civilian government sectors, for example, also incorporates the US military. When the Secretary of Defense in the Pentagon places a telephone call, it is likely that a commercial telephone company will be providing the service. It has been estimated that over 95 per cent of defence communications in the United States rely on the public telephone system.[1] According to a recent *Washington Post* report, during autumn 2002 a Californian detective began investigating a suspicious pattern of surveillance against Silicon Valley computers. Unknown browsers from the Middle East and South East Asia were said to be exploring the digital systems used to manage San Francisco Bay Area utilities and government offices. The FBI's San Francisco computer intrusion squad was alerted and, together with the Lawrence Livermore National Laboratory, trails of a broader reconnaissance were traced. A forensic summary of the investigation, prepared in the Defense Department, said that the bureau found 'multiple casings of sites' nationwide. Routed through telecommunications switches in Saudi Arabia, Indonesia and Pakistan, the 'visitors' were said to have studied emergency telephone systems, electrical generation and transmission, water storage and distribution, nuclear power plants and gas facilities. It was said that some of the probes suggested planning for a conventional attack. Others were reported to have homed in on a class of digital devices that allow remote control of services such as fire dispatch and of machinery such as pipelines. Information about such devices – and how to program them – were reported to have been discovered also on recently captured al Qaeda computers. This poses the prospect of new information-based threats different from familiar financial disruptions by hackers responsible for viruses and worms. It is posed instead at the informational interface between computers and the physical structures that they control. Specialised digital devices are used by the distributed control systems (DCSs) and Supervisory Control and Data Acquisition Systems (SCADA) of what is now called 'critical national infrastructures'. The simplest ones collect measurements, throw railway switches, close circuit-breakers or adjust valves in the pipes that carry water, oil and gas. More complicated versions sift incoming data, govern multiple devices and cover a broader area of the close-coupled systems of network societies nationally and internationally. The electronic/information frontier does not follow territorial boundaries and they are often not designed with security in mind. Should you wish to attack electronic power generation, transmission and distribution, oil and gas storage and distribution, banking and finance, transportation systems, water supply facilities, emergency assistance resources and so on, you may or may not choose to operate in cyberspace. As 9/11 illustrated, all the information you may require would be available in American Airlines' flight schedules.

Traditional forms of conquest, as well as traditional measures of national capability, land or raw materials thus begin to recede somewhat in significance under the dynamics of global liberal governance and network-centric warfare. Here is both war and economy without boundary. Territorial conquest and domination is not what they are about, albeit traditional geo-strategic factors may still be very much in play as well. The object is less to seize territory, or to free it, as in the Gulf War at the beginning of the 1990s. One reason is that the enemy is no longer readily identifiable and easily associated with a single place, regime or system of power. The enmity that global liberal governance encounters is as widely disseminated as is its own globalised networks of power through which resistance itself also moves. Resistance occurs then within the very capillaries of global liberal governance, as much in its heartlands as in its borderlands. To speak of insides and outsides in this way is, however, also to be in danger of missing the point about how liberal governance functions in many power plays sometimes directed at populations sometimes ordered into states of the Westphalian system, sometimes ordered in altogether different ways in terms, for example, of the global poor, economic migrants, refugees, globally available pools of cheap labour, global consumer markets, trans-nationally organised crime, and so on.

Awareness of such widespread counter-networking 'asymmetric threat' has also brought about a peculiar shift in the new strategic discourse of network-centric warfare. First articulated in detail by Arquilla and Ronfeldt, it was commended as a strategy to be adopted by the United States, and subsequently also its allies, not simply to exploit the RMA but to effect a wholesale re-engineering of western strategic policy as well as military operational concepts and doctrines (Arquilla and Ronfeldt, 1993, 1996 and 1998). The focus of attention has, however, shifted noticeably. It now offers 'netwar' as a generic account of the ways in which resistance to global liberal governance manifests itself. By this means a very significant conflation of radically different kinds of activities takes place, including activities such as that of the landmines campaign that might well be interpreted as a classical example of global liberal governance itself.

Arquilla and Ronfeldt now say that netwar is an emerging mode of conflict, in which a whole variety of protagonists, ranging from terrorist and criminal organisations to militant social activists and Princess Diana-inspired arms control movements, use network forms of organisation, doctrine, strategy and technology attuned to the information age against the power of global liberal governance. The practice of netwar, they claim, is well ahead of theory, as both 'civil' and 'uncivil' society actors increasingly engage in this way of contesting the operational power of global liberal governance. Strategists and policy-makers, in Washington and elsewhere, they note, have begun to discern 'the dark side of the network phenomenon', especially in the wake of the 9/11 attacks. Their concern is directly reflected in, and further circulated through, the torrent of papers and institutional reforms that have been produced in the United States, especially since 9/11.[2] It now also refers to an emerging continuum of conflict and crime at levels short of traditional military-warfare in which the protagonists use network forms of organisation and related doctrines, strategies and practices to target asymmetrically the vulnerabilities of global liberal network societies. These protagonists are likely to consist, they say, of dispersed organisations, small groups and individuals who communicate, co-ordinate, and conduct their campaigns in a networked manner, often without a central command. Thus, netwar is said to differ from modes of conflict and crime in which the protagonists prefer to develop large, formal, stand-alone, hierarchical organisations, doctrines and strategies. Netwar, they say, is about the Zapatistas more than the Fidelistas, Hamas more than the Palestine Liberation Organisation (PLO), the American Christian Patriot movement more than the Ku Klux Klan and the Asian Triads more than the Cosa Nostra (Arquilla and Ronfeldt, 2001).

US military strategists in particular anticipate that this will become the major operational mode of network-based conflict and crime in the decades ahead. Many actors, they say, are already evolving in this direction, including traditional adversaries who are modifying their structures and strategies to take advantage of networked designs. The examples provided offer a revealing insight into liberal governance's new rogues' gallery. These include: 'transnational terrorist groups, black-market proliferators of weapons of mass destruction (WMD), drug and other crime syndicates, fundamentalist and ethnonationalist movements, intellectual property pirates, and immigration and refugee smugglers' (Arquilla and Ronfeldt, 2001). Such fears are further detailed and elaborated by a host of new organisations including: the US National Infrastructure Protection Center (NIPC); the Critical Infrastructure Assurance Office (CIAO); the National Infrastructure Assurance Council (NIAC) and Information Sharing and Analysis Centers (ISACs). Above them all now is the new department of Homeland Defence. All note one way and another with varying foci of attention how urban gangs, back-country militias and militant single-issue groups in the United States and elsewhere have developed a netwar orientation. The netwar spectrum, they insist, also includes a new generation of social revolutionaries, radicals and activists who are beginning to create information-age ideologies, in which identities and loyalties may shift from the nation-state to the transnational level of global civil society. New kinds of actors, such as anarchistic and nihilistic leagues of computer-hacking 'cyboteurs,' may also engage in netwar. Recent cases of social netwar by activist NGOs against state and corporate actors are also cited. The International Campaign to Ban Landmines (ICBL), they suggest, is also a prime case of a social netwar developed by NGO activists whose network eventually included some government officials, in a campaign that one prominent organiser, Jody Williams, called 'a new model of diplomacy' for putting pressure on the United States and other recalcitrant governments:

> It proves that civil society and governments do not have to see themselves as adversaries. It demonstrates that small and middle powers can work together with civil society and address humanitarian concerns with breathtaking speed. It shows that such a partnership is a new kind of 'superpower' in the post-Cold War world.... For the first time, smaller and middle-sized powers had not yielded ground to intense pressure from a superpower to weaken the treaty to accommodate the policies of that one country.[3]

Here then is the underside of global liberal governance – its dissenting alter ego – a side that exposes its radically ambivalent relation to the very self-regulating freedom that it promotes. Some net warriors good, other net warriors bad. Differentiating between different kinds of network structures and types, such flatness and openness may be impossible for terrorist, criminal and other violent netwar actors who, it is said, depend on stealth and secrecy; cellular networks and/or hierarchies may be imperative for them, along with hybrids of hierarchies and networks. Here they also refer to the Earth Liberation Front (ELF), a radical environmental group of unclear origins. The ELF may in fact have only a small core of true believers who commit its most violent acts, such as arson and vandalism at new construction sites in naturally wild landscapes (such as Long Island, New York). But according to ELF publicist, Craig Rosebraugh, the ELF consists of a 'series of cells across the country [the US] with no chain of command and no membership roll'. It is held together mainly by a shared ideology and philosophy. 'There's no central leadership where they can go and knock off the top guy and it will be defunct.'[4] In other words, the ELF is allegedly built around 'autonomous cells' that are entirely underground.

It is also noted that one of the most sophisticated doctrines for social netwar comes from the Direct Action Network (DAN), which arose from a coalition of activists dedicated to using non-violent direct action and civil disobedience to halt the WTO meeting in Seattle. DAN's approach to netwar epitomises swarming ideas. Participants are asked to organise, at their own choice, into small (5–20 people) 'affinity groups': 'self-sufficient, small, autonomous teams of people who share certain principles, goals, interests, plans or other similarities that enable them to work together well'.[5] Each group decides for itself what actions its members will undertake, ranging from street theatre to risking arrest.[6] Where groups operate in proximity to each other, they are further organised into 'clusters': but there may also be 'flying groups' that move about according to where needed. Different people in each group take up different functions (such as police liaison), but every effort is made to make the point that no group has a single leader. All this is co-ordinated at spokes-council meetings where each group sends a representative and decisions are reached through democratic consultation and consensus (in yet another approach to leaderlessness). This approach generated unusual flexibility, mobility and resource sharing during the Battle of Seattle and they bolster their point with an eyewitness account:

> In practice, this form of organisation meant that groups could move and react with great flexibility during the blockade. If a call went out for more people at a certain location, an affinity group could assess the numbers holding the line where they were and choose whether or not to move. When faced with tear gas, pepper spray, rubber bullets and horses, groups and individuals could assess their own ability to withstand the brutality. As a result, blockade lines held in the face of incredible police violence. When one group of people was finally swept away by gas and clubs, another would move in to take their place. Yet there was also room for those of us in the middle-aged, bad lungs/bad backs affinity group to hold lines in areas that were relatively peaceful, to interact and dialogue with the delegates we turned back, and to support the labour march that brought tens of thousands through the area at midday. No centralised leader could have coordinated the scene in the midst of the chaos, and none was needed – the organic, autonomous organisation we had proved far more powerful and effective. No authoritarian figure could have compelled people to hold a blockade line while being tear gassed – but empowered people free to make their own decisions did choose to do that.[7]

The year 2000 brought an advance in US government thinking about networking trends among its adversaries, and in considering new options for dealing with them. Government and military-related research institutes paid the most attention.[8] But high-level policy making became involved as well. The US State Department's annual report for 1999, *Patterns of Global Terrorism: 1999* provides a good example. 'U.S. counterterrorist policies,' it noted, 'are tailored to combat what we believe to be the shifting trends in terrorism.' One trend it logged was the shift from well-organised, localised groups supported by state sponsors to loosely organised, international networks of terrorists. 'Such a network supported the failed attempt to smuggle explosives material and detonating devices into Seattle in December. With the decrease of state funding, these loosely networked individuals and groups have turned increasingly to other sources of funding, including private sponsorship, narcotrafficking, crime, and illegal trade.'[9] By December 2000, observation of this trend (and of the growing link between crime and terrorism), became even more pronounced in the report of a US interagency group on global crime. While noting that most criminal organisations remain hierarchical (they still have leaders and subordinates), the US International Crime Threat Assessment found that:

> International criminal networks – including traditional organised crime groups and drug-trafficking organisations – have taken advantage of the dramatic changes in technology, world politics, and the global economy to become more sophisticated and flexible in their operations. They have extensive worldwide networks and infrastructure to support their criminal operations... Much more than in the past, criminal organisations are networking and cooperating with one another, enabling them to merge expertise and to broaden the scope of their activities. Rather than treat each other as rivals, many criminal organisations are sharing information, services, resources, and market access according to the principle of comparative advantage.[10]

In sum, liberal governance not only anticipates that it will be resisted, it configures resistance in ways that directly reflect its own emphasis on networks. That way a wide variety of different and diverse social, protest, criminal and political movements are increasingly being conflated into a single security problematic for global liberal governors. Just as the liberal state has been re-engineered via governmental practices so also has the liberal face of war. Network-centric warfare theorists claim that the same multiplier effects said to follow from the information and communication revolution and its allied forms of network organisation will secure for global liberal governance a global military superiority to match its current economic hegemony.

Conclusion

In response to the dialectic of power and resistance, global liberal governance has therefore been elaborating its own complex demonology. In one sense it is a highly diverse demonology. In another sense, especially since the 9/11 attacks, it threatens to become a massive hyperbolic conflation of widely different kinds of social, economic, political and criminal activities. At least one important issue that becomes very evident here is that of the extra discursive sources driving resistance to global liberal governance beyond the discursive regime of global liberal governance itself, especially those including its emerging discourse of net, information and cyber war.

To note the powerful correlation of resistance and power is not to claim that resistance is a mere creature of power and its discursive formations. It is not. As other chapters in this collection testify, all instances of resistance possess their own drivers, their own discourses and their own trajectories. They are also motivated by diverse and perhaps even also divergent responses to the objective material conditions that the economic, political, social and cultural practices of global liberal governance have been inscribing upon the world. But there is necessarily an interface between power and resistance. That interface is configured neither by power nor by resistance alone but by the complex and violent correlation of the two. Recall that global liberal governance has been described as a remedial regime continuously engaged in critical re-evaluation of its own many and varied practices. It is remedial because it continuously fails. And one reason why it continuously fails is that it deals with forces, circumstances and dynamics that ultimately always exceed its powers of control. Its programmes are never fully realised. Its changing ambitions are never wholly achieved. Its values are never fully subscribed. Its practices misfire. Its peace is never tranquil and its military might is never wholly dominant. The reason is that in all instances it applies itself to local conditions and historically situated circumstances that can never be fully understood in advance, not least because they immediately undergo change in response to the very interventions that the practices of global liberal governance make upon them. That is why, in *reflecting* upon the resistance to global liberal governance, it is equally important to take stock of how that resistance is figured by global liberal governance. The wars that it will fight, the violence that it will perpetrate and thereby also the further resistance that it will engender will, in part at least, remain a function of how it construes the responses of a plural, diverse and dynamic world to its will to govern more efficiently, more intensely and ultimately – despite its own diversity – more homogeneously.

Notes

1. Joint Security Commission, Redefining Security: A report to the Secretary of State for Defense and the Director of the CIA, 28 February 1994: http://www.dss.mil/seclib/jcs.htm#c8.
2. See for example the latest collection of essays in Security in the Information Age, Joint Economic Committee of the US Congress, May 2002.
3. Jody Williams: http://www.wagingpeace.org/articles/%20nobel_lecture_97_williams.html (10 December 1997).
4. http://firstmonday.org/issues/issues6_10/ronfeldt/#note27.
5. Ibid., note42.
6. Ibid., note43.
7. Starhawk, How We Really Shut Down the WTO, December 1999, www.reclaiming.org/starhawk/wto.html. See http://firstmonday.org/issues/issues6_10/ronfeldt/#note44.
8. Ibid., note27.
9. Ibid., note55.
10. Ibid., note56.

3
Global Governance and State Collapse

Christopher Clapham

Introduction

At the core of the project of global governance lies a particular conception of the relationship between statehood and global order. In place of the now unsustainable idea that 'sovereign states' form the autonomous building blocks from which an anarchical international system is constructed, states have been reconceptualised as the key intermediaries between the norms according to which the new global system is expected to operate, and the implementation of that system on the ground. Despite the increased salience of other organisational forms, including non-governmental organisations and international regimes, and despite the characteristic hiving off to other agencies of what were previously seen as essential state functions, there is no alternative to the state as the key regulatory agency at the local level. The 'failure' or complete collapse of states therefore arouses deep concern among the core states of the modern global order, as the actual or potential site for threats to systemic stability – a concern that has been massively enhanced in the aftermath of the attacks on 11 September 2001. As a result, the period since the end of the Cold War has been marked by attempts on the part of core states and associated institutions to reconstitute states that were seen as having 'failed', in accordance with a doctrine of statehood that is compatible with the legitimising principles of the new global order.

But while the universal coverage of the inhabited areas of the world by effective states is regarded as necessary, it has paradoxically been undermined by the project of global governance itself, and more broadly by the wider social, political, and economic developments of which that project forms part. The problem of how to conceptualise, legitimise, and operate a state that remains awkwardly suspended between the global norms that is it expected to embody, and the local populations from whom it must draw its support (but over whom it is at the same time expected to extend its control), remains unresolved. Nowhere is this relationship between statehood and global order more problematical than in those parts of Africa where state capacity has been severely threatened, and where in places the state has effectively ceased to exist. This chapter accordingly explores the paradoxes of the project of global governance, and the varied resistances that have impeded its implementation, in a part of the world in which, on the one hand, it has been most energetically pursued, but in which, on the other, its problems and deficiencies are most glaringly apparent.

Origins and bases of the governance dilemma

In a broad sense, projects of global governance encompass *any* hegemonic conception of international order, which must in turn embody a conception of how the constituent elements of that order should be constructed, whether that construct consist in the feudal system of medieval Europe, a constellation of Leninist party-states linked by 'proletarian internationalism', or a community of liberal multiparty democracies coexisting in accordance with democratic peace theory. Given the peculiarly dependent nature of Africa's incorporation into modern global politics, the continent has continuously been subjected to a succession of norms, derived from those forms of governance that were regarded as universally legitimate by the international hegemonies of their time. The current project of global governance, in a narrower sense of the term, is but the latest of them.

The first of these, in the modern era, was European colonialism, from which African states in their present form – and in significant parts of the continent, states in *any* form – still overwhelmingly derive. The rapid partition of the continent between European colonial powers in the last two decades of the nineteenth century was driven by the conviction that the entire inhabited surface of the world *ought to be* divided between states, not merely in order to facilitate access to raw materials, but in order to promote the blessings of 'civilisation' – the extirpation of the slave trade, the spread of Christianity, and all the benefits of 'development' – for which states provided the essential structural precondition. Outside a very few areas, states of the kind required could only, in the estimation of their new rulers, be provided by colonialism, and colonialism itself effectively consisted in a process of state formation, with the demarcation of external and internal boundaries, the establishment of hierarchies, and the creation of structures of control and (much more modestly) social services and economic development.

The most obvious immediate deficiency of this project was its externality. Indigenous people were at most allowed only subaltern roles in its implementation, and in the aftermath of the Second World War, its political base was fatally undermined by the combination of local resistance and a changed global setting that challenged its legitimacy. The problem could however at least apparently be resolved, to the satisfaction of almost all the interested parties, by adopting a second governance formula, which sought to remedy the problems of the old one by extending independent sovereign statehood to the colonial territories, under the direction of indigenous regimes. In place of the old legitimating principle of 'civilisation', this rested on the new one of 'self-determination', while continuing to uphold the central features of the state construction project, including notably the preservation of the territorial units which had rapidly and haphazardly been put together by the incoming colonialists. The principal colonial powers – with Portugal as the sole exception – were willing if not happy to withdraw from colonial commitments, which offered decreasing rewards at an increasing price. And the new dispensation likewise met the demands of the post-war global order, in the form both of the superpowers and of the principles established by the United Nations.

Over the three decades that followed independence in the late 1950s and early 1960s, this second form of global governance itself came under challenge. First and most obviously, the economic basis of independent African states proved increasingly difficult to maintain, though the extent to which this was due to their dependent role within the global economy, as against the extent to which it could be ascribed to domestic mismanagement, was strongly contested. From the early 1980s, the African debt problem – which was itself no more than a symptom of a much deeper economic malaise – led to the imposition by the World Bank and allied institutions of 'structural adjustment' policies, which constituted the first systematic attempt to impose external governance on African states, albeit initially only in the limited area of economic policy. By the end of the decade, however, the World Bank (1989) had come to the view that much more basic reforms were required.

Second, the political structures of most African states were rapidly centralised in the hands of often autocratic rulers, and lost the capacity to respond to demands from their societies; the characteristic form of response, through what came to be known as 'neopatrimonial' systems under the control of heads of state, placed further pressure on the economy. As state capacity diminished, and resistance increased, threatened African states called on the international system for support, and in the Cold War era, this was expressed through economic, diplomatic and military assistance from global patrons, whether superpowers or former colonial rulers. Though ostensibly state strengthening, this assistance – especially when it took a military form – eventually subverted the very states that it was intended to uphold. From the mid-1970s, the brutality of a number of African rulers, symbolised by Idi Amin in Uganda and Jean-Bedel Bokassa in the Central African Republic (or Empire, as it briefly became), helped to undermine the legitimacy of the idea of unrestricted sovereign statehood in Africa, and to provide a moral basis for projects of external supervision.

Finally, from the mid-1980s onwards, Africa came to be regarded by the dominant states in the international order as a 'problem', in which political failure was accompanied by humanitarian and environmental disasters, creating what came to be known as 'complex emergencies' that demanded an external response. The Ethiopian famine of 1984 marks a clear step in this process, though it was not until the end of the Cold War in 1989 that the policy space was created for an integrated attempt to tackle the related problems of declining state capacity, civil war, autocracy, human rights abuse, and environmental decay that were identified as the key ingredients in the complex. The centrality of statehood to the problem was underlined when the complete collapse of government in Somalia after the fall of Siyad Barre in January 1991 left a vacuum in which nothing resembling a state could be discerned.

In the post-Cold War global order, these problems could be seen as issues of legitimate external concern. Africa regained its place on the global moral agenda, redolent of the missionary enterprise of the mid-nineteenth century, as a dark continent in which external actors had not merely the right but the obligation to intervene, in the interests of humanity as a whole – a belief expressed in the *droit d'ingérence* or right of intervention articulated by the French humanitarian campaigner Bernard Kouchner, who became a minister in successive *Parti Socialiste* administrations in France. This approach was most vividly illuminated by the willingness of the United States to commit some 25 000 troops to 'Operation Restore Hope' in Somalia. But in addition to its most obvious humanitarian manifestations, the decline of state capacity presented a series of further 'threats' to the core states of the global system. One of these was unrestricted population movement. Africa has over the last two decades had easily the highest proportion of refugees to population of any region of the world; and these were not only a source of major concern to neighbouring states, but also led to a stream of illegal immigrants and asylum seekers seeking refuge in the West. Another was disease, especially since Africa was the source of AIDS, of which it likewise had by far the world's largest infected population. Terrorism was a third, not so much because any significant terrorist movements emanated from the continent, as because any area outside the control of states was seen – especially after September 11 – as potentially dangerous. And – given that Western perceptions of Africa are significantly affected by its wildlife and associated tourism – the environmental movement had its own distinctive continental agenda.

The new project of global governance

Political and economic failure in Africa therefore came to be seen in the core states of the new global order, especially after the end of the Cold War, as an appropriate setting for the application of integrated programmes of governance reform. The all too evident problems of the continent could readily be explained as the outcome of governance failure. Africa's economic decline, in sharp contrast to apparently successful development in other parts of the developing world such as eastern Asia, had already been ascribed by the World Bank and others not only to the failure to implement the correct economic policies, but much more broadly to the inability of existing political structures to generate the *kind* of government that would have an interest in economic reforms, and that could mobilise the political constituencies needed to put them into effect. The absence of democracy – and no government in continental Africa was peacefully removed from power and replaced by an opposition party during the three decades to 1990 – could be regarded not only as an evil in itself, but as the source of other governance problems, including corruption, inefficiency, and human rights abuse. The civil wars in which much of the continent was mired, together with attendant evils such as refugee flows, were readily explicable as the outcome of unaccountable regimes, often heavily based in particular ethnic sections of the population, whose abuse of power understandably drove excluded communities into flight and rebellion. A general lack of state capacity, all too visible in the decay of health and educational systems, deprived even those regimes that sought to address basic problems of the ability to do so.

One of the most distinctive features of the new governance agenda was then the creation of a supportive coalition within Western states and societies. In sharp contrast to the strongly contested impact of globalisation on Western societies themselves, which gave rise to the internal forms of resistance encapsulated in the anti-globalisation movement, Western support for the global governance agenda in Africa was virtually universal. A leading role both in the public promotion of this agenda in the West, and in its implementation in Africa, was indeed played by non-governmental organisations (NGOs) which articulated the concerns of Western civil societies, and acquired the status of the missionaries of the new global order. Many of them were indeed associated with the churches, which abandoned their interest in proselytisation and transcendental goals in order to take part in a developmental enterprise geared to welfare – a reversal classically expressed in the fund-raising slogan of the British NGO Christian Aid, 'We believe in life *before* death'. An extraordinary number of specialised organisations were engaged in conflict resolution, human rights monitoring, protection of pastoralist communities, nature conservation, and other tasks. These were particularly well placed to further the broader aims of the governance agenda by engaging with (and, indeed, often creating) 'civil society' organisations within African states which – to continue the missionary analogy – acted as the local congregations of global faith-based concerns. They also gained direct inputs into the governments of donor states, which in turn channelled much of their aid funding through NGOs, a process which confirmed the 'humanitarian' status of their aid, avoided the need to establish their own implementing agencies, and enabled them to exercise a measure of leverage over the recipient organisations. Though engagement of international organisations such as the European Union, and UN specialised agencies such as UNICEF, was to be expected, more surprising members of the coalition were the World Bank, and even individual transnational corporations. Despite the inevitable variations in interests and emphases that occur within any coalition, these shared broadly similar concerns. To take one striking example, the World Bank became closely engaged in articulating explanations for civil wars in Africa, and providing funds for the demobilisation and social reintegration of former combatants, activities which would once have been regarded as well beyond its mandate (see Coletta *et al.*, 1996; Collier and Hoeffler, 1999; Collier, 2000).

The substantive content of the global governance agenda not only encompassed the belief that states were necessary, but extended to a clear idea of what such states should look like, and how they should be created. This was based on the assumption that the Western liberal democratic state provided a universally valid model for reconciling domestic political order with a peaceful and responsible engagement with the international system, individual liberty and respect for human rights, and the achievement of social and economic welfare. The first requirement for implementing this model was the resolution of armed conflicts in those states where they presented a major challenge to statehood, and this was to be achieved by bringing the conflicting parties together under external mediation, and inducing them to agree to a compromise settlement, that would then at some point be validated by an internationally monitored election. Such processes of attempted mediation were undertaken in a large number of states,[1] with almost universally unsuccessful results, the sole major exception being the peace settlement in Mozambique (see Clapham, 1998; Alden, 2001; Lyons, 2003).

In those cases where serious internal conflict was not a major problem, the three key elements of the governance agenda were economic liberalism, democratisation, and good governance. The first of these had indeed been implemented since the early 1980s, in the form of the 'structural adjustment' programmes imposed by the World Bank and International Monetary Fund as the price for assistance to indebted African states. The second benefited enormously from the upsurge of popular protest against corrupt and undemocratic regimes that broke out as soon as the collapse of the Soviet Union and the evident reluctance of the Western powers made clear that these would no longer receive the level of repressive external support to which they had become accustomed; it could also readily (and not entirely inaccurately) be presented as support for indigenous African demands. It likewise tied in closely with new Western approaches to conflict resolution: whereas previously, external patrons had supported 'their' African client states against 'rebels' who characteristically gained support from neighbouring governments backed by rival patrons, within the classic logic of bipolar politics, now the former rebels were regarded as legitimate actors, who were to be incorporated into national political structures that were established as the result of roundtable negotiations, and validated by multiparty elections. The 'good governance' leg of the troika started with respect for basic human rights, and extended to transparency, accountability, the eradication of corruption, and the establishment of a lean but efficient state machinery that was capable of maintaining basic order and essential public services.

This agenda, however, was not merely imposed on recalcitrant Africans by a dominant global hierarchy. Many Africans shared it, and indeed had good reason to. They, far more than Westerners, had been the principal victims of bad governance: one of the most invidious features of quasi-statehood had been the implicit acceptance that African rulers – however brutal and corrupt they may have been, or however they had gained power – 'represented' the people whom they sought to control; and once those people were given the chance to express their own opinions, they frequently demonstrated how false this assumption was. Though some of the indigenous NGOs formed as part of the new agenda could be characterised as 'rentier NGOs', which were established in order to capture the rents made available by external aid programmes under the guise of creating an indigenous 'civil society', others reflected genuine aspirations, and were often staffed by individuals of enormous courage and dedication. Public opinion surveys confirmed that multi-party democracy was overwhelmingly the most favoured political system (see Bratton *et al.*, 2001). A plausible case could be made that 'good governance' was both favoured by most Africans, and could lead to a significant increase in constraints on government in much of the continent.

Even many African governments were co-opted into these programmes. Indeed, given the difficult balancing act that they had to maintain between domestic and international pressures, and their common dependence on external aid, African rulers of necessity became extremely adept at appropriating donor agendas, while from the donor viewpoint, it was equally important to recruit African 'partners', and to present their governance initiatives as coming from 'Africans themselves'. Favoured regimes, amongst which those of Ghana and Uganda attained a special status, could gain considerable additional funding and diplomatic support, together with the turning of a benevolent blind eye towards deficiencies in their own governance, by adopting the appropriate postures. Even when elected opposition leaders sought – as happened in Zambia and Malawi – to limit their own subordination to the pressures that had brought them to power, their capacity to do so was limited.

This chapter, accordingly, does not suggest that the 'good governance' agenda was entirely wrong, misconceived, or unsuccessful. Any claim that external powers had no right to intervene in the internal affairs of sovereign African states was belied by the heavy dependence that these states in any case had on the international order, and by the ways in which this dependence had operated during the Cold War period, when external powers had not only tacitly supported dictatorships of the most brutal kind, but had supplied them with the weaponry and other resources needed for them to stay in power. If it had been acceptable for Western powers to support dictatorship, it was difficult to argue that it was unacceptable for them to support democracy, even when this involved abandoning the very leaders whom they had previously upheld. Equally, the same basic formula that was applied in Africa had achieved significant successes in much of the rest of the world, and it was at least plausible to suppose that it could do something to ameliorate the generally dismal condition to which two or three decades of misgovernment had reduced many Africans. Nor do I accept arguments, generally put forward for the most transparently self-interested reasons, that Africans are in some way unsuited to democracy, and must be kept, for their own good, under some tutelary autocracy. Furthermore the new agenda, especially when it could be implemented in favourable circumstances, and chimed with the aspirations of significant sections of the indigenous populations, did indeed help to bring about improvements in the quality of government in quite a number of African states. Whatever the inadequacies of the crude indicators of 'freedom' produced by external monitoring organisations (see Freedom House, annual), the overall shift since about 1990 is striking, unidirectional, and corresponds to real changes on the ground.

Sites of resistance

This agenda, regardless of the arguments that could be made in its favour, could not be expected to achieve universal acceptance and unproblematic implementation. At numerous points, it encountered not only explicit resistance, but more importantly a series of diverse *resistances*. Given the hegemonic status of the proponents of the governance agenda, it was in any event always likely that its opponents would resort to the 'weapons of the weak' (Scott, 1985), and seek to subvert it through covert action, obstruction, and non-compliance, behind a façade of acceptance. Many of the obstacles, however, were even less explicit than this, and could best be characterised as resembling the resistance on an electrical circuit, that steadily saps the ability of the current to deliver anything close to the original charge at the far end of the wire. Nor were these resistances exclusively the result of African opposition to, or incompatibility with, demands made on the continent from outside; compliance was also undermined by the very mechanisms through which Africa had been incorporated into the modern global system. The discussion of resistances is therefore most conveniently divided into three main sites, deriving first from explicit forms of opposition, second from the nature of the encounter between statehood and indigenous social structures, and finally from the contradictions of globalisation itself.

Explicit resistance and the claim to sovereignty

Overt resistance to the governance agenda in Africa largely derived, unsurprisingly, from those actors who had most benefited from the alternative governance project which it sought to displace. In just the same way that Portugal and the *apartheid* regime in South Africa continued to cling to forms of legitimisation derived from the colonial project, long after this had given way in the global system as a whole to new norms of self-determination and African independence, so rulers threatened by the new agenda clung to what had by that time become the outmoded norms of sovereignty. These norms had provided a convenient formula that chimed in both with the aspirations of African successor elites, and with the formal structure of the international system that they were joining (see Clapham, 1999). The rules of 'sovereignty' were enormously supportive to African rulers, allowing them privileged access to the international system on the one hand, coupled with complete freedom of action in the domestic political arena on the other. The new governance agenda threatened both their monopoly of external linkages, and their control over the internal arena, and it was perfectly understandable that they should resist it. In addition, the idea of sovereignty was much more broadly internalised by African elites, for whom it constituted an essential defence against external pressure. Though they could readily identify misgovernment inside their own countries, any 'attack' by either Western states or intergovernmental organisations on the autonomy of African rulers was almost automatically conceptualised in terms of the fundamental cleavage between 'Africa' on the one hand, and an outside world that was conceived as hostile and dominating on the other.

The 'first generation' resistance of entrenched autocratic rulers to the new norms of governance was for the most part soon overcome. Even President-for-Life Kamuzu Banda of Malawi was pressured into accepting multi-party elections, which he then – to his astonishment – lost, while President Mobutu Sese Seko of Zaire was overthrown in 1997 by an ostensibly internal insurgency that was tacitly or explicitly supported by the great majority of his neighbours. Of the dinosaurs, as they came to be known, by the year 2000 only Daniel arap Moi of Kenya and Robert Mugabe of Zimbabwe remained. Moi maintained himself until the end of 2002 by sharp political manoeuvring against a divided opposition, while Mugabe – who until the South African transition of the early 1990s had been protected by the international community's desperate need to present Zimbabwe as a 'success story' – found himself increasingly embattled. Across much of Africa, at least reasonably fair elections took place, and even though some of the newly elected leaders attempted to entrench their own continued tenure of power behind the barrier of sovereignty, their capacity to do so was limited.

It nonetheless proved extremely difficult to create an African continental or subcontinental consensus behind the norms of good governance. Unlike, for instance, Latin America or central Europe, where civil society campaigners were able to create extremely effective cross-national linkages in support of regional political reform, African pro-democracy activists remained largely immured within their own domestic political systems.[2] Even though insurgent movements forged multiple connections across state frontiers, enhanced by their need for base areas and their dependence on covert support from neighbouring states, I know of no case in which opposition political parties or civil society organisations established equivalent relationships. In part, this reflected the very different physical environments in which these different actors operated: guerrilla movements developed in the ill-controlled borderlands between zones of state government, and mobilised the frontier as a political resource; democratic political parties and professional organisations, on the other hand, were geared to the very different politics of cities, and especially of the capital city. But to a large extent, too, it resulted from established norms of 'non-intervention' in the internal affairs of other states, which retained their resonance in some forms of politics, even after they had lost it in others.

At the intergovernmental level, the problems were still greater. Any African support for governance projects necessarily had to operate at the subcontinental or regional level, since a continent of over 50 states was simply too large and diverse to provide any effective reference group. Africa is indeed diplomatically divided into regional groupings – North, West, Central, Eastern, and Southern – within the Organisation of African Unity, several of which have further internal clusters of closely associated states. Of these, however, only West Africa (through the Economic Community of West African States (ECOWAS)), and Southern Africa (through the Southern African Development Community (SADC)) possessed regional organisations with any pretension to promote common standards of governance for member states; and in each of these peer pressure was undermined by internal divisions, and the reluctance of other states to accept the leadership of the respective would-be regional hegemons, Nigeria and South Africa. As a result, pressure for governance reform remained enmired in the global politics of North–South relations.

Even when African states were formally incorporated into North–South alliances that ostensibly sought to promote the governance agenda, there were inevitable tensions between African objectives, geared largely to gaining access to financial and other resources, and Western ones, geared largely to control. These were enough, for example, to undermine ambitious proposals such as the African Crisis Response Initiative, which was intended to provide Western (and especially United States) backing for African peacekeeping forces which would help to maintain order in the continent, thus obviating the need for direct and politically unsustainable interventions by Western forces (see Omach, 2000). The New Partnership for Africa's Development (NEPAD), a plan developed especially by President Mbeki in South Africa and Prime Minister Blair in the United Kingdom, was beset by similar constraints. Resting on an exchange, in which the African partners would guarantee the achievement of good governance in the continent, while the Western ones would provide development funds, it effectively foundered on the failure of the SADC to provide more than token efforts to address the situation in Zimbabwe – a classic case of bad governance if ever there was one.

The flawed bases of domestic statehood

Even if there had been a reasonably coherent constituency dedicated to securing 'good governance' in Africa, however, it was by no means clear that this could actually be constructed on the foundations provided by African states. The global governance agenda largely took it for granted that the postulated convergence of domestic political stability, democracy, governmental effectiveness, and fidelity to global norms could be achieved by the application of a broadly standard set of reforms. In some cases, as already noted, such reforms did help to promote significant improvement in standards of governance, marked in particular by peaceful transfers of power from outgoing regimes to incoming ones after 'free and fair' elections. It may sometimes even be possible to discern underlying changes in social attitudes, of the kind that have underpinned democratisation elsewhere (see Bratton *et al.*, 2001; Vengross and Magala, 2001). Over much of the continent, however, the 'broadcasting of power' in the form required for effective statehood is extremely problematical (see Herbst, 2000), and raises issues for the sustainability of statehood that go well beyond the impact of particular policies or institutional arrangements.

At the heart of the problem lies the difficulty of creating effective political structures in areas with very sparse populations, and correspondingly weak economic and transport infrastructures. Simply extracting from the economy the resources needed to run an effective state – and states are expensive organisations to run – is beyond the capacity of many African governments; indeed, the attempt to extract a level of resources greater than the economy could bear was a significant contributor to African economic decline. Beyond that, moreover, one can plausibly argue that societies inhabiting areas that lack any indigenous tradition of statehood must of necessity develop their own alternative mechanisms for ensuring security and social control, and that these in turn may be deeply inimical to the social values that underlie states of any kind, let alone those subject to the demands of modern Western conceptions of good governance. Somali social values, to take one extreme example, are admirably adapted to the demands of survival in a harsh physical environment, where nomadic pastoralism provides the most effective mechanism for exploiting the very limited available resources; the collapse of the Somali state equally demonstrates how ill-suited these values are to the conceptions of hierarchy and obedience, let alone those of Weberian bureaucracy, that a 'modern' state requires. One characteristic mechanism for the maintenance of social order in the absence of states, replicated in varying degrees through much of the continent, is the very high value placed on the mutual obligations of kinship – obligations which run sharply counter to the assumptions of autonomy and neutrality that underlie the conception of statehood advanced by the good governance agenda. Another, still more controversial, consists in the forms of spiritual control that are commonly (though simplistically) lumped together under the heading of 'witchcraft'. Though this can indeed be used to maintain authority – and a great many African leaders have sought to associate themselves with occult forces – it is not a kind of authority that lends itself to the limitations on power associated with the governance agenda, let alone with democracy and human rights (see Ellis, 1999). States, in short, are not universal institutional contrivances that can be imposed on (or imported into) any human society, and made to work with equal effectiveness. They are, rather, the product of particular social and economic circumstances and historical epochs, and can disappear almost as readily as they can be created (see Tilly, 1990; Herbst, 2000). Given that in much of Africa, the state itself was an organisational form exclusively derived from the imposition of an external colonialism (even though there are also parts of the continent in which statehood did have a historical resonance), there is no *a priori* reason to expect it to survive, once the specific historical conditions that created and maintained it have disappeared.

In the clearest cases of state breakdown in Africa, collapse has been triggered by the state-subverting actions of the state's leaders themselves. Individuals such as Siyad Barre in Somalia, Samuel Doe in Liberia, and Siaka Stevens and his successors in Sierra Leone, set about undermining the institutional basis, such as it was, that the state required. Robert Mugabe in Zimbabwe has engaged in a very similar exercise, within a state that, at the outset, had one of the most effective institutional structures in Africa. Given that leaders may normally be expected to sustain the institutions that provide their own source of power, this paradox points to the dilemmas of survival in weak states (see Reno, 1998). One element in the problem is simply financial: when resources are extremely restricted, and leaders need to assure their survival by the discretionary allocation of benefits to individuals whose support they need, they are under a strong incentive to restrict payments for state services, such as education and health services, which confer no immediate political benefits on the ruler; these cuts fall most heavily on outlying and rural areas, which are in the worst position to bring direct political pressures on the regime, and in the process rot the state's administrative capabilities, and destroy its legitimacy. Another element is that state institutions that operate according to the rational–legal logic of a Weberian democracy, as required by the dictates of 'good governance', or political institutions that require regular multi-party elections, constitute a threat to the ruler himself. Siaka Stevens secured the murder of a governor of the national bank who protested at his abuse of the basic principles of sound financial management; Siyad Barre subverted an army that might otherwise have ousted him from power; Robert Mugabe was prepared to destroy the Zimbabwean economy, and undermine its judiciary, in order to retain power in an election that he had no chance of winning by legitimate means.

African states must also contend with the problems created by the extraordinarily arbitrary nature of the partition imposed by external conquest. African state territories generally correspond to no social or geographical logic, but instead often split indigenous societies apart, while simultaneously lumping very different peoples together into the same political unit. Their frontiers are often quite ridiculous.[3] One result is that virtually all of the larger African states, such as Angola, DR Congo, Ethiopia, Nigeria, and Sudan, have suffered from major problems in creating any sense of national identity that could provide a social and moral base for good governance. In Europe, it has been considered perfectly normal to unite or divide political units in such a way as to fit most of the members of particular 'nations' into a single state, while dividing them off from their neighbours, as happened, for example, in nineteenth-century Germany and Italy, post-First World War central Europe, and the former Soviet Union after 1991: in all of these cases, the creation of states based on popular consent was deemed, without serious argument, to entail the redrawing of their boundaries. There has however been no equivalent project for the reterritoralisation of Africa; and though it could certainly be doubted whether this would overcome many of the basic problems of African statehood, there are certainly cases where it would have been beneficial, and where the possibility of creating more effective and accountable states has been closed off by the continental taboo on territorial change.

The ambivalent impact of globalisation

Without a doubt, the formal project of global governance favours the maintenance of states, provided at least that these can meet the minimal conditions that it lays down, and Western governments and international organisations have been deeply concerned about the implications of state decay. Without much question, too, the impact of the outside world on modern Africa, from the colonial era through to the present day, has overall had the result of creating and strengthening states. Nor is there any plausible case that Western states are seeking to subvert or destroy African states, since these states remain central to their own objectives in Africa, both for averting the 'threats' that Africa is regarded as presenting, and for achieving such objectives as they have within the continent itself. Access to raw materials, for example, is at the very least made vastly cheaper and easier by the existence of a structure of political order; and 'capacity building', in one form or other, remains a central objective of aid programmes. The impact of the modern global order on Africa is nonetheless thoroughly ambivalent, and there are significant ways in which this impact serves to undermine the very project of statehood that its principal actors seek to uphold.

For a start, although Africa forms an integral part of the modern global system, it has been incorporated into that system on terms so dependent and subordinate as to make it extremely difficult for African states and societies to reap the benefits that global liberalism in principle has to offer. This in turn has a negative impact on those states themselves. Their revenues, which are essential to their survival, derive very heavily from international trade, which is sustained by exports that retain an almost unchanged dependence on primary products, which are first subject to high fluctuations in export prices, and second affected by the long-term decline in the prices of primary products, relative to other visible and invisible trade. Though management failures within African states are certainly an important element in the problem, the poor economic performance of African states undermines their capacity to provide the public goods needed to sustain their legitimacy, and makes them overly dependent on external aid. The resulting political conditionalities are certainly intended by the donors to create the prerequisites for effective governance, and on quite a number of occasions have certainly done so; but they require a shift in the whole basis of government, from neopatrimonialism to Western-style accountability, which is virtually impossible to manage in the face of a recalcitrant leadership.

But the global economy also subverts African states in more insidious ways, through the escape of traded commodities from state control. At its simplest, smuggling across virtually unpoliceable frontiers has been endemic in Africa for a very long time, as producers take advantage of more favourable prices on the other side of the border, or importers seek to evade the high tariffs on manufactured goods. However, these informal trade routes become much more dangerous when they are associated with rival political forces that seek to challenge state control. The clearest example is that of smuggled diamonds, which have recently (as 'blood diamonds') become the subject of attempts at international control, that have fuelled civil wars especially in Angola and Sierra Leone. Both the long-lasting UNITA insurgency in Angola, and the operations of the Revolutionary United Front (RUF) in Sierra Leone, have been funded to a large extent through diamonds, which – as easily transportable and exceptionally high value commodities – provide the perfect source of funding (see Global Witness, 2003). Charles Taylor in Liberia managed to fund his NPFL insurgency, before taking over as Liberia's elected president after the July 1997 elections, through the export of such bulky items as tropical timber, which was shipped out through Côte d'Ivoire. Though narcotics exports have not reached the levels found in Colombia and other parts of Latin America, their transshipment (especially through DR Congo and Nigeria) appears to have grown rapidly. Even famine relief can become a source of support for insurgencies, most evidently in the Horn, while several armed opposition movements – notably the EPLF in Eritrea prior to 1991, and the RPF in Rwanda before 1994 – have systematically taxed the incomes of their supporters in the diaspora. In short, the international economy only sustains African statehood, for so long as African states are capable of maintaining control over transactions into and out of Africa; and even though external economic actors would generally (outside the drugs trade) prefer to deal with 'legitimate' markets and suppliers under the control of states, if only because these are normally much more reliable than underhand deals mediated through guerrillas or dubious middle-men, they are quite prepared to engage in whatever deals are needed to get hold of essential supplies: coltan, which is an essential ingredient in the manufacture of mobile telephones, has for example been smuggled out of opposition-controlled areas of eastern DR Congo, through the states, principally Rwanda and Uganda, that support the movements that control the zones of production (see Global Witness, 2002). The engagement with the international economy that provided the impetus for the imposition of colonial state systems on Africa in the first place, can equally provide the means to undermine the states that it established.

The very institutions that serve as the agencies for global governance themselves subvert the autonomy and accountability that states must acquire, if they are to achieve the effectiveness and legitimacy that the governance agenda requires. States whose actions are all too clearly identifiable as the products of external pressure can scarcely be account-able to their own populations in any very meaningful way; while the attempt to establish accountability by encouraging 'ownership' by African governments of the reform programmes urged on them by exter-nal donors is inherently contradictory. This has been the basic problem underlying the NEPAD initiative. Non-governmental organisations not only promote their own agendas, and channel resources into recipient countries for programmes that the state would not otherwise be able to (and might well not wish to) put into effect, but very often act as substi-tutes for state agencies in their implementation. These problems, more-over, are not specific to Africa, or even only to areas of weak states: they are inherent in the process of globalisation itself, and resonate with problems of non-accountability and political alienation even in the core states of the developed world.

Conclusion

This chapter does not seek to contest the broad moral legitimacy of many of the principles which, in the name of 'good governance', the global donor community has sought to impose on African states. Nor does it seek to contest the desirability of an effective state system in Africa, where state collapse has generally been accompanied by appalling levels of bloodshed and human misery. The project of statehood itself, in the form in which it has been developed under the banner of global governance, likewise appears to me to be broadly legitimate – more so, certainly, than either state destruction, or a rigid adherence to principles of state 'sovereignty' that have in practice provided international cover for some thoroughly brutal dictatorships. The project of accountable statehood, moreover, is not merely an expression of external power over weak and dependent Africans, but itself promises benefits to, and enjoys support from, substantial constituencies within Africa: to take one currently topical example, it seems to me highly likely that the vast majority of Zimbabweans would prefer the forms of governance promoted by the Western-led international community in Zimbabwe, to those imposed by their own government.

I nonetheless remain deeply sceptical about the *capacity* of the project of global governance, as this has been pursued in Africa, to incorporate the whole continent into the structure of effective, stable, peaceful, democratic, rights-respecting, terrorism-controlling, ecologically sustainable and economically liberal statehood that the ideal and idealised relationship between global order and local identity requires. Not only is this project itself riven with ambivalence, but it is also peculiarly difficult to implement under the conditions that Africa provides. Given at least its partial failure – and this chapter has of necessity concentrated largely on the areas of the continent that remain most problematic, at the expense of those where an enhanced level of good governance has been achieved – much of Africa is likely to remain messy, insecure, ill-governed, and in a condition to present a 'threat' to those parts of the world that retain the greatest commitment to the project of global order.

Notes

1. Including Western Sahara, Sierra Leone, Liberia, Chad, Sudan, Ethiopia/ Eritrea, Djibouti, Somalia, Rwanda, Burundi, Congo/Zaire, Congo-Brazzaville, Angola, Mozambique, and Lesotho; the South African transition, in some respects analogous, was achieved through an internal political process.
2. This is illustrated by the strikingly different regional responses to the March 2002 elections in Zimbabwe on the one hand, and the April 2002 attempted overthrow of President Chavez in Venezuela on the other. In Zimbabwe, pressures for 'free and fair' elections came overwhelmingly from non-African actors, while the response of neighbouring African regimes was at most muted, and often obstructive; in Venezuela, regional states protested at the would-be overthrow of an elected government, while the United States (which disapproved of the Chavez regime) turned a blind eye.
3. For examples, one need only look at The Gambia, whose territory is inserted like a worm into the side of Senegal, or the area of the Democratic Republic of Congo that nearly bisects Zambia.

4
Global Governance and Conflict Prevention

Hugh Miall

Introduction

Conflict prevention is an intrinsic feature of good governance in well-ordered societies. Legitimate institutions and accepted procedures allow contests over resources, values and authority to be settled through political channels, instead of through violence. Within states, common governance can be a preventor of conflict, especially when it is linked to a sense of political community and provision of public goods. Between states, common institutions and co-operation can help to overcome the conflicts of interest and security dilemmas that are inherent in anarchical systems. Ever since the Brundtland Commission published its report (World Commission on Environment and Development, 1987), it has been argued that there is a pressing need for sound and legitimate global governance, to anticipate the conflicts of interest that are developing in a rapidly globalising system, to address poverty and to deal with global environmental change (Falk, 1995; Tickell, 1998; Pogge, 2002). Conflict prevention would be a key element in such a system.

In practice the contemporary system of global governance ameliorates some conflicts but exacerbates others. On the one hand, conflict prevention is emerging as an international norm, to which major states and international organisations give rhetorical support and limited institutional backing. On the other hand, major states frequently fuel regional tensions and democratisation can destabilise transitional societies. Some aspects of globalisation and global governance are themselves among the root causes of local conflicts.

Conflict prevention therefore encounters resistance from above and from below. From above, major states and international organisations may be unwilling to engage in prevention or may have national interests at stake in prosecuting conflicts. From below, nationalist leaders and spoilers resist because they are unwilling to compromise their objectives or because they have something to gain from prosecuting violent conflict. Both from above and from below, dissimulation is widespread, as governments and parties subscribe to international norms but fail to adhere to them in practice.

This chapter aims to elucidate the relationship between global governance and conflict prevention and to review the evidence about whether certain practices of global governance prevent or aggravate violence. In particular, it draws on quantitative research to explore the global relationships between democratisation, good governance and armed conflict. It goes on to illustrate these themes by taking central and eastern Europe as a site where conflict prevention has been both accepted and resisted. It will be argued that the mixed experience with structural and operational conflict prevention to date illustrates the tension between normative conceptions of 'genuine' global governance and the 'distorted' form of global governance that is actually emerging (Held and McGrew, 2002: 13–14).

Conflict prevention as a site of global governance

Conflict prevention is a rather recent arrival as an international norm.[1] The idea of deliberately intervening in conflicts at an early stage was promoted by early peace researchers like Quincy Wright and Kenneth Boulding, who promoted the idea of 'social data stations' to collect indicators of 'social temperature and pressure', to 'predict cold or warm fronts'. Rupesinghe (1998), Lund (1996) and others (Miall, 1992) argued that early intervention in conflicts could be more effective and less costly than efforts at conflict resolution after armed conflict have broken out. Boutros Boutros-Ghali took up the call for conflict prevention in his *Agenda for Peace* in 1992.

At about the same time the first steps towards institutionalisation took place, when the members of the Organisation for Security and Cooperation in Europe ((OSCE), then the CSCE) undertook to intervene in an early stage in potential conflicts, and set-up the institution of the High Commission on National Minorities. By 2001, the UN, the EU, the G8 and the majority of international regional organisations (such as the OAU, the OAS, ASEAN) had committed themselves to conflict prevention, and many had set-up some form of conflict prevention machinery (Lund, 2002). Major states followed suit, although the institutional investment often lagged behind the rhetoric. For example, the British Government set up a Global Conflict Prevention Fund, administered by the Foreign Office, the development ministry DFID and the Ministry of Defence, with a wide-ranging brief covering peace-keeping, peace-building, security sector reform, light arms and a wide range of crisis regions. The budget was £60 million, of which half was for existing commitments. Although institutional and financial commitment remained slight, conflict prevention made rapid progress as an international norm.

Since global governance is both emergent and contested, it is not surprising that there are different views of the role of conflict prevention within it. Three in particular can be distinguished.

The realist view is that states are still, in the last analysis, the crucial actors. They will act on the basis of their interests whatever the international constraints. Only the threat or use of force will forestall violence, and early intervention may simply trigger violence rather than contain it (Stedman, 1995). According to this view, which is quite widely held in the foreign ministries of the major states, conflict prevention in particular and global governance in general are more expectation than reality. Conflict prevention policies may be advanced when they meet the interests of the major powers, but sacrificed when they contradict them.

Another view, held by structuralists and post-structuralists, argues that conflict prevention is part of an overall strategy of Northern security and development policy, and reflects the policy of excluding and containing the societies of the South. Conflict prevention is one of the nodes of the emerging 'cross-cutting governance networks involving state and non-state actors from the supranational to the local level'. Such networks bring together 'state and non-state, military–civilian and public–private actors' in pursuit of the aim of global stability (Duffield, 2001: 8–12). Conflict prevention activities by non-governmental organisations (NGOs) and liberal wars waged by the major powers are two sides of the same coin. Paradoxically, they tend to sustain the very patterns of conflict and subjugation they are ostensibly concerned to transform.

A third view, that of its advocates, is that conflict prevention is a norm that deserves a higher priority. But its implementation needs to be improved (Lund, 1995, 2002). Conflict prevention may have positive or negative impacts, depending on the measures and the context. It can only be effective if it works with the grain of existing institutions and cultures. Governance can be a preventor of conflict, but only if it gains legitimacy and offers public goods.

There is some truth in all three views. The extent to which they elucidate the nature of global governance, conflict prevention and resistance will be examined in the analysis that follows. There is no doubt that a form of global governance is developing rapidly, driven by radical social, economic and political changes affecting the entire world system (Castells, 1997). There is also little doubt that western traditions of conflict resolution are being prioritised in this process. Whether they are imposed from outside, or resisted, or adapted to local circumstances and complemented by local traditions, will shape whether conflict prevention becomes simply another tool of western hegemony or a more widely shared ethos.

The nature of conflict, as well as governance, is changing under the impact of globalisation. There has been an evolution from 'protracted social conflicts', internal conflicts over ethnicity and government (Azar, 1990), to 'international social conflicts', protracted social conflicts that spill over into regional conflict complexes and attract international intervention (Ramsbotham and Woodhouse, 1996). Resistance to major power interventions may now be engendering a new generation of 'global local conflicts' – conflicts fuelled at local sites by resistance to global trends and spilling over into attacks on global targets.

Local and regional conflicts are, more than ever, enmeshed in global conflict formations. So it is difficult to address local sources of conflict without taking account of wider sources of conflict in the global order. Conflict prevention can be interpreted either as a practice of contemporary global governance or as a norm about how global governance should be practised. The tension between these two interpretations underlies the difference of views about what the practice of conflict prevention is now and how it relates to global governance.

The developing practice of conflict prevention

Preventive diplomacy already had a long pedigree before the end of the Cold War. The United Nations Security Council was empowered to recommend procedures or terms for settling inter-state conflicts, and the Secretary General sent special representatives to trouble-shoot potential crises, in some cases with good effect. A significant tradition of non-governmental mediation also developed. But the central antagonism of the Cold War limited progress.

The ending of the Cold War gave a spur to the idea that violent conflict could be prevented by co-operative security measures, and that Europeans could manage their conflicts together and inhabit 'a Single Home'. With the adoption of CSCE principles, it became possible for states to begin to hold each other to account over their internal practices in human rights. There thus developed, quite rapidly, the institutions of a commissioner for minority rights, long-duration missions, a conflict prevention centre and an active policy of early warning and preventive diplomacy. NGOs which had been pressing for conflict prevention as a form of early conflict resolution now found common cause with states which supported innovation in the CSCE. The major powers, however, remained quite cautious. The United States and Britain, for example, initially opposed the Dutch proposal for the creation of a High Commissioner for National Minorities at the Helsinki Summit of 1992.[2] At this stage, conflict prevention was not perceived to be a particularly important strategic interest of the North.

A distinction developed in the literature between 'light', or 'operational' conflict prevention, oriented to averting the breakout of violence, and 'deep' or 'structural' conflict prevention, oriented to avoid situations developing which might have the potential for violence (Carnegie Commission, Miall *et al.*, 1999: 97). 'Light' prevention involves early warning and fact-finding, to anticipate the likely sites of potential conflict and the ways in which escalation might be triggered (Davies and Gurr, 1998). It also involves diplomatic pressure, mediation, long-term missions on the ground and interventions by national, international and non-state third parties.

'Deep' conflict prevention is usually taken to involve democratisation, the introduction of human rights, improvement of governance, the establishment of effective systems of justice and administration, citizens' rights, a free media, civil society and economic and social entitlements that meet basic human needs. There are good grounds for arguing that, in principle, these measures should tend to prevent conflict. For example, effective democracies based on real citizen rights should enable potential conflicts to be addressed through institutionally agreed procedures (Wallensteen, 2002: 140–4).

However, when these measures are introduced from outside, they can be intrusive and can constitute, as Duffield remarks, a form of social engineering. Connie Peck (1998: 45) characterises the 'building blocks of sustainable peace and security' as 'well-functioning local, state, regional and international systems of governance, which are responsive to human needs'. To introduce them from outside does indeed constitute global governance.

If these institutions are introduced without real substance or local commitment, they may exacerbate conflict rather than prevent it. Similarly when societies rapidly open their markets without either a solid domestic economic base or social protection for their citizens, economic and social dislocation is likely. A number of major armed conflicts, in central and eastern Europe, Africa and elsewhere can be considered to be 'wars over liberalisation' as much as internal or ethnic conflicts (Lund, 2002).

This chapter analyses the global impact of two types of 'deep' conflict prevention – democratisation and good governance. It also examines 'light' conflict prevention in the context of central and eastern Europe.

Democratisation and the incidence of armed conflicts

We can get some idea of the success of and resistance to 'deep conflict prevention' by examining the relationship between democratisation and good governance and the incidence of armed conflicts. If, in general, democratisation does tend to prevent armed conflicts, then democratic governance is an appropriate norm for a normative global governance project. If, on the other hand, democratisation or resistance to democratisation triggers armed conflicts, the promotion of democratic governance is inconsistent with conflict prevention, at least in the short term.

The main quantitative studies of violent conflict suggest that the amount of armed conflict underway in the world has fallen since the end of the Cold War (Gleditsch, 2001; Wallensteen and Sollenberg, 2001). There is, however, some evidence of a slight upward turn again at the end of the 1990s.

Alongside this decline in the number of armed conflicts, there has been a significant increase in the number of democracies. According to the work of Gurr (2001), the number of democracies overtook the number of autocracies just before 1990. Since then the number of autocracies has fallen sharply, while the number of democracies and transitional regimes has increased.

Is there an association between the increase in the number of democracies and the decline in armed conflicts? Gurr (2000; Gurr and Khosla, 2002) makes this claim, but the evidence is mixed.[3] We can get some purchase on it by examining the conflicts which have been ended or begun since 1989. The states in which armed conflicts were terminated in the period 1988–2000 by peace agreements according to the Uppsala data (Gleditsch *et al.*, 2002) are listed by Wallensteen (2002: 80). Two main groups of cases have been associated with a change of polity. First of all, in conflicts like the Central American trio (Nicaragua, Guatemala, El Salvador), elections and democratic politics have been established or re-established following peace agreements. Here war endings led to democratisation, and the establishment of democratic institutions was a significant mechanism for channelling conflict into political institutions. In others a change of polity, from communist to post-communist, has been associated with the outbreak of wars (in former Yugoslavia and the former Soviet Union). In the African cases there has sometimes been a return to multi-party elections following peace agreements. But as Christopher Clapham notes in his chapter, outwardly democratic institutions in African countries do not necessarily imply substantive democratic governance.

According to the democratic peace proposition, an expanding zone of democracy should prevent conflict between states that are democracies. However, the democratic peace proposition does not show that democracy is a preventor of interstate war. Democracies fight just as many wars as other types of polity. Major powers that are democracies tend to fight more wars than minor powers that are autocracies. The significant finding is that, with few exceptions, democracies have not fought other democracies. They tend to fight more wars against autocracies than do other autocracies. Raknerud and Hegre (1997) show that the tendency of democracies to join in coalition wars against autocracies explains the apparent discrepancy between their abstinence from war with democracies and their propensity to fight wars in general.

An important question is whether as democratisation progresses, new democracies will also be peaceful, or whether the inter-democratic peace will break down if states with serious conflicts between them become democracies. Doyle (1986) and Russett (1993) argue that democratisation will extend the area of inter-democratic peace. Ward and Gleditsch (1998) argue that the transition period has unsettling effects. The recent experience with the eastern enlargement of the EU has had mixed consequences but does not dis-confirm the inter-democratic peace proposition. In some cases it has produced political conflicts which have not escalated into armed conflict (e.g. Hungary–Slovakia, Hungary–Romania). In others a clash between democratisation and autocracy has led to war (former Yugoslavia). The NATO war against Yugoslavia became a classic example of a liberal inter-state war, fought between a large coalition of democracies and a lone autocracy. Contested democratisation appears likely to increase the risk of armed conflicts between democratic states and autocracies, without necessarily threatening the inter-democratic peace.

The evidence for a domestic democratic peace is also significant, though less strong than for the inter-state democratic peace. Democratic states have not avoided civil wars. But settled democracies have been less prone to them than other regime types. Stable autocracies also experience relatively few civil wars. It is semi-democracies and transitional regimes that have the highest incidence (Hegre *et al.*, 2001). This is partly because such polities tend to be unstable, and political instability and regime change clearly increase the probability of civil war. But even allowing for this effect, a higher level of civil war is found in 'semi-democracies'.

The implication of this finding is that democratisation will tend to result in a higher level of internal conflict and civil war. Therefore an expanding area of democracy is likely to produce internal wars on its periphery. In the longer term, however, if the new democracies become settled, their internal conflicts will tend to settle down.

In multi-ethnic societies, democratisation and quasi-democratisation can readily stimulate inter-ethnic conflict. This was common in eastern Europe, where the majority nations tended to claim their own identity for the state, and in Africa, where control of the state is often the prize for the dominant ethnic group. Gurr's studies on conflicts involving minorities indicate that settled democracy tends to inhibit ethnic rebellion, but democratic transitions may trigger them. He finds a low incidence of ethno-national protest and rebellions between 1986 and 1998 among old democracies (Gurr, 2000: 44–5). In new democracies (established after 1980 without relapsing into autocracy) there is a tendency to greater discrimination against minorities, and greater opportunity for resistance. Both factors encourage a substantial increase in ethnopolitical protest, but this protest can sometimes be channelled into political institutions (Gurr, 2000: 154). New ethnic rebellions occurred in a number of new democracies (e.g. Georgia, Moldova) while they have been mitigated elsewhere (e.g. Nicaragua). It can be calculated from Gurr's data (2000: 155) that in 1985–98, 47 per cent of the ethnopolitical groups in democracies (44 per cent in old democracies, 50 per cent in new democracies) had neither protests nor rebellions in 1985–98, compared with 40 per cent of the groups in transitional regimes and 30 per cent in autocracies.[4]

The incidence of internal conflict in different types of regimes since 1989 can be gauged by using the Uppsala/PRIO dataset on armed conflicts (Gleditsch, 2001) and the Polity database on regime types (Jaggers and Gurr, 1995). Taking the 116 countries which have politically significant minorities, as listed by Gurr (2000: 289–94), and the data on minor, intermediate and major armed conflicts from the Uppsala/PRIO dataset, it is possible to examine the association of democratisation with armed conflict at the global level.

Table 4.1 shows that old democracies are much more likely to avoid internal conflicts and new democracies, although they have more internal conflicts than old democracies, are less prone to major conflicts than transitional regimes or autocracies. Eleven of the 32 transitional regimes experienced major wars some time during the decade. But autocracies were even more prone to internal warfare during this period, with 14 of the 26 autocracies experiencing major conflicts. Some of these conflicts are continuations of wars that predate the end of the Cold War. Nevertheless, there is an indication here that globalisation and the post Cold War pressure for democratisation has created a wave of turbulence, which extends to non-democratic regimes. However, once societies have consolidated democratic institutions, they tend to be less prone to internal armed conflict.

In many cases, the issue of what kind of democracy is to be established may be as important as whether a polity is democratic, especially if the society is multi-ethnic. Democratic institutions are sometimes a matter more of form than of substance, as in some central and eastern European countries (Schöpflin, 1994) and many African countries (Clapham, 1999). Appropriate political institutions are particularly important in multi-ethnic societies. Marta Reynal-Querol reports a study

Table 4.1　Armed conflicts by regime type, 1989–99

Regime type	None	Minor	Intermediate	War	Total
Old democracies	19	2	2	2	25
New democracies	24	4	1	4	33
Transitional regimes	16	3	2	11	32
Autocracies	10	0	2	14	26
Total	69	9	7	31	116

Note: Old democracies are countries whose democratic political institutions were established before 1980 and that had not reverted to autocratic rule. New democracies are countries whose democratic institutions were established between 1980 and 1994 and that had not reverted to autocratic rule since 1980. Transitional regimes are countries with a mix of democratic and autocratic features plus countries that made a transition to democracy after the 1970s that subsequently failed. Autocracies are countries with autocratic institutions that did not attempt democratic transitions. Armed conflicts are counted as contested incompatibilities involving the use of armed force and at least 25 battle-related deaths, with one of the parties being a government. Each country is coded by the largest internal armed conflict that occurred between 1989 and 1999. Minor armed conflicts are those with at least 25 battle-related deaths per year and fewer than 1000 battle-related deaths in the course of the conflict. Intermediate armed conflicts are those with at least 25 deaths per year and an accumulated total of at least 1000 battle-related deaths, but fewer than 1000 in any given year. Wars are armed conflicts with at least 1000 battle-related deaths per year.

of 138 countries between 1960 and 1995, in which she finds no cases of ethnic civil war where a proportional system is in place (Reynal-Querol, 2001: 22).

To conclude, democratic governance has tended to be a structural preventor of conflict over the long term, but the democratisation process has been a short-term contributor to armed conflicts. Imposed or dissimulated democratisation may do little to avert violent conflicts, but democratic institutions that develop strong social roots do appear to have a preventive effect.

Good governance

Edward Azar (1990) developed an influential theory of conflict, modelled on the experience of his home country, Lebanon. He saw the internal wars prevailing since the 1970s as constituted by interrelated failures of domestic governance, distorted development, militarised politics and the denial of human needs. Armed conflict in turn degrades governance, deforms institutions and destroys development. Hence, a protracted cycle of social conflict can set in, leading sometimes to complete state failure.

Conversely, a more benign cycle could prevent conflict through good governance, development, civil politics and helpful external policies. Since the association of armed conflict with failures of governance and state failure is well-established, I have investigated the evidence for the contrary proposition, that good governance is a factor that tends to prevents internal conflict. Cross-national indicators of the quality of governance have recently become available. For example, Kaufman *et al.* (1999) collected comparative data for six concepts related to good governance: voice and accountability, political stability, government effectiveness, regulatory burden, rule of law and control of corruption. Using these indicators with Gurr's data on rebellions, in a study of 113 countries, it is possible to observe a clear association, as one would expect, between 'good governance' and prevention of violent rebellion. Table 4.2 shows the results.

Seventy per cent of the countries ranked in the top third on quality of governance indicators experienced no violence in their minority conflicts, and only 5 per cent had large-scale violent minority conflicts. Of the countries ranked in the bottom third on quality of governance, only 37 per cent experienced no violence and 29 per cent experienced large-scale violence. The figures suggest that good governance, or some characteristics associated with its measure in these studies, helps to prevent violent ethnic conflict.[5]

Table 4.2   Quality of governance and incidence of violent ethnic conflicts in 113 countries, 1995–98

	No violence	Small-scale violence	Large-scale violence
Top third of countries on governance indicators	26 (70%)	10 (27%)	2 (5%)
Middle third of countries on governance indicators	17 (45%)	16 (42%)	5 (13%)
Bottom third of countries on governance indicators	14 (37%)	12 (32%)	11 (29%)

Note: Author's calculations based on Kaufmann *et al.* (2000) and Minorities At Risk (MAR) data. The findings represent 113 countries with data available in both sources. A composite indicator of quality of governance was based on the mean of each country's ranking on six governance indicators. Countries were grouped into three equal groups on this indicator. Figures for armed conflict are derived from the 'rebellion' variable in the MAR dataset. MAR indicators were aggregated into no violent conflict, small-scale conflict (between 2 and 6 on the MAR scale, that is a local uprising to a small-scale guerrilla war) and major deadly conflicts.

Good governance, of course, needs to be distinguished from global governance. Further studies investigating particular attributes of external global governance are needed to establish whether the effects of externally imposed changes in governance are benign or malign. A more fine-grained approach is needed to examine the effectiveness of measures like elite accommodation, autonomy, federalism and electoral systems that give incentives to multi-ethnic co-operation. I therefore turn now to a case study of conflict and conflict prevention in one region, central and eastern Europe.

Conflict prevention and resistance to conflict prevention in central and eastern Europe

The transition in central and eastern Europe, from communist rule under the domination of the Soviet Union, to a post-communist society under the influence of Western political and economic forms, has triggered a wave of political conflicts. In central and eastern Europe,

Table 4.3   Central and eastern Europe: armed conflicts by regime type, 1989–99

Regime type	None	Minor	Intermediate	War	Total
Old democracies	0	0	0	0	0
New democracies	9	2	0	1	12
Transitional regimes	4	0	1	4	9
Autocracies	2	0	0	1	3
Total	15	2	1	6	24

however, the prevalence of armed conflict has been lower than elsewhere. This can be ascertained by comparing Table 4.3, which shows regime type by level of armed conflict in central and eastern Europe, with Table 4.1. Here the proportion of armed conflicts, and of wars, is somewhat less than in the global case. In central and eastern Europe, the majority of wars took place in transitional regimes.

There is no doubt that the combined impact of the collapse of communism and the intrusion of Western-style states and democratic forms had highly disruptive effects. The wars in Bosnia, Croatia, Kosovo, Trans-Dniestr, Chechenya and Abkhazia were all wars over secession and state integrity, influenced by the growth of nationalism and the quest of national groups to establish their own, Western-style states.

On the other hand, a significant number of conflicts over ethnicity or government that had the potential to become violent did not do so. They include the end of communist rule in the GDR, Czechoslovakia, and elsewhere, the lack of violent conflict in the political disputes over citizenship in Estonia, Latvia and Lithuania, the peaceful divorce between the Czech Republic and Slovakia, the non-violent conflicts over Hungarian minorities in Slovakia, Romania and Voyvodina, the absence of violent conflict involving the Greek minority in Albania and the Muslim minority in the Sanjak, the mainly peaceful development of the conflict between Albanian-speakers and Slav Macedonians in Macedonia, the largely peaceful dissolution of the Soviet Union, the lack of violent conflict between Russian-speakers and the governments of most of the Newly Independent States, other than Trans-Dniestr and the progress of the conflicts in Ajara and the Crimea.

The extent to which the non-violent development of conflicts can be attributed to deliberate conflict prevention varies. The OSCE had a significant interest in conflicts throughout this region, and was active especially in the Baltic States, Albania, FYROM, Kosovo, Croatia, Macedonia, Molodova, Romania, Hungary, Slovakia, Georgia, the Ukraine and in

Kazakhstan, Kyrgyzstan, Uzbekistan and Tajikistan. The conditionality involved in the EU's *acquis communitaire* appears to have been a significant factor in a number of central European countries. However, domestic political developments and conjunctions were also important, as some particular cases will illustrate.

Estonia

Estonia, for example, is often taken as a prime case of successful conflict prevention. The High Commissioner for National Minorities (HCNM) was active in the crisis over citizenship, and the broader influence of the OSCE and other external authorities also had an impact. The HCNM's success in defusing the crisis in the northeast in 1993 may have prevented a possible outbreak of violence. However, although he succeeded in securing some amendments to Estonian legislation on citizenship and language, the Estonian government resisted most of his suggestions, and the majority of the Russian-speakers in Estonia remained stateless. The fact that the conflict did not develop along more violent lines was due more to the failure of Russian-speaking parties to mobilise a vigorous opposition. This was due in part to the fragmented character of the Russian-speaking minority and in part to the inconsistent support of the kin state. Another highly significant factor was the development of the political system in Estonia, which gave incentives for cross-ethnic co-operation. When the Estonian Supreme Soviet had considered the electoral system for the introduction of multi-party elections, a disagreement developed between the communists who wanted a majoritarian system and the Popular Front of Estonia which favoured a list PR system. After some haggling, a Single Transferable Vote system had been adopted, as in the Republic of Ireland. It turned out that this system gave incentives for Estonian parties to seek support among the Russian-speakers, and one party in particular, the Centre Party, became a channel for the Russian-speakers to pursue their interests, even though it was led by Estonian politicians. Khrychikov and Miall (2002) has shown that this domestic political capacity played a vital part in the accommodation of the conflict over the long term. It can be concluded that the role of global governance in the prevention of violent conflict was limited, and that the prevention of conflict was attributable to a conjunction of external and internal circumstances. It is notable that the Estonian nationalists have continued to resist many of the HCNM's proposals, even though they are now likely to be accepted for EU membership.

Macedonia

The Macedonian case is another frequently cited case of successful conflict prevention. There is no doubt that after the dissolution of Yugoslavia, Macedonia was heavily protected by the international community. The deployment of UNPREDEP effectively placed an international guarantee on Macedonia's territorial integrity. However, for all the efforts of the OSCE, the HCNM, the UN and a host of NGOs, the Albanian community and the Slav Macedonians remained unable to overcome their differences. The crucial factor which kept them together, as in the Estonian case, was tactical political co-operation. Between 1993 and 1998 the Albanian and Slav Macedonian parties were in coalition in parliament, even though the divisions over status, education and local government came close to boiling point. After 1998, the ethnic situation grew more polarised, but a new coalition developed between the Macedonian nationalists (VMRO-DPMNE) and the more radical Albanian party (the DPA).

The situation reached a crisis with the war in Kosovo and the expulsion of the Kosovar Albanians into Macedonia. The Albanian community openly supported the KLA and NATO, while the Slav Macedonians opposed the NATO bombing. After the US bombing of the Chinese embassy in Belgrade, China vetoed the continuation of UNPREDEP. Sharp tensions arose between NATO and the Macedonian government, especially over the Macedonian treatment of the Kosovo refugees. These were not helped by the incident in which a Macedonian minister was killed by a NATO vehicle. It was the hospitality of the Albanians in Albania to their kinfolk, and the end of the bombing campaign which allowed the Kosovar Albanians to return, which eased the crisis. Even when KLA forces re-entered Macedonia from Kosovo, a development that the NATO forces in Kosovo were unable to prevent, Macedonia still avoided outright conflict. Preventive diplomacy worked as well as it could, but it was subject to vagaries over time, influenced by differences among the major states and affected by the shifting priorities of the international community.

Albania

Albania was a less successful story. Here the international community was deeply engaged in supporting Albania's government, yet the state came close to collapse in early 1997. Four main dimensions of conflict could be identified in the early 1990s (Miall, 1997). The most important was the polarisation between the two main parties, the Democratic Party, led by President Berisha, and the Socialist Party, whose leader Berisha had imprisoned. Another was the economic dislocation caused by the abrupt transition to an unregulated free market from Hoxha's system of agricultural collectives and central planning. Rapid growth of ghettos around Albanian towns, as the landless peasantry fled the countryside, was a clear threat to public order. A further potential source of conflict was the diversity of religious and regional identity groups. A fourth was the contested status of the small Greek minority in the south.

As a backward, impoverished country close to the heart of Europe, Albania at first received priority treatment from the institutions of global governance. Financial support flowed in for the new state, which seemed to be making a remarkable success of its economic transition following the privatisation of the land. Small teams of American advisers could be found installed at the heart of several ministries, including the Ministry of Justice. President Berisha's centre-right stance found favour from British Prime Minister Margaret Thatcher and the German Christian Democrats.

The HCNM did have considerable success with the Greek minority issue. The local Soros committee did what it could to support multi-party politics, for example, supporting conferences and services for Mayors and local government. But the major Western states were slow to realise that the leader they were backing was becoming an autocrat. When Berisha moved against the opposition and the free press after losing an important referendum in 1994, he received little criticism from important quarters. The Council of Europe took the unhappy decision to admit Albania after Berisha had sacked two judges. Only when Berisha flagrantly rigged the 1996 elections, in the context of the financial crisis caused by the collapse of the pyramid schemes, did the Western governments unite in criticism. Berisha then made his resistance clear by accusing the OSCE monitors of being 'former collaborators of the dictatorial regime of Enver Hoxha'.

The OSCE proceeded to organise a successful rescue operation, sending Franz Vranitzky, the former Austrian chancellor, to negotiate with the Albanian government and opposition. With armed civilians in control of the streets, Berisha was forced to call for armed intervention from the West. Vranitzky then secured agreement on a government of national unity and fresh elections. Italy led an *ad hoc* force to create a secure environment for humanitarian assistance. The crisis eventually eased following the defeat of Berisha in the new elections.

But large areas of Albania fell out of effective government control and the underlying problems of weak governance, polarised politics and economic deprivation remained intractably in place.

Kosovo

Kosovo is a case where the international community failed to pursue a sufficiently deeply engaged conflict prevention policy with significant vigour. Weller (2000) has analysed the missed opportunities. At the time that Milosevic swept away the autonomy and institutions of Kosovo's republican government, the Western response was to do nothing in practice. The West's policy was to promote 'autonomy plus', but this was resisted both by Milosevic who was not prepared to consider autonomy, and by the Albanians who would have nothing but independence. Faced with this impasse, Western diplomats merely repeated the 'autonomy plus' formula, and failed to explore possible ways out of the crisis with sufficient determination. For much of the time, Kosovo was subordinated to the priority of Bosnia, which required co-operation with Milosevic.

The West gave a low priority to Kosovo because the Albanian resistance was non-violent. It is a sad reflection on international policy towards conflict prevention that it is violence, and not non-violence, that wins attention. When Rugova's appeals for international support were ignored at Dayton, the founders of the KLA drew their own conclusions.

In the light of what developed later in the crisis, and the obduracy of the Serbian regime regarding Kosovo, it may seem naive to suggest that other outcomes might have been possible. Yet the conflict was not always in a state of escalation. The Serb side deliberately reduced the level of human rights abuses in 1995–96. It is during this period, before the formation of the KLA and the massacres in Drenica, where a more inventive conflict prevention policy, less wedded to a predetermined solution, might have found some scope for movement.

A number of non-governmental organisations then took up 'track-two' interventions to try to break the deadlock. For example, the Comunita Sant-Egidio and the Bertelsmann Foundation explored possible options in workshops with the Albanian leaders, and less senior Serb representatives. The former achieved an agreement on the education system, the latter explored some interpretations of self-determination that found some common ground. Others worked with the civil societies on both sides, especially student groups who were politically prominent in both Serbia and Kosovo. The Norwegian Nansen Academy supported by the Peace Research Institute at Oslo and the Richardson Institute at Lancaster University held workshops with student leaders which demonstrated that common ground could be found.

The resistance here consisted of unyielding positions on the Serbian and Albanian parties, while the international community remained locked into a favoured solution that would not work. As the crisis came to a head, conflict prevention was abandoned for threat and then coercion. The short-lived effort to introduce an OSCE monitoring force was too late to check the development of fighting between the KLA and Serb forces. When the NATO bombing began, it cut away the remaining possibilities for accommodation. First the Albanians, then the Serbs, were expelled from Kosovo. Following the war, the province has become an international protectorate. Subsequent efforts to introduce some forms of democratic governance and peace-building, administered by a variety of NGOs and international bodies, have few prospects of success while the issue of status remains unaddressed. There was little peace to build, apart from between the rival Albanian factions, for almost all the Serbs had left apart from the people of Mitrovice who needed heavy and permanent NATO protection to avoid the retribution of the Albanians.

Conclusion

The east European cases reviewed here show that commitment to democratisation and conflict prevention has not been a top priority for the agencies of global governance. Although these are accepted as norms, the major powers have been willing to abandon conflict prevention (as in Macedonia and Kosovo) when it clashed with other priorities. They have also been prepared to support politicians who have undermined the substance of democracy while sustaining its forms (as in Albania). Although this chapter has not covered case studies in the South, it casts doubt on the thesis that conflict prevention is a major strategic interest for the North in its relations with areas on the margins of the central areas of economic and political power.

When imposed from outside, democratic institutions and good governance do not necessarily take root. But when appropriate forms of electoral system or political institutions are adapted to local circumstances (as in Estonia), they may form an effective element of conflict prevention. Harnessing domestic support and legitimacy for conflict prevention is essential to its success. When measures associated with conflict prevention are accompanied by other public goods (as when accession to the EU was in prospect), structural conflict prevention can be effective, even if it involves some fundamental changes in systems of governance. The view that conflict prevention is a chimera and that only the threat of violence can be effective in preventing conflict does not accord with the positive cases.

We are left with the view that conflict prevention remains potentially important but it is still a fledgling instrument for a 'genuine' form of global governance. Actual global governance in this area remains tentative, experimental, fragmentary, sometimes effective in conjunction with favourable domestic circumstances, but sometimes ineffective and even counter-productive.

Resistance to conflict prevention has come not only from governments and parties unwilling to adopt external proposals for how they should settle their conflicts, but also from the major powers themselves. Despite the rhetoric, commitment to conflict prevention in practice has been partial and conditional. Agencies of global governance have demanded democratic institutions and improvements of governance, but these demands can be set aside if other foreign policy requirements override them. The findings reported in this chapter suggest that established democratic institutions and good governance do tend to prevent violent conflict, but also that such institutions need to be appropriate to the local circumstances.

The difficulty of promoting conflict prevention as a norm of global governance is that it is enmeshed with other policies and practices which sometimes themselves contribute to local conflicts. This means that the conflict formations at the global level need attention, quite as much as local conflicts. If it is true that democracy, human rights, good governance and development are associated with structural prevention of conflict, then these desirable values must be sought at the level of world society as well as in local societies. For this reason, conflict prevention ultimately has a transformationist agenda. It requires a transformation not only of local conflicts but of the system of global governance itself.

Notes

1. For the idea of global governance as a set of norms, see Christopher Clapham's chapter in this volume and Vayrynen (1999).
2. Personal interviews, Helsinki, 1992.

3. There was a rise in the number of armed conflicts up to 1992, and the number of democracies was rising over the same period.
4. Author's calculations.
5. William Easterly, 'Can institutions resolve ethnic conflict', unpublished, World Bank, February 2000, reaches similar conclusions using different sources of data. Easterly argues that quality of institutions (based on the International Country Risk Guide) lessens war casualties on national territory and lessens the probability of genocide.

5
Against Global Governance? Tracing the Lineage of the Anti-Globalisation Movement*

Peter Wilkin

> In human social systems, the most complex systems in the universe, therefore the hardest to analyse, the struggle for the good society is a continuing one. Furthermore, it is precisely in periods of transition from one historical system to another one (whose nature we cannot know in advance) that human struggle takes on the most meaning. Or to put it another way, it is only in such times of transition that what we call free will outweighs equilibria. Thus, fundamental change is possible, albeit never certain and this fact makes moral claims on our responsibility to act rationally, in good faith, and with strength to seek a better historical system.
>
> (Wallerstein, 2001: 3)

Introduction

In order to analyse something as apparently diverse and unmanageable as that which has come to be known as the anti-globalisation movement (hereafter, AGM) it is necessary to make some initial clarification. In this chapter my intention is to focus on that part of the AGM that is seen as being concerned, broadly speaking, with issues of social justice. In short, those groups who have sought to carry on the mantle of progressive social change that has marked earlier internationalist movements such as liberalism and socialism. I make this distinction precisely because to be 'anti-globalisation' is potentially to be aligned with groups that possess radically contradictory agendas. Thus I distinguish those concerned with social justice from what I would classify as the self-consciously reactionary wing of the AGM. By this I mean those groups that have sought to oppose globalisation and global governance on the belief that it is a threat to their nation or, more pointedly perhaps, their race. For example, the by now well known US white militia movement have a general critique of global governance and the new world order that places them firmly in the AGM camp (Ronson, 2001). However, there are two crucial differences between the reactionary and the progressive AGMs: first, the former base their critique upon a need to preserve a form of political separatism. Thus it is the white race or community that is under threat, at the most general, the white US community in particular. Second, their critique is built around an elaborate conspiracy theory that in some variants sees global socialism as the ultimate goal of the world's political and economic elites. By contrast, the AGM that I am concerned with in this chapter are those that are not seeking to privilege *particular* groups but whose ambitions are more universal, with an improvement or transformation in the general condition of humankind as their goal(s) (Luard, 1990). It is at once that simple and that ambitious. This is not to say that what I (non-perjorativley) describe as the reactionary wing of the AGM are not worthy of analysis in themselves, but serves merely to narrow the focus of this chapter.

Having narrowed the scope of my inquiry, the structure of the chapter is as follows. In order to analyse and offer a reasonable interpretation of the AGM I will address a number of pertinent questions. Initially I will consider the question as to why they have emerged on the world scene, providing an historical context for their coming into being, before setting out a brief empirical history of their rise to prominence. However, my aim here is not merely to list one event after another. For those wishing to find detailed empirical accounts of the vast range of activities that the AGM has been involved in I would recommend a visit to any of the numerous AGM web sites, but perhaps most usefully that of the People's Global Action (PGA) web page and in particular their section on 'Actions against Globalisation', which offers an extensive list of such activism. On the contrary, the task of this chapter is to offer an interpretation of this movement in the context of the rise of global governance, not to provide a calendar of the events that they have been involved in. Having set out this historical overview I will consider the agenda of the AGM and how it relates both to global governance and older protest movements, what Wallerstein, Arrighi and Hopkins usefully termed as anti-systemic movements (Arrighi *et al.*, 1989). From here it will be possible to evaluate the aspirations of the AGM and the extent to which it presents any kind of significant challenge to the ongoing project of (neo-liberal) global governance. There are, unsurprisingly, substantive criticisms of the AGM from the political left and right, and some of the more salient ones need to be considered here. I want to begin, though, by turning to the historical context in which the AGM has emerged.

Part one: after the revolutions

The apparent spontaneity of events that overtook the world media and politicians alike in November–December 1999 at Seattle need to be considered in their historical context. The spontaneity was, in many respects, both well prepared and some time coming. Although the 'Battle of Seattle' is regarded by many as the turning point for the AGM, the first time that they had seriously dominated the world's political, economic and media institutions, even a cursory inquiry into the AGM reveals it to be a complex, structured and organised movement that had very carefully sought to prepare the grounds for its dramatic emergence onto the world scene (Gilham and Marx, 2000; Wainwright *et al.*, 2000). In order to explain how they reached the battle of Seattle it is initially necessary to backtrack to the beginning of the 1990s to set out the backdrop against which the AGM developed.

The end of the Cold War and the Velvet revolutions of 1989–91, which transformed Eastern Europe and beyond, ushered in a new era that subsequently came to be known as the New World Order. Aside from the changing geopolitical framework that emerged in the 1990s, the end of the Cold War saw the movement towards the consolidation of a new global architecture that had its roots in such processes as the liberalisation of global finance in the late 1980s and the transformed role of International Financial Institutions such as the IMF and the World Bank earlier in that decade (Thomas, 2001). The collapse of state socialism led many commentators to speak, once again, of an end of ideology, echoing Mrs Thatcher's famous acronym of TINA (There Is No Alternative). Only now it seemed that there really was no alternative. The institutions of global governance that were consolidated over the ensuing years were rooted in a commitment to a neo-liberal agenda that proffered a universal blueprint for peace, prosperity and freedom. Simply, the liberalisation of trade coupled with a commitment to political democracy would provide the ultimate framework for world order, maximising the possibilities of economic growth and political liberty (Kegley, 1994; Steans and Pettiford, 2001; Wilkin, 2001). It very quickly became apparent that old established alternatives to this powerful neo-liberal formula were being abandoned by political parties around the world. The meaning of political concepts appeared to be undergoing radical revision as conservatives, social democrats and communists alike all subscribed to this new orthodoxy, replacing Nixon's dictum that 'we are all Keynesians now' with the phrase, 'we are all (neo) liberals now' (Giddens, 1994). In response to this, political opposition took increasingly polarised forms with the revival of frequently aggressive and xenophobic nationalist movements and the deepening of forms of theocratic politics, all of which shared hostility to liberal freedoms and, to a lesser extent, that indefinable phenomenon, the West. There is little reason to doubt that the early 1990s was a triumph for neo-liberalism as a global political and economic force that had seemingly transformed the world. Its self-professed achievements were colossal, winning the Cold War and transforming the global economic order to usher in a new era of global governance in which the relationship between states, markets and citizens could be restructured through a commitment to the new global troika: privatisation, liberalisation, deregulation (MacEwan, 1999; Wilkin, 2001).

By contrast, for those opposed to the apparent triumph of capitalism, there seemed in this period to be only disarray and defeat, though there were some significant exceptions to this (Callinicos, 1991; Wallerstein, 1995). The revolutionary momentum of 1968 had been a high watermark for those committed to social justice and it had receded significantly into the past. Indeed, many of the figures associated with that period had themselves become part of the institutional political processes around the world. In their own way, Bill Clinton, Joschka Fisher and Jack Straw were all 1968-ers who had come full circle by the early 1990s (Berman, 2001). This is not to argue that in the early 1990s there was an absence of oppositional voices, movements or ideas. On the contrary. But it is the case that this particular period represents an interregnum for those social forces committed to the idea of social justice as a *general* improvement in the condition of humanity. That which is being witnessed now with the rise of the AGM has in significant part emerged from this historical juncture.

Aside from the momentous political and economic changes that were transforming the world in the late 1980s and early 1990s it is crucial to stress the importance of a range of technological developments that were taking place that have been of profound importance to the process of global governance and, conversely, to the AGM. The Information and Communication Technology (ICT) revolution of the past two decades has, through the introduction and proliferation of computers, satellites, fibre optics, robotics, the internet, mobile phones, digitisation and the like, served to help build this era of global governance. The ICT revolution has provided the infrastructure for states, however uneven this is in practice, to increasingly organise and coordinate their activities on such diverse issues as tracking the spread of disease to the planning and practice of warfare. It has also helped companies to transform their processes of production as well as their capacity to monitor and survey changing patterns of demand. To clarify, the social changes that have been wrought through the implementation of this ICT by states and corporations have been far-reaching and profound (Comor, 1994; Corbridge *et al.*, 1994; Friedland, 1996; Cox, 1998; Dickens, 1998; Castells, 2000a,b). This is not to make the case for a form of technological determinism, though. The technology itself has myriad uses and does not determine social outcomes. As will be shown, the technology is often, though not always, capable of being used for more authoritarian or more libertarian purposes. The AGM itself has been able to use much of this technology for its own ends and in many respects it is hard to imagine that the AGM would be possible if it had not had access to such ICT. This, then, is the backdrop to the emergence of the AGM. It is a period in which established political orthodoxies have been seriously called into question or fundamentally rejected and one in which a framework for (neo-liberal) global governance was being established. As bold commentators once again forecast the end of history, a range of disparate and uncoordinated voices around the world were preparing to offer an alternative point of view.

Part two: arrival

The lineage of the AGM is far from straightforward. It is clear that many involved in the movement have been actively campaigning around many issues to do with peace, social justice, human rights, and fair trade, for many years. So there is a clear connection that can be drawn between the AGM and past social movements (Ray, 1993; Melucci, 1996; Della Porta *et al.*, 1999a,b; Bircham and Charlton, 2000; Cohen and Rai, 2000; Starr, 2000; Hamel *et al.*, 2001; Welch and Chesters, 2001). However, it is also the case that there are important differences in the way that the AGM has sought to organise itself thus far and there are numerous voices from the older established social movements who view the AGM as composed of dangerous anarchists who have little to offer progressive politics (Macintyre, 2001). Further, despite criticisms that it is simply a form of rainbow politics, attempting to hold together a series of irreconcilable views and demands, there is a reasonably coherent series of themes that recur in the AGM that relate directly to global governance. I will turn to these in more detail in part three when I consider the agenda of the AGM but, for the moment, it is sufficient to clarify that despite the plurality of voices within it, I would argue that there are three broad areas that tend to connect these disparate groups to a greater or lesser degree, and they are all aspects of global governance. The globalisation of the economy is one strand that connects the AGM. Specifically, it is a concern with what the AGM see as the enhanced power of capitalists and TNCs to control the world's resources for private gain rather than public good. This tendency towards the privatisation of decision-making has profound implications for democracy, protection of the environment and culture alike. The globalisation of politics is the second main strand of concern that connects the AGM. As the Belgian PM Guy Verhofstad concedes, the world's political institutions seem increasingly remote from democratic control and increasingly willing to sacrifice democratic governance to private interests (Verhofstad, 2001). The expansion of corporate power and the deepening of capitalist social relations have served to undermine the ability of ordinary citizens to control the institutions that are nominally there both to represent them and which derive their power, legitimacy and authority, from them. For the AGM, democracy is under threat by the privatisation of decision-making taking place under the guise of global governance. The final area of global governance that connects the AGM is that of culture. The commodification of culture and the standardisation of cultural products is a pervasive theme in the AGM (Klein, 2000). Ironically, the markets that are said to be the best mechanism for promoting choice and plurality are encouraging the triumph of the biggest and most powerful cultural commodities, not necessarily the best. Private power, the end of democracy and the end of cultural diversity are all powerful criticisms of a global governance that is attempting to instil a more rigorous form of self-discipline upon the world's populace. All of these points are contentious and need to be rationalised and I will examine them in detail in the next part of this chapter. Nonetheless, I take them to be central to the coherent agenda that the AGM is establishing.

A common criticism of the kind of groups involved in the AGM is that they are the products of a relatively prosperous, relatively free and liberal Western world. Where else would people have the time, resources and freedom to organise such complex events. These charges are usually made with a subtext as to the political immaturity of the groups involved who will one day, perhaps, wake up to the follies of their youth and assume the mantle of political responsibility. Such charges usually come from former activists turned politicians or from those who never held such convictions to begin with and should thus be considered in that context. This is not to say that there are not important criticisms to be made of the AGM. There are. It is merely to defend the idea that rebellion and revolt are normal and healthy parts of a democratic society. At the very least, the AGM should be recognised as such in an era of neo-liberal global governance and the end of ideology. More substantively it is interesting to note that the initial charge against the AGM that its impulse springs from the post-materialist age in which the core capitalist-states and their populations are now said to reside is quite simply wrong. The key inspirations for the AGM in the 1990s have come from groups based in states that are peripheral to the capitalist economy, not at its core. It is the landless peasants movement in Brazil (MST), the Indian farmers of Karnataka state and the Zapatistas of Chiapas, who have set out many of the broad themes that connect the AGM (Corporate Watch, 2000). It is from sections of the world's ultra-exploited in the periphery that the initial inspiration for the AGM emerges. In the early 1990s protests took place around the world against the final GATT Round, drawing together farmers and peasants in the periphery to protest a liberalisation of trade agenda that was being driven by the core capitalist states and the major corporations. They were starkly aware that they would not have the power to 'compete' with such organisations, if indeed, 'free trade and open competition' was the real objective. There is a strong case to argue that the agenda being pursued was never one of simple free trade for all so much as mixture of free trade in areas where companies in the core would dominate (intellectual property rights, pharmaceuticals) and protectionism in areas where they might not (textiles, agriculture) (Wilkin, 2001). As these initial protests revealed, neo-liberals rarely practised what they preached. In truth, the core capitalist states and companies sought power and control, not an abstract 'competition' with the periphery that they might lose.

These trends culminated in the North American Free Trade Agreement (NAFTA) that, on one reading, sought to liberalise trade between the United States, Canada and Mexico on 1 January 1994. Another reading suggests that it was also to enable US corporations ultimately to dismantle Canada's public services under the guise of unfair competition (after all, these services were subsidised by the state) and to use cheaper Mexican labour and environmental regulation as a stick with which to dampen down wage inflation in the domestic US market (MacArthur,

2000). The emergence of the Zapatistas movement on the day that the NAFTA treaty came into being was at the time a huge shock to the institutions of global governance that underpinned the institutional and normative framework of the New World Order. Indeed, so great was the shock to the financial architecture of global governance that the Mexican currency collapsed as the virtues of a Mexican economy which had seemed so real to capitalist investors only 24 hours earlier were rapidly undermined. If this could happen in Chiapas, perhaps powerless groups throughout Mexico could do the same? This was hardly the docile public body that capitalist investors had been hoping for with the NAFTA treaty and so, in a rational panic, they withdrew their investment in droves. The unintended consequence of this was to exaggerate and strengthen the impact of the Zapatistas uprising, the very thing capitalist investors wanted least. As a propaganda coup this was an impressive feat by the Zapatistas. Utilising ICT to disseminate its message whilst allied to a classic guerrilla-style campaign in Chiapas, the Zapatistas burst onto the world's political consciousness with as imaginary a piece of political theatre as had been seen since the time of the Situationists. The by now well-known figure of Sub-Commandante Marcos distributed an initial message via the internet to the world's news agencies and myriad sites around the world in which he set out a new agenda of resistance that situated the struggle of the Zapatistas as part of a global struggle against all forms of oppression. At once the movement was specific to the region and also global in its identity and ambition. The Zapatistas, despite the appearance of a spontaneous uprising, had been active in the region for decades and had consciously and painstakingly built up support in local communities, developing their ideas in response to the successes and failures of orthodox leftist groups of the era (NACLA, 1991, 1994; Smith, 2001). They very quickly became a magnet for all kinds of interested parties and a succession of conferences followed in which they sought to extend their reach and develop new forms of solidarity with groups from all over the world. The agenda was a clear one and was set out by the Zapatistas in their second declaration in June 1994 which states that 'the struggle of the EZLN is not only for the Zapatistas, it is not only for the Chiapanecos, not only for the Indians. It is for all Mexicans, for all of those who have nothing, for the dispossessed, for the greatest in poverty, ignorance and death'. So what specific lessons have the AGM learnt from these protests in the periphery that have enabled them to take the battle for social justice to the core capitalist states?

The AGM began to develop in the wake of these events of the mid-1990s as disparate groups began to organise their activities in a systematic manner. One important example within the AGM is the emergence of the group known as People's Global Action (PGA) who serve as a useful example of the way in which the AGM has developed as a network. In order to develop a framework for its activities the PGA organised a meeting in Geneva in February 1998 that brought together representatives from social movements from all continents, with 300 delegates from 71 countries. The aspiration to present some kind of coordinated opposition to neo-liberal global governance meant that a structure of sorts was required in order for such a movement to function at all. The history of New Social Movements is a large, well documented and growing field but it is not one that is simply applicable to the AGM. Indeed, many within the AGM have consciously sought to learn from what they see as the weaknesses of past NSMs in order to build a stronger foundation for the AGM. Whereas past NSMs focusing on issues such as gender, the environment, and human rights, have acted as formal institutions, with staff, buildings, income and so on, mirroring in some respects their party-political counterparts, the AGM has sought to avoid these tendencies whilst still having a sense of structure. Thus, the group that emerged out of the Geneva meeting and that has subsequently come to be known as PGA has no staff, no offices, no regular income and no leaders. In practice the PGA is a highly decentralised umbrella organisation that allows the various subgroups within it to organise their own activities. It exists as an instrument to help coordinate activities and to encourage as many people to participate as possible. It has followed up the original meeting with subsequent PGA meetings in Bangalore in 1999 and Cochabamba in 2001. These conferences are due to take place every two years. Its initial statement of principles (what it calls its 'hallmarks') are not unreflective of the AGM as a whole and are worth setting out here:

(1) A very clear rejection of capitalism, imperialism and feudalism; all trade agreements, institutions and governments that promote destructive globalisation;

(2) We reject all forms and systems of domination and discrimination including, but not limited to, patriarchy, racism and religious fundamentalism of all creeds. We embrace the full dignity of all human beings;

(3) A confrontational attitude, since we do not think that lobbying can have a major impact in such biased and undemocratic organisations, in which transnational capital is the only real policy-maker;

(4) A call to direct action and civil disobedience, support for social movements' struggles, advocating forms of resistance which maximise respect for life and oppressed peoples' rights, as well as the construction of local alternatives to global capitalism;

(5) An organisational philosophy based on decentralisation and autonomy.

The problem of co-optation is a familiar one in political thought. Those involved in the AGM have thus far been very conscious of this and their organisational framework has specifically been built with a view to minimising such a possibility. No single group or individual really speaks for the AGM. Under PGA its members speak for themselves and to each other. This plurality of voices is often a criticism of the AGM as was clear in the Seattle Press after the WTO meeting in 1999. An editorial in the *Seattle Press* newspaper observed that 'during the conference the anti-WTO community did not present an identifiable and accountable umbrella organisation, nor a coordinated position on what it was for or against, nor reconcile positions that various groups and individuals presented that appeared to be in conflict' (Slater, 2000).

The PGA network has a distinct advantage over its classic NSM forebears, owing to the impact of the earlier mentioned ICT on political organisation. Through the use of the internet, mobile phone and computers, activists have been able to develop this very flexible sense of structure that is sufficiently solid to enable them to organise very complex and intricate social protests. Despite much of the media coverage of events such as the battle of Seattle and Genoa, the AGM is not geared-up for acts of political violence and mayhem as the adequate response to global governance. (Indeed, if the question of political violence is to be raised here it is quite clear that the worst violence at Genoa was caused by the police forces that systematically sought the most peaceful and non-violent protestors, safe in the knowledge that they would be least likely to fight back.) (*The Guardian*, 2001; *The Independent*, 2001). At Seattle, for example, the Seattle area Direct Action Network (DAN) took responsibility for organising the protests against the WTO meeting but more than this sought to organise an array of events to go with the protests. The carnival-like atmosphere of many of these events has been commented upon by a number of journalists and writers (Cockburn and St Clair, 2000). In addition to the more creative side of political opposition manifesting itself in street theatre and artistic performance, at Seattle the local DAN, affiliated to PGA and in turn as part of the overall AGM, organised a range of public meetings between themselves, the local community and representatives from the political and economic elites taking part in the WTO summit. In this respect it is a multiple form of political opposition that seeks to use all aspects of human ingenuity to challenge the agenda of neo-liberal global governance; from entertainment, to mass protest to serious debate. As I say, this is possible in significant part precisely because of the ICT that provides the organisational infrastructure for such activism. For those fearful of the decline of the public sphere in an age of ever-converging media networks of ownership and control, this movement can be seen as part of a defence of that classic liberal ideal.

What seems reasonably clear is that although the AGM in general and PGA in particular present a new form of social movement with a different kind of structure from that seen in NSMs generally, they have at the same time grown out of this tradition of social movement. Of course, a critic might chide that there is no AGM, *per se*, that there are, in fact, many groups with lots of ideas but that there is nothing as coherent as a movement. There is some truth to this claim. However, it fails to take account of the way in which new and complex information networks have emerged in the past two decades, fuelled by ICT, the impact of which has been to allow for radically new forms of organisation. Social movements in the twenty-first century need not look like social movements have in the past. Indeed, it would be somewhat odd if they did. The activists involved in what I have described as the progressive wing of the AGM are not bound by past ideologies that fix their sense of political identity in terms of nation, geography or ideological orthodoxy. In some respects the links that are often drawn between anarchism and the AGM are pertinent if we take anarchism to be a series of ideas about the potential for human freedom rather than a fixed ideological tract that stands above time and place (Guerin, 1970). It is this flexibility, this ability to resist being simply reduced to a single aspect of human experience that is a strength of the AGM thus far. It is also potentially a weakness and having established both the context in which the AGM emerged and the manner of their arrival onto the world scene as a challenge to neo-liberal global governance, I want to turn now to the agenda that they have set out.

Part three: the agenda

In an era shaped by the so-called 'Washington consensus' that has sought to embed neo-liberal truths in the major institutions of global governance, the act of dissent should be welcomed in its own right

(Soederberg, 2001). Any democratic order requires meaningful dissent in order for it to function, a point which Belgian Prime Minister Verhofstad, for one, clearly recognises. Indeed, from within the institutions of global governance itself there have been voices of dissent in recent years, including the much discussed departure of chief economist Joseph Stiglitz from the World Bank, leaving in his wake a trail of criticism about the intellectual inadequacy of the organisation (Atkinson, 2000). Not everyone welcomes dissent of course, and in sections of the business-press the emergence of the AGM has been viewed with much disgust. Familiar forms of 'abuse' including, Luddite, romanticist/ utopian, irrational, through to the more familiar labels of extremist and more recently terrorist, have all appeared (Achieng, 2001). As a focus for dissent against neo-liberal global governance, the AGM has clearly played a significant role thus far. However, the question has to be asked whether there is anything substantive to this dissent, or is it more an expression of political frustration at the apparent ongoing and deepening process of neo-liberal global governance? In short, have they got anything to say? In my view they clearly do have a number of important critiques to make of global governance and its ongoing development. To evaluate these claims I will return to the three broad areas of concern that can be argued to connect the AGM: the globalisation of the economy, politics and culture, before considering a range of criticisms made against the AGM from both the left and the right. There is a sense in which the AGM does not easily fit into a left–right dichotomy and some figures within the movement such as the political journalist Alexander Cockburn have written that it is best viewed through a libertarian versus authoritarian political framework. My conclusion is that there is something to the substantive points made by their critics, but that the strength of these criticisms must be qualified by the fact the AGM is new, developing and at present, the only progressive and fundamental challenge to neo-liberal global governance on offer.

To recap, the progressive wing of the AGM are opposed to what they see as the death of democracy through the privatisation of political processes; the extension of private corporate-power over more areas of cultural life and the global economy. By contrast, they are in favour of extending democracy to the economy, decentralising political decision-making where possible, and promoting a genuine plurality of cultural practices. Neo-liberal global governance, it is argued within the AGM, promotes the opposite of this.[1] These are general points that can be said to connect the AGM, but within the movement there is debate and dissent as to what this would mean in practice. This is hardly surprising given the sheer spread of the movement and the speed with which it has grown in the past five years. Perhaps the most effective way of examining these themes is by taking some of the major criticisms levelled against the AGM as a counterpoint. There are three major criticisms that are useful to consider here and I will address them in turn, some of them connecting critics from the left and defenders of neo-liberal global governance alike. They are: anti-globalisation as reactionary or romantic politics with an inadequate understanding of capitalism; the internal incoherence of the movement; a lack of democratic credentials in the AGM itself. These are serious charges to which a reasonable response can be given by the anti-globalisation movement.

Anti-globalisation as reactionary or romantic politics

> It is hard to know which was worse – watching the militants dress parade their ignorance through the streets of Seattle, or listening to their lame-brained governments respond to the 'arguments'. (*The Economist*, Editorial, 'Clueless in Seattle', 4 December 1999)

> Second, remember universal brotherhood? You know – concern for the world's poor and downtrodden? As Paul Krugman recently noted in *Slate*, free trade gives millions of people a step up the ladder. Yes, that may mean working in a sweatshop. But these people manifestly prefer that to their prior condition. (Robert Wright, 'We're all one-worlders now', *Slate*, 23 December 99)

> It meets my tests of reactionary utopianism. (Christopher Hitchens, Interview with *The Stranger*, 17–23 January 2002)

> But we can hardly say 'capitalism' anymore, much less socialism. Instead, we say 'globalisation,' and 'technology'. And that's bad for both intellectual analysis and transformative politics. (Doug Henwood, 'What is globalisation anyway?')

The quotes from Hitchens and Henwood come from the political left while those from *The Economist* are from proponents of neo-liberal global governance. What they share in common is a view that the AGM is, at least in some guises, anti-progressive and anti-modernity. This is a serious charge that I think arises because of the very name by which the movement has become known: anti-globalisation. I will take the critique from the left first. For many writers with long established leftist credentials the AGM has proven to be a problematic entity. As Henwood asks in his article, what does it actually mean to be anti-globalisation? Along with Hitchens he argues that in part it must mean to be anti-modernity and anti-cosmopolitan, with all that this entails. Thus, it means at best a romantic or nostalgic political agenda, at worst a reactionary one. I feel that this criticism has some weight on two grounds. There are undoubtedly strands within the AGM who are hostile to technology and modernity and who argue that progress is to go back to a small-scale more humane form of social relations. At worst there are some within the deeper green movements who have argued for a form of social Darwinism as a solution to many of the world's problems. It is difficult to see how solutions to the kind of problems starkly addressed by the AGM, matters such as global poverty, ill health, malnutrition, could be found without the use of the benefits that modernity has bought us: science, technology, large-scale forms of production, organisation and distribution. Perhaps the problem is with the name 'anti-globalisation' itself? David Korton, for example, a major figure within works on anti-globalisation is, in essence, a defender of small-scale capitalism under the principle that: big is bad. Others within the AGM are clearly, and defiantly, anti-capitalist in their views. So there is an undoubted tension within the movement over this issue (Korton, 1996).

From the neo-liberal global governance camp the critique is different though it shares a focus on the anti-modern aspects of the AGM. The problem is cogently set out by Paul Krugman in his defence of slave-wages in the periphery. The AGM, for Krugman, do not understand history, progress or capitalism. In something like a classic defence of modernisation theory he accuses the AGM of wishing to deny the impoverished millions in the periphery the opportunity to become slightly less impoverished. There is no way, as Krugman and other commentators suggest, to buck the laws of capitalist development. For the AGM the response has been to point out the ultimate absurdity of an economic system in which human need is subordinate to these kind of amoral abstractions. The world is awash with resources of all kinds; the problem is not one of being unable to produce to satisfy human need. On the contrary, there are crises of overproduction. The problem is with capitalism itself and its prioritising of private power over human need. Such a system is morally unacceptable in an age where the technology and resources are available to challenge such massive global inequalities. Indeed, what kind of choice is it that neo-liberals are really offering those in the periphery other than a very marginal one? There is, of course, more to be said on this issue, but suffice to note for the moment that for the AGM, global capitalism is not the solution to global poverty.

The internal incoherence of the movement

> To put several hundred such people in a big hotel with instructions to 'determine the facts behind the assertions of anti-globalisation protesters' and 'recommend policies to address the most contentious issues' would be great fun for outsiders. It would be like watching scorpions in a bottle. It is wrong to imagine that the protesters agree even among themselves. (Martin Wolf, 'Responding to the anti-globalisation protestors', *Financial Times*, 4 September 2001)

The quote illustrates a particular problem with the AGM, as a plurality of voices it is riven with contradictions and dissent. For the above proponent of neo-liberalism, this amounts to so much hot air. These people exist by not having to talk to each other in a serious manner, if they did, they would fall apart. This is an important criticism but I think it is invalid on two grounds. First, the dissent within the movement that emanates from a plurality of voices is not necessarily a sign of weakness. There is a strong argument to be made that the vitality of the movement will not come from some kind of institutionalised intellectual consensus (such as with the 'Washington consensus'). The trajectory of the movement is more likely to be a progressive one provided that dissent and argument are there in abundance as such a process will undermine the possibility of more authoritarian elements within the AGM being able to impose themselves by dint of some claim to epistemic privilege (Hitchens, 2001). After all, there is no stronger epistemic claim in the current era than the prescriptions of neo-liberal global governance itself. If that is what consensus amounts to then it is not the kind of aspiration that fuels the AGM. Second, despite the fractious nature of many of the debates within the AGM, such as those taking place around the legitimate or illegitimate use of violence as a tactic of resistance, it is (contrary to what the writer above suggests), quite possible for groups which appear to have nothing in common, to find grounds for solidarity and agreement on some basic but important principles. Seattle was a good illustration of this with links being consciously fostered between trade unions, environmentalists and other opposition groups. As one demonstrator from the Topless Santa Cruz Lesbian Avengers said at the time: 'When we got here, the steelworkers weren't very queer-friendly. As the week wore on, they got more comfortable with us. My nipples stand in solidarity with the steelworkers and the Teamsters and all the labouring peoples' (Henwood, 1999). Despite the pessimistic view of the neo-liberal commentator the plurality of voices within the AGM need not necessarily be a source of weakness. Experience and practice show thus far that it is a potential source of dynamism within the movement and that agreement on many broad themes is possible. It should be remembered that the AGM is both young and composed of many young people who are not bringing any particular historical or ideological baggage with them. It is far too early to say that the contradictions of the AGM cannot be lived with and accommodated by its members. This remains an open question.

Democratisation

> Are they a dangerous shift of power to unelected and unaccountable special interest groups? (*The Economist*, Editorial: 'The non governmental order', 1 December 1999; Applebaum, 2001)

This, once again, is an important criticism of the AGM that goes to the heart of current debates about global governance. Democratisation has been one of the major themes within global governance and as the writer above argues, it is an issue that must be of central importance to the AGM. The argument levelled against them is quite straightforward, governments exist to represent the people, and have a democratic mandate to do so. Social movements such as the AGM possess no such legitimacy and therefore have no greater right to influence the political process than any other voice. Indeed, perhaps their claims are less legitimate given the violence that has accompanied the protests thus far. There are two aspects to this criticism that are important to the AGM and that will play a large part in determining its future. The first is over the issue of democracy within the AGM itself. Thus far it has sought to promote discussion, participation, decentralised organisation and a generally inclusive approach to its activism. The ethos of the AGM, drawing from anarchist political thought and practice, amongst others, has generally tended to be anti-elitist. Nonetheless, as the AGM develops it will have to find ways to incorporate wider numbers of people within a fairly loose structure and organisational process.

The second strand of the argument about democracy reflects not on the AGM itself so much as it does on its critics and is something that the AGM has stressed thus far: they are trying to defend and extend democracy, not undermine it. The AGM has arisen in part as a response to the perceived failures of democracy in the era of neo-liberal global governance. The lack of accountability and trust in politicians, the global tendencies towards corruption, the questioned legitimacy of states, the outright failure of states in the periphery, none of this is the work of the AGM, they are problems that it has been confronted with. For the AGM, neo-liberal global governance is exacerbating these tendencies towards the erosion of democracy by consolidating private corporate-power and eroding the capacity of states to deliver on the welfare demands of the electorate. For the AGM, existing political parties are too heavily compromised by the system of global governance to be of much use in resisting the erosion of democracy and therefore the onus is upon ordinary people to defend and transform democracy, not in itself a particularly radical idea. For the AGM, the processes of democratisation being promoted under global governance are essentially elite driven and reflective of elite interests. They do not extend meaningful participation to the populace so much as invite electorates to make choices from pre-packaged alternatives, all of which offer some variant on the neo-liberal agenda. I do not intend to resolve this argument so much as establish it. Suffice to say the tendencies towards which the AGM point are ones that have been observed by political commentators across the political spectrum.

Conclusions: trajectory?

So how does this leave the analysis of the AGM with regard to its future developments? Social science is not in the business of making predictions but I would note that there are a number of tensions and contradictions within the movement that serve both to propel it forward and that might equally at some point see it fragment. It offers a substantive challenge to neo-liberal global governance because it is the first global political movement to have emerged in the post-Cold War period. Its significance can in part be measured by the desperation with which the business press have sought to attack it and define it as an essentially irrational and violent rabble. Similarly, politicians have done their part by using the ongoing war on terrorism to introduce legislation around the world that is so all embracing as to catch the AGM quite comfortably in its net. This somewhat crude tactic actually reinforces the point made by the AGM that democracy is being drained in the era of neo-liberal global governance, and that states and corporations have been willing participants in this process.

The strength of the AGM is its essentially libertarian principles. It is open to any and all to join and no rigid ideology is to be imposed upon those who take part. It is an evolving global forum for debate and activism. At the same times its weakness can be measured not just by the international dynamics I have set out earlier but also by the power of those institutions that it wishes to challenge and transform. In effect, neo-liberal global governance itself. For the AGM it is the major political and ethical issue of the global age.

Notes

* Thanks to Alison Edgley, Lloyd Pettiford and Clare Richards for their help in this chapter.

1. For a critique of neo-liberalism and its attendant problems see the PGA manifesto at http://www.nadir.org/nadir/iICTiativ/agp/en/PGAInfos/manifest.htm.

Part II

Global Governance in Post-Conflict Zones

6
Global Governance and Resistance in Post-War Transition: The Case of Eastern Slavonia and Bosnia

Judith Large

Introduction

For people living in post-war societies under international/UN mandates, the term global governance is not abstract. Administrative authority and nominal rule of law amid disruption and destruction may be experienced (or perceived) as being in the hands of those outsiders who reside in compounds with white cars and a particular flag. Access to food relief, to identity papers, to the means for reconstruction, transport or medical care may depend on this imported infrastructure, while a state is literally re-built. This was the case in Eastern Slavonia in 1996, and in Bosnia following the Dayton Agreement. In Eastern Slavonia, the UN team undertook to oversee the legal re-integration of a break-away Serbian enclave (autonomous zone) back into the state of Croatia (which in turn had broken away from Yugoslavia) during a specific transitional period. Violent disintegration in Bosnia led to three parties being brought to a US sponsored negotiating table in Dayton, Ohio, with a tripartite but UN protected 'statelet' invented and occupied by transition authorities. In Bosnia the post Dayton governance project is long term and incomplete. Seven years after the treaty a British national newspaper summed up the role of the new UN high representative: 'On the advice of the peace implementation council, he will have the power to dismiss officials who obstruct the Dayton peace process and *impose laws when necessary*' (Norton-Taylor, 2002).

In post-war transition the global governance project resembles a blueprint for the creation of pluralistic liberal democracy based on a market economy. This is typically sought through processes of demilitarisation, improved police and judicial systems, monitoring of human rights, free elections, general 'democratisation', reconstruction and economic development through privatisation and wider market forces.

As Clapham states elsewhere in this volume, it is not the intention here to suggest that such aspirations for the reconfiguration of the State are in themselves misplaced. Indeed, there were individuals in the war torn ruins of the former Yugoslavia who thought that human rights, the rule of law, protection of minorities, 'democracy' and economic revival would be a 'good thing'. The objective is rather to explore reaction to the governance project, particularly in the intersection between attempted implementation of global governance structures and norms, and experience/resistance of the local population. There is evidence of localised forms of resistance to benign international occupation through classic 'weapons of the weak' embedded in everyday struggles for survival, supporting James Scott's (1985) formulation of 'foot dragging, dissimulation, false compliance, pilfering, feigned ignorance, slander, arson, sabotage' and more. The broader analysis draws on work by Michael Pugh (2000a) arguing that in place of pre-war statist orders, international agencies and local corporate commands assert control and negotiate areas of collaboration. 'From a critical theory perspective in which "the state" is demoted, one can thus speak of "intermestic manipulation" – the term "intermestic" being defined by Alan Bullion as "the intermingling of domestic, regional and international factors that overlap or intersect and that can transcend traditional state-centric (realist) notions of sovereignty"' (Bullion, 1995).

This concept of intermestic manipulation is an assertion that in a protectorate there is a common ground between international and domestic parties as well as friction and resistance. Eastern Slavonia (ES) was under international jurisdiction for a limited time and then reverted to Croatian statist as well as local government centres of authority and power. Bosnia (BiH), however, is increasingly seen as caught in a protectorate limbo where neo-liberal reform is almost impossible to achieve. Within such configurations are various levels of counter-movement. The warlord in ES, the nationalist mafias in Bosnia, will also have local oppositions, manifesting in non-cooperation or active resistance. The latter in turn can draw on international norms and donors for support.

For members of the international community engaged in the region there is an assumption that external actors wield the ability and moral authority to bring about the peaceful change that local communities failed to do. If international diplomacy failed to prevent the onset of conflict, then, the presumption follows, external actors should at least make concerted efforts to pick up the pieces and regenerate societies in ways that ensure better governance. 'These hubristic assumptions are not sufficient, however, to endow external actors with superior techniques for dealing with peaceful change. Nor does the evident destruction and dislocation they confront represent a *tabula rasa* on which external scribes can write a peaceful future' (Pugh, 2000b). Far from being a *tabula rasa*, the society in question will hold not only scars but also memory, context-based, historical and structural influences of its own.

This chapter examines the structural and normative reconfigurations attempted through global governance mechanisms. It suggests limitations in receptivity by target populations, contradictions inherent in implementation by directive, and manifestations of resistance on a spectrum from partner elites (as per 'simulation' discussed by Selby) to regional profit and patronage networks, traditional authorities, collective and individual attitude and stance.

Small geographically and governed for a fixed period, Eastern Slavonia presents a very specific case study of measures undertaken and results or aftermath. It is a micro-study alongside the macro-enterprise of establishing and administering BiH, with its tripartite leaderships (Bosnian, Croat and Serb), and massively displaced populations. The Bosnian case study is a thematic exploration of the contradictions inherent in imposing 'democracy' from above, hindrances to refugee return and protection of minority rights, privatisation and the informal economy. Global governance is structured but challenged in BiH.

Eastern Slavonia and interim governance: the United Nations Transitional Administration for Eastern Slavonia (UNTAES)

Eastern Slavonia is located at the easternmost tip of Croatia (bordering Serbian Vojvodina, south of Hungary), extending approximately 30 kilometres from east to west and 140 kilometres north to south. Intersected by the river Drava, it is known for agriculture, with fertile plains stretching to join the Danube valley in the east. Its villages and towns, notably Borovo Selo, Vinkovci and Vukovar, were the scene of early (1991) armed skirmishes and later the full scale assault on civilians which came to symbolise the brutality of war in Yugoslavia.

Fierce fighting led by ethno-nationalists in 1991 resulted in forced population exchanges over the Drava, some 70 000 Croats and ethnic

Hungarians fleeing from the newly established Serbian Autonomous Zone in Baranja to the North, and Serbs fleeing north from Croat dominated Osijek and surrounds. Some 75 000 Serbs, many refugees from other parts of Croatia, subsequently moved in to the region. In spring of 1992 UN 'Blue Helmets' arrived by agreement, to stabilise (some say freeze), and police the divide. While local nationalist Serbian leaders looked to Belgrade for eventual reward and incorporation, they were nonetheless negotiated away, back to Croatia in the final stages of the Dayton Agreement. The region would be returned to Croatian sovereignty. At the time that UNTAES assumed control, the population was approximately 160 000.

The 14-point agreement signed in Dayton in November 1995 provided for a year-long transition period for the re-incorporation into Croatia. The document allowed for a possible one-year extension, and for local elections, but precluded a referendum. Eastern Slavonia was effectively on war-alert as late as January 1996. The city of Osijek (which remained Croatian during the war) was heavily sandbagged and boarded. Serb artillery and tanks were in evidence on the other side of the Drava which had become a political demarcation line. As the deals were being signed, the majority of local residents repeatedly made clear their belief that any agreement would not hold. Most remained convinced that force would still be needed to resolve the Eastern Slavonian question.

It was this climate which the UNTAES mission entered, with personnel comprising 5000 military peacekeepers and 20 civil affairs staff members. While the former undertook the supervision of demilitarisation and the provision of essential security, it was left to the latter to design and conduct, so far as possible, a peaceful and co-operative re-integration of infrastructure, institutions, and people. UNTAES would work with break-away Serb authorities and newly legitimate Croatian ones to forge viable relationships and infrastructure. Representatives were mandated to convene meetings of the former enemies and draw up agreements and work plans. The global governance challenge was literally to forge new local administrative structures – in the judiciary, education, telecommunications, agriculture and health – with norms and mechanisms allowing the Serb and other minority populations to remain, and the Croat (majority refugee or displaced) to return. Key words in the UNTAES mission document included 'confidence building measures', 'tasks relating to civil administration' and 'highest standards of human rights' for all local residents irrespective of their ethnic origin.

Joint Implementation Committees (JICs) sought to bring the two sides together to negotiate and agree to the process of transition to ensure that it was as inclusive, orderly and efficient as possible. Initially the JIC processes set new precedents and gained important ground for a minority (Serb) former break-away population facing absorption into the majority (Croat) state. UNTAES JICs were made operational for: police, civil administration (customs, taxation, licences), the restoration of public services (roads, water, communications), return of refugees and displaced persons, provision for human rights, elections, records, education, health and the judiciary.

In the case of the JIC on police, new officer appointees and trainee police were removed from the highly charged immediate environment and given training in Budapest, with seemingly good results. The list of recruits itself had the prior approval of each political (outgoing Serb and incoming Croat) administration. Areas like roads, electricity and telecommunications required practical reconnection, and there was little opposition to mixed work crews. Mixed crews (international, Serb and Croat) conducted flying missions for mosquito spraying and carried out de-mining work. UNTAES sponsored an open market on what was once a war time front line and found tens of thousands of mixed population thronging there every Saturday to trade, visit and renew associations. This was a positive sign that populations themselves were not adverse to renewed exposure or transactions.

Ceremonies held in Vukovar on 15 January 1998 marked the completion of UNTAES and the assumption of full Croatian sovereignty over the region. However, January and February also witnessed an increase in incidents directed against Serb displaced persons in the region and a crisis of confidence regarding the Government's commitment to safeguard their rights and safety. This triggered the movement of Serbs to the Federal Republic of Yugoslavia or further afield to Norway, Canada, and elsewhere.

According to reports of UN monitors (UNHCR, 1998), the period from 15 January to 25 February saw 201 reported incidents relating to housing, including 169 incidents of intimidation. Some 68 ethnically motivated incidents were reported, including the murder of two elderly Serbs in separate incidents. Police could not intervene effectively without the backup of local authorities. Mixed families (those intermarried, Serb/Bosnian/Croatian/Hungarian, and so on) who had remained on either side of the divide watched developments with a mixture of concern and *déjà vu*. Local peace and human rights groups monitored and offered as much advice and shelter to those seeking help as possible, as did international agencies still present.

Given the overall aim – the peaceful reintegration of peoples, and of the region back into Croatia – a study was commissioned the following autumn to examine outcomes. Findings indicated that in the judiciary, '[a]ll courts are now cleared of Serbs. There are no Serb judges or clerks' (Large *et al.*, 1998). For lawyers who practised outside the Croatian legal system from 1991–96 there was now a re-registration fee of 10 000 DM, in a region of grossly high unemployment where average-to-good salaries are pegged at between 250 DM and 350 DM a month. This made inclusion and re-entry for Serbian legal professionals virtually impossible.

In the field of education, recommended pluralist measures such as equal representation of language and religion in primary classrooms had collapsed completely. Settlement patterns deem most villages to have clear majority groups. In mixed areas returnee vengeance was targeted at minority teachers. For higher education, Croatian language exams were now a prerequisite to university entrance. Students who studied from 1991 in ES, using the Cyrillic alphabet and spoken Serbian, were at an immediate disadvantage – a reason to move across the border and look east to linguistically compatible Novi Sad or Belgrade for higher education.

Access to care and livelihood: more legal labyrinths

It is my experience that the state legislation now systematically applies every bureaucratic labyrinth possible to exclude and intimidate specific groups without resorting to brute force. (Woman lawyer interviewed by the author in Osijek November 1998)

It was not only hardliner groups which offered resistance to UNTAES-led reform in the new Croatia. There ensued a Kafka-like administrative and legal labyrinth for citizens to manoeuvre for citizenship, employment, access to health care, pensions, passports, and so on (Large 1999).

The new law on 'Convalidation' required that measures agreed under UNTAES be implemented in accordance with the Croatian Constitution and in line with regional authority interpretation and resources. It allowed for individuals or institutions to bring clauses of the negotiated agreement for local court scrutiny and judicial testing, when there was legal interest in doing so. The scope for blockage of previously agreed measures (such as keeping on Serb public servants in employment) was enormous, time consuming and perfectly legal. An employee claiming unfair dismissal (according to the Affidavit on Employment Rights signed 16 December 1996) could take his case to court, where average processing time of such appeals was quoted as eight years.

Although the Croatian government promise of entitlement to pensions was one of the first official commitments made to the population of ES, according to lawyers in Osijek 5000 people who nominally qualified in Baranja were receiving no benefits in winter of 1998/1999. People needed their pensions or employment status and salaries in order to receive health care, due to the introduction of privatisation in health care. In Baranja alone approximately 50 per cent of the population were unemployed, and an unknown number working for no salary.

Contracts negotiated regarding the state agriculture collective were in disarray, with high unemployment levels. According to a lawyer at the Baranja human rights centre there was manipulation of dates on contracts, claiming expired or out-of-date status and non-eligibility for health insurance or benefits. Small farmers wishing to purchase segments of land from this formerly nationalised venture are met with incomplete privatisation laws, lack of procedure and/or exorbitant prices to broker informal deals.

New legal procedures presented barriers. 'Nostrification' meant the process of ratifying earlier training in order to assure employment at levels equivalent to current standards. Many argued that the nostrification system was used by Croatia to screen those trained in other countries, now including other parts of the former Yugoslavia. Prior to 1991 all training institutions in the former Yugoslavia had essentially the same programme and their degrees were accepted in all parts of the country. In the aftermath of the conflict, however, this requirement for nostrification became a targeted mechanism for screening out Serb professionals. A complex set of regulations and requirements is associated with the nostrification procedures, as are high fees for setting long exams. In particular, nostrification affected young people who were not employed before 1991 and who took their state exams or higher diplomas in FRY. It was therefore perceived as a barrier specifically for the Serb population. It became another incentive to leave, to seek employment where qualification was honoured and recognised, that is FRY.

Following UNTAES' withdrawal the United Nations was represented by a small number of civilian police who monitored the Croatian police. Monitoring of human rights was the responsibility of the OSCE who reported in turn to the Council of Europe. Widespread evictions of Serbian and other minority populations were reported, often referred to as a silent exodus. UNTAES estimates had put the number of remaining Serbs in early 1997 at between 120000 and 130000. Early 1999 OSCE estimates of the Serbian population were as low as 50 000. Two way returns had not been realised, and Croatian returnees frequently brought back with them hard line attitudes. Most international NGOs left the area, following trends and funding first to Bosnia and then to Kosovo and its periphery. Local NGOs did their best, as anti-war and human rights activists embraced ideas of 'development' and attempted to work for a multi-ethnic society.

The UNTAES experience points to limits to intervention. Reconciliation cannot be programmed, and states will certainly pass laws and formulate legislation, as is their right to do. There was, after all, no final bloodbath in East Slavonia. In the handover of a once Serbian mini-state back to the state of Croatia, collective violence was tempered, the population spared the application of total force. Now legal labyrinths disempower, permits and application forms are not forthcoming, people are politely disqualified from rights to identity, to livelihood and citizenship. In the aftermath of armed conflict, legalities and administrative procedures prove an effective means of resisting norms and standards supposedly imposed by the international community, and may ultimately bring about the very ethnic division which was a war aim in the first place.

Eastern Slavonia and Bosnia and Herzegovina as linking systems

In any examination of 'governed' populations, inter-relationships between regions and people are striking and further complicate post-war recovery. Bosnian Serbs who fled to ES generally did not want Croatian citizenship, but to return to Bosnia. They could not cross the new border without a passport, but they could only obtain a passport in Bosnia. Thus were the catch 22s (falling outside the designated remit of global governance) which froze the pockets of the displaced and marginalised.

Similarly, in Bosnia and Herzegovina for years after Dayton, the internally displaced and refugees were thwarted by the need for official documents in order to reclaim their homes. People who had fled under fire or forcible eviction were requested by state authorities to present their birth certificates, title deeds, proof of state leasing and so on. Eventually the Office of the High Representative with UNHCR took the initiative of organising the Commission for Real Property Claims to fast-track returnee applications. Cutting through bureaucratic red tape and refining procedures is their mandate. There are those who charged them with undermining local authority capacity, but local authorities often proved intransigent, or impossibly cumbersome. In both cases resistance is entwined with self-preservation, old orderism and control, fear of more change, or indeed, inter-ethnic pay-back and unfinished business.

Considering Bosnia: democracy by direct rule?

The signing of the General Framework Agreement for Peace in Bosnia and Herzegovina (GFAP) at Dayton on 14 December 1995 marked the end of a devastating three-and-a-half-year war which caused 1.2 million refugees to flee abroad and displaced a further 1.1 million.

The Dayton Agreement initially established its interlocking network of international policy-making forums as part of a one-year transition to limited Bosnian self-government. But in December 1997, just one year into this extended consolidation period, the international administration became an open-ended commitment, with no clearly defined point at which even limited Bosnian self-government could be realised.

This extended process of international regulation has involved a top-down approach to post war recovery and governance. Governing representatives at municipal, canton, entity and state levels have little choice but to follow international policy under the threat of being dismissed or having sanctions imposed. This level of external regulation was extended to the international take-over of the state-run television station in Republika Srpska and the UN High Representative deciding the national flag of the new country. Some aspects, such as the imposition of uniform passports or car licenses, have been received positively by the local population. David Chandler argues that while Bosnian politicians are fully accountable to international peacekeepers, there are no mechanisms making international policy-making accountable to the Bosnian people.

To Chandler this is democratic accountability reduced to 'transparency'. Teaching democracy ends up being a call for international institutions to make widely known their future plans and policy goals for the region. This does not alter the fact that the Bosnian people have no active role in decision-making, and are potentially reduced to the role of passive onlookers. He argues that the extended peace-building approach not only failed to build support for political alternatives, but also provides *carte blanche* for international administrators to override democratic processes, on the grounds that Bosnian voters are not responsible enough to have the rights granted to citizens in Western states. The implication of this approach is the end of formal democracy, of legitimacy through accountability to the electorate. Democracy is redefined as its opposite, adherence to outside standards, not autonomy and accountability.

Anti-hegemonic and inter-group resistance

There has been visible popular resistance to the imposition of specific outside standards, such as mass demonstrations in Sarajevo (2000) over changes in labour law which reduced maternity leave and brought in 'reforms' thought to contravene workers rights under the old communist regime. International observers were taken aback by the vehemence of demonstrations in Banja Luka (a Serbian stronghold in the war) against laying the first flagstone for the rebuilding of the Ferhadija Mosque in May 2001. In an act of deliberate provocation and disrespect, protesters slaughtered a pig and spilled its blood on the site. This was a violent show of opposition to ideals of religious tolerance or multi-cultural society. It was also a statement, saying to potential Muslim returnees to Banja Luka that they were not welcome.

The new governance project for Bosnia stipulated an almost entirely novel state structure, which incorporated very few pre-existing institutions. The international community (Office of the High Representative, UNHCR, other UN operatives such as the WHO, UNICEF, UNDP, the World Bank, IMF, OSCE, military peace-keepers, and every imaginable NGO – international, national, local) would operate through newly created local structures and a complex distribution of power and competence. UNHCR works alongside 14 legislators at state, entity and canton level in the Federation of Bosnia and Herzegovina. At state level, each Minister has two deputies and consensus is required for any decision. Institutions at entity and cantonal level are influenced by still-dominant ideologies of ethnic separation and by party politics which obstruct the functioning of state institutions. Indeed, the settlement froze lines of confrontation between Bosniak Bosnia, Croatian Herzegovina, and Serbian Republika Srpska and acknowledged the consolidation of ethnic occupations, while 'the accord's principal backer pledged to equip and train the army of only one of the three parties, the Bosnian dominated central government' (Cousens and Kumar, 2001). Equally daunting, each of the three dominant identity politics aimed to 'govern' its own. For several years after the war, Bosnia operated with three different legal systems; three sets of license plates; three international telephone exchanges; three currencies; two alphabets; increasingly, three languages; and three school systems. Such conditions contravened Dayton's specific guarantees that Bosnia's residents should have freedom of movement, could return voluntarily to their prewar homes, have their basic human rights protected and have confidence in a future increasingly respectful of democratic participation. Jacques Paul Klein, senior UN representative since 1997 (a leading figure in the UNTAES operation previously in ES), described in February 2002 the steps imposed to push for a unified polity: a single passport, currency printed tactfully with alternating Latin and Cyrillic script, a single uniform car license plate, insistence on freedom of movement and the national flag by international decision:

> We assumed that if we stopped the violence, that would be enough. But the war went on bureaucratically, with obfuscation and delay. Nothing fundamentally has changed, in that 50% of the population – most of the Croats and Serbs – don't believe they are citizens of the state. (Quoted in Brooks, 2002)

Refugee return

The Dayton Agreement was meant to create an overall framework to reconstruct the country and reverse ethnic cleansing. By late 2001, according to UNHCR estimates, some 300 000 Bosnian refugees were still in need of a durable solution and a further 518 252 people still registered as displaced. The ethnic map created by the conflict has not changed significantly as Bosnia remains effectively divided along ethnic lines (Englbrecht, 2001).

The UNHCR and the international community (including 'bilateral players') have given post-war recovery and in particular, refugee return in Bosnia, the highest priority. According to the Forced Migration Review web site fact page, European Union Emergency Assistance to former Yugoslavia was four times the amount given to the Africa/Caribbean/ Pacific states. In 1999 donor governments gave $207 for every person in need in former Yugoslavia and $8 per head for those in need in DRC.

UNHCR officials informally cited 1996 as the year of 'If/whether return can take place', 1997 as 'How' and 1998 as 'When'. Many individual officials worked tirelessly to unblock the myriad of regional knots preventing return. Whole population transfers had taken place, many of these negotiated exchanges over borders to Croatia and FRY. Minority return became a particular concern. Wartime property laws actively discouraged return and mobility was dependent on compensation for property. Access was frequently denied to personal and official records, to reconstruction and business loans, and to basic services like education and medical care. As in the former Yugoslavia, jobs, pensions, social services, housing and education remained largely a state prerogative; administrative authorities therefore wielded considerable capacity to deny a range of civil and economic rights to minority populations or opposition figures.

Guy Hovey (2000) documents findings on resistance to return encountered from the leadership of the Displaced Persons group itself. His example is the non-elected leaders representing the interest of those displaced from Sipovo. Their power arose from the perception of members that those in leadership could influence the allocation of assistance. Development of direct links between implementing NGOs and their membership threatened the leadership and brokerage role to which they had become accustomed. Minorities were understandably nervous about going back to an area from which they had been forcibly evicted. Many refused to do so.

To increase returnee confidence, security was often reinforced with a large SFOR presence and regular International Police Task Force patrols. At the same time attempts were made to deem host area local police ultimately responsible for the safety of returnees. Fear worked both ways. While minorities were anxious about returning, majority populations were fearful of the implications of minority return and the risk of revenge attacks against those thought to have participated in ethnic cleansing. Many individuals opted for their own paced voluntary return, with a few men going back to the former home ruin at weekends only to rebuild a wall or plant a field, then checking on whether these improvements were allowed to stay untouched until next visit. This type of gradual reconstruction was less difficult than the nightmares involved in trying to evict a new occupant, who had in turn been evicted from a village three hundred miles away where their home was also occupied, and so on. 'Reluctance to return was also based on worries about schooling, employment and how to get by without humanitarian aid. Although eventually better-funded programmes provided returnees with agricultural and other inputs, the first returnees were underfunded' (Hovey, 2000).

By the end of January 1998 some 30 minority (in this case Muslim) families had returned to Sipovo Municipality. Hovey's description is classic, and will be echoed all over Bosnia:

> Return followed a pattern: older members returned first, followed
> by younger members as confidence increased. Problems occurred
> and … continue to occur. Houses owned by minorities had windows

smashed, threats were made and one house was burned. Local police were uncooperative and only made sham investigations of incidents. (Hovey, 2000)

In this case, co-ordinated and robust action by the international community, together with co-operation from local authorities and the general public, largely countered these incidents and these initial returns led to many more minority families returning.

Majority return was not straightforward either, particularly to rural areas. Forced migration for many meant exposure to urban life and new life styles, possibly new opportunities. The return of refugees and IDPs is a gradual, painstaking process throughout. Areas with human resources available to assist with re-integration, such as Travnik, became well known. Where a minority mayor had been elected in the 1996 elections, as in Drvar, tensions resurfaced continually. (People were allowed to vote in place of origin.) Residents in Sarajevo resented assistance given to returnees, whereas those who had stayed and survived the siege felt disadvantaged and so on.

Privatisation

Critics argue that the privatisation programme imposed on Bosnia was misconceived from the start (ICG, 2001). Based on an already discredited model used in Russia and the Czech Republic, USAID hired PricewaterhouseCoopers to create a voucher-based scheme that would enable the state not only to liquidate its assets, but also to pay its debts to its citizens. The voucher model does not attract fresh capital, but merely changes ownership on paper. As a consequence, it does not bring the technology and know-how transfers necessary to boost both the production and productivity of worn out or war-torn plants.

The privatisation legislation, written and sponsored by USAID in 1998, created an entity-based scheme involving 12 privatisation agencies: one for the RS, one for the Federation as a whole, and one for each of its 10 cantons. From the very start this institutional and regulatory framework was open for exploitation, and offered politicians the chance to confirm the effects of ethnic cleansing by means of ethnically exclusive privatisations. It also afforded them a large measure of control over most aspects of the process. One obvious conflict of interest was that the legislation permitted the managers of each state company to create the privatisation programme for their own firm.

Pugh (2000a) speaks of a 'clientist/nationalist economy', explaining how political and economic interest worked hand in hand in dividing spoils of the war. In the banking sector, the nationalist parties divided jurisdictions and recreated their own mini-versions of the old Yugoslav Payments Bureau (PB) for monopoly over financial transactions. The new PBs have become powerful, controlling election campaign funding and linking directly to financial police in each canton. This makes it easy to control the opening or closing of new businesses, not to mention targeted auditing.

Privatisation enhanced ethnic politics, since entity governments were allowed to distribute disproportionate numbers of vouchers to their war veterans, which discriminated against citizens who had fled or been forcibly removed from their homes during the war. In both entities almost half the vouchers (by value) issued thus far have gone to war veterans. After a phase of resistance to privatisation from 1996 to 1998, the nationalist parties sought to control both the process and the asset holding. Ownership and management of telecommunications and energy were divided on party lines to provide major sources of revenue for the nationalist parties and their vertical structures. Influence extends to the commercial banking sector. In April 2001 the High Representative ordered SFOR raids on the Hercegovacka Banka headquarters and 10 other branches in Mostar, meeting stiff resistance from 'mob violence and police complicity' (Gutman, 2001). A subsequent audit for the OHR confirmed suspicions of major diversion of funds.

In order to obstruct or circumvent privatisation – and to limit the damage it would do to vested interests – local governments dragged their feet, stripped assets, accorded preferential treatment to favoured buyers and devised means to maintain their control over companies even after their privatisation. In addition, in creating privatisation packages, local politicians often scared off potential investors by insisting that an unreasonably large number of workers must be kept on the payroll. Political obstruction was and is most apparent in profitable, publicly owned companies enjoying monopolies or particularly favourable market positions and whose boards consist of government appointees. The power utilities, tobacco factories, telecommunications firms, water companies and forestry commissions serve as sources of cash and patronage for the ruling parties and offer rewards for colleagues now out of office. Given the huge revenues generated by such enterprises, it was not surprising that, following the November 2000 elections, new entity governments moved quickly to install their loyalists on the governing boards.

Inverse privatisation

Thriving regional black markets abound for would-be Bosnian entrepreneurs interested in trading guns, drugs, people or stolen cars.[1] Cars moving south, drugs moving north; this has been the pattern since the end of the war. Bosnia lies across long established heroin smuggling routes between the Middle East and Europe. Gun running fuelled the wider Yugoslav war itself. Recently Bosnian police intercepted a shipment of 318 assault rifles, 1008 mortar grenades and 512 hand grenades destined for Kosovo. According to local media the smuggling ring in question involved senior Bosniak and Bosnian Serb officials and local business tycoons (Prenda, 2001). Increasingly, people smuggling is recognised as a major source of illicit revenue in Bosnia, providing a conduit for hopeful would-be immigrants.

Such high profile transactions reflect a sharp end of non-taxable profit, demand and supply. The black market functions in far more convivial ways, supplying cigarettes, soap, toilet paper, chocolate, pens, counterfeit CDs and tapes, clothing and even tinned food. Asked why the public is silent on the issue of reconciliation, the sociologist and publicist Slobodan Nagradic answers: 'For our politicians who win voters by their rhetoric of national homogenisation, reconciliation is a dangerous subject and they are unwilling to accept it … It is absurd, but [black market] smugglers did more for reconciliation than politicians' (Englbrecht, 2001).

Black market activity is the ideal free market; mafia activity represents both competition and dividends. The stall holders with their small goods, the supplier of domestic products who calls at the block of flats, the seller of cigarettes on the street corner – all are at once beneficiaries and links in the chain of transactions. Undeclared work, a simultaneously highly formal and informal economy relates directly to inadequate welfare provision. As argued earlier, it is hard enough to claim a pension or medical care if you hold recognised employment. If you have nothing, or if you barter for bread each day, who provides? The shrewd observer in Sarajevo, in Banja Luka, or Tuzla will see the taxi driver paid in cash passing cigarette money out the window to the old man on the corner. When visitors arrive in a train station or airport they will be offered lodging in the comfort of a family flat – for cash. Remittances from abroad find their way to the elderly and to relations left back home. In the words of Boris Divjak (2001), 'The trade and smuggling of humans, narcotics, arms, and other illicit and excise goods; finally – prostitution, drug addiction … often just the consequences of the futureless situation in BiH.'

Divjak goes further, however, to point out that it is not only the black market entrepreneurs who avoid paying taxes and social contributions. This has been the practice of the international community 'from their first day onwards, not just for the ex-patriots but for the local employees there. Would that not be avoiding the fair game at the labour market, particularly now that an agreement exists with the Entity Governments on the payment of taxes? A local enterprise faces a less competitive starting position if it were to employ national experts, as it bears a greater fiscal burden.'

Newly articulated resistance

Divjak's pointed observation that the International Community (IC) does not pay taxes either is representative of emergent resistance articulated on lines of accountability and double standards. If IC representatives misbehave or are themselves corrupt, by which democratic process may they be removed? Which international companies are making profits from contracts which Bosnians themselves could fulfil? If a mobile phone contract is awarded, what are the terms, and do nationals have a say in this? Sarajevo leaders seized on a series of international scandals to press the West into giving them more control over the country. Kebo (2001) cites a report that the OHR was ready to hand out the job of printing new Bosnian identity cards to the giant Siemens company. The project, designed to establish the first proper register of all Bosnian citizens, was said to be worth about 50 million German marks. This caused such an outcry that the deal was never finalised.

Conclusion

Peace-building is nothing less than the reallocation of political power; it is not a neutral act (Bertram, 1995). The claim that there are objective standards of human rights and of democracy to which all parties may be held may be ethically compelling. But in the highly politicised context of creating or re-creating a state's institutions, it is politics and power that dictate who will interpret or impose such standards and how. Roland Paris (1997) argues that the principal flaw in the current official approach to peace-building is that 'market democracy' is prescribed as a remedy for civil conflict without adequately anticipating the side effects of this remedy: Chandler (1999) argues that while Bosnian politicians are fully accountable to international peacekeepers, there are no mechanisms making international policy-making accountable to the Bosnian people.

When the IC have favourites among leaders or politicians who espouse desired liberal values, this is no different than party cronyism of the past or ethnic alliances or mafia configurations now. The global governance project is to transplant democratic politics to a society where the previous Yugoslav regime had for years a law banning any verbal attack on the government, including jokes. With the legacy of this penal code, not to mention the development of violent ethno-nationalism, it is perhaps not surprising that democratic opposition is not immediately forthcoming.

Resistance in the form of blocking refugee return, tax avoidance, twisting privatisation mechanisms or oiling black market routes will stem from a multiplicity of standpoints: genuine fear, lack of trust, hatred, petty abuse of power, coercion from dominant power holders in the form of ethnic elites and strong men. If the IC hold nominal authority in Bosnia they lack a legitimacy in their position. Many of the population not only wish for the liberal dream, but also engage with the project, learning English, working as translators or drivers, restoring links with other groups, mending badly broken human links and literal bridges. The police in Mostar, Bosniak and Croat, agree finally to work together. Serb IDPs wait in Banja Luka remembering when they also lived in Mostar. If manifest blockage and subterfuge is hindering the governance project, then new voices directed towards the IC may be a sign of a different kind of leadership, a shift in perceiving and dealing with liberator/occupier.

This chapter has explored two contrasting cases of global governance in post-war transition, normatively similar but different in scale and intended outcome. In ES intervention to assist transition played a distinct role in avoiding a bloodbath, and in easing the pathway of those who lost in the struggle between identities. A self-proclaimed dissident region was returned to Croatian sovereignty. But the intended peaceful and just re-absorption of its Serb community was thwarted by hard-line intimidation, by in-built disadvantages and legalities designed for navigation by non-Croats.

Among the ES and BiH populations are also 'muted groups': those rendered silent or inarticulate (or numb) by structures of dominance. Their silence may come from dependence, from fear or a timeless focus on sheer survival. They view the debate on neo-liberal globalisation with incredulity. In this sense, their own non-compliance, their evasiveness, also slows down a governance project deemed unwieldy by its own contradictions. Celia McKeon worked in the region for four years, latterly in Sarajevo. She comments on the acute sense of dis-empowerment felt by the majority of citizens with 'so little faith in their own potential'. Networks of local education and advocacy groups working for reform 'have commitment and genuine aspirations, but lack engagement with political structures'.[2]

The instruments and aims of global governance in ES and BiH were effectively resisted by non-cooperation and open obstruction. Co-opting the agenda of rights, authorities made clever use of legal niceties, legislation and administrative technicality directed against minorities. The government of Croatia currently interacts with international financial institutions in securing loans, adapts domestic production standards to EU regulations in hope of future membership, and no doubt shows a legal framework for the protection of its minorities. In Bosnia effective partition continues. Refugee return targets held by the IC do not always match the aspirations of the displaced who have resettled elsewhere, or cannot face return. Minority return has met considerable resistance, overcome when sustained commitment, conditionality and incentives are cultivated. Privatisation measures remain deliberately blocked, denying much needed investment and revenue.

Global governance operates vertically, imposing measures on host populations, who in turn respond with horizontal strategies based on kinship, patronage and profit networks. They resort to time honoured practices of barter, gifts, support systems reciprocal obligations of kinship, localised economic distribution and cross border, informal trade. The black market and grey economy thrive, resisting market controls. Ethno-nationalist elites still hold sway over groups prepared to make visible demonstrations against their former neighbours, against external interference, against the arrest of well hidden leaders. Given the dynamics of group mobilisation, the ultimate site of resistance is surely the individual, the means of forging identity, survival, recovery, eventually over time perhaps change of allegiance or loyalty. If 'democratic oppositions' require a consensual operational base, it may be that this will only emerge over time in Bosnia and Herzegovina through resistance in part to global governance itself. For now there is no civil war, but an uncivil peace.

Notes

1. In 1998 a poster seen in southern Germany quipped: 'Come to Mostar: your car is already there.'
2. Conversation with Celia McKeon, 2 March 2002. As early as 1996 a report on the NGO sector in BiH was commissioned by CARE, resulting in a now classic

study by Ian Smillie: *'Service Delivery or Civil Society? Non Governmental Organisations in Bosnia and Herzegovina'*. Smillie identified emergent trends which are still problematic; donor funded projects which provided specific services (once a realm of state provision) or advocacy with no strong community base or engagement with local structures, competition for funds and the replications of specific project forms were according to external stipulations. Long-term sustainability was questionable.

7
Governance and Resistance in Palestine: Simulations, Confrontations, *Sumoud*

Jan Selby

Introduction

With the Madrid peace conference of October 1991 and the subsequent Israeli–PLO Oslo Accords of 1993, the West Bank and Gaza became established as key sites for the project of liberal global governance. Following the 1991 conference, multilateral working groups were set up to address region-wide problems such as economic development, the environment and arms control, these bringing together both core Middle East parties and a range of state, inter-state and non-state actors from outside the region, especially Europe and North America (Peters, 1996). With the 1993 Accords (Israel and the PLO, 1993) the level of international involvement grew even greater. The accords themselves established a framework for a five-year 'interim period' of Palestinian self-rule within the West Bank and Gaza, during which time various territorial, administrative and security powers would be progressively transferred from Israel to the Palestinians. This period would be brought to an end through the signing of a 'permanent status agreement' based on UN Security Council Resolution 242, which had called for 'withdrawal of Israel from territories occupied' in the 1967 war, and 'the termination of all claims or states of belligerency'. None of this would be possible, however, without the support of the international community, since the PLO was in the midst of a financial crisis, and the West Bank and Gaza had been both economically 'de-developed' (Roy, 1995) and politically de-institutionalised (Sayigh, 1997; Frisch, 1998) during the course of Israel's occupation. Responding to these realities, the international community immediately began formulating plans for the development and reconstruction of the West Bank and Gaza, and for the construction of autonomous Palestinian institutions. Within days of the Rabin–Arafat handshake in Washington, the World Bank had published a six-volume report, *Developing the Occupied Territories: An Investment in Peace* (1993), which outlined its assessment of the economic situation in, and the policy, institutional and investment needs of, the West Bank and Gaza. This report subsequently informed an October 1993 Bank-sponsored international conference, at which donors pledged US$2.1 billion of aid to the Palestinians for the five-year interim period (Brynen, 1996: 46). With additional pledges, that figure had increased to over US$4 billion by late 1998; and during that same year, donors offered a similar level of support for a further five years (necessary given delays in the Oslo timetable). To place these figures in some perspective, in 1996 the West Bank and Gaza were in receipt of the highest ever per capita aid sums of a developing world post-conflict area (Brynen, 2000: 74–8). As the Council on Foreign Relations (1999) put it, 'in both absolute and per capita terms, the donor effort for the Palestinians has been one of the largest ever undertaken by the international community'. It can be taken as read that, just as the West Bank and Gaza have been major recipients of international aid, so more generally have they witnessed a wide-ranging attempt to establish governmental institutions and infrastructures in accordance with internationally accepted principles of good governance.

If we can switch tack for a moment, another key arena of contemporary global governance is the developing world's growing water problems. Water issues first rose up political and development agendas during the 1970s, under the stewardship of the United Nations, and on the back of the then emerging sensitivity to international environmental problems (Young, 1994). More recently, new institutions such as the International Water Resources Association (IWRA), the Global Water Partnership (GWP) and the World Water Council (WWC) have begun to take the lead in establishing consensus over priorities and best practice for water management, these institutions being sponsored not so much by the United Nations and its member states as by the World Bank, and being informed above all by the Bank's neo-liberal economic and policy doctrines (Biswas, 2000: 280). Specifically, the global governance agenda for the water sector has come to argue for (1) institutional separation of water supply and regulatory functions, with the former being conducted by the private sector, the latter by public state institutions; (2) full-cost pricing of water, such that subsidies are eradicated and the true costs of production, supply and management are borne by the consumer;

(3) demand as well as supply management, wherein efforts are devoted not simply to modifying 'water's behaviour', but also to modifying 'human behaviour and perceptions' (Ohlsson and Lundqvist, 2000: 195); (4) 'integrated water resources management', such that the various strands of water policymaking cohere, and are co-ordinated with other policymaking areas; (5) joint and co-ordinated management of all trans-boundary water resources, and integrated river basin management, such that river basins are managed as single hydrological units; and (6) a raft of broad good governance themes, such as recognition of poverty issues and the role of women, promotion of transparency and accountability, and commitment to the establishment of 'partnerships' between governments and 'stakeholders' in the making of water policy (e.g. World Water Council, 2000). Broadly accepted by most inter-state, state and non-governmental organisations, these principles constitute the foundation for the majority of current interventions in the governance of water in the developing world.

This chapter will examine governance and resistance at the intersection of these two quite distinct 'global governance complexes' – considering governance and resistance, that is, both in relation to the Oslo process as a whole, as well as more specifically in relation to attempts to reconstruct and refashion the Palestinian water sector in accordance with the imperatives of the World Bank's neo-liberal blueprint (the chapter will focus principally on the West Bank, much less so on Gaza). Since 1993, the challenge of reconstructing the Palestinian water sector and improving water supplies has been one of the major priorities of development organisations working in the West Bank and Gaza. Both of these territories face severe water crises, with Gaza's shallow aquifers increasingly depleted, polluted and saline (the latter as a result of inflow from the Mediterranean), and the West Bank's Palestinian communities enduring regular and protracted supply cuts, often of more than three months at a time (Lonergan and Brooks, 1994; Elmusa, 1997; Rouyer, 2000; Selby, 2003b). Responding to these increasingly dire realities, donors saw water and wastewater improvements as vital both in providing the necessary infrastructure for economic development, and for confidence building purposes. The World Bank, for one, placed water alongside transport as the sector most in need of investment (World Bank, 1994: 8–9). Similarly, the US Agency for International Development (USAID) defined the water and wastewater sectors as one of three 'strategic' investment areas, and has devoted the major part of its financial support for the Palestinians to the water sector (USAID, 1999). Led by these two donor organisations, though with the support of many others, over 10 per cent of all official aid money to the Palestinians since 1993 has gone to water and wastewater programmes (Rouyer, 2000: 229).

The project of promoting good governance of water – and good governance in general – within the West Bank and Gaza has met with considerable resistance, however. My aim in this chapter is to chart three such types of resistance, 'simulation', 'confrontation' and *'sumoud'*. By 'simulation', I refer to resistant activity which simulates adherence to the internationally accepted norms and principles of the global governance agenda, but which in reality, and under the surface, is barely informed by such ideas and ideals. This is a form of covert resistance, practised by political actors who seek to convey a commitment to internationally accepted norms, but whose actions are in reality governed by the dictates of power and political interest. By contrast, 'confrontation' denotes resistant activity at its most bold and conspicuous, when powerful apparatuses of governance are openly challenged and opposed by resistant actors. Finally, by *'sumoud'* – the Arabic word for 'steadfastness', and one that is central to the Palestinian vocabulary of resistance – I refer to resistant activity which is devoted to getting around power, to bypassing it and to coping quietly in the face of adversity. I consider all three of these to be distinct forms of resistance. This does not mean, it should be said, that global governance as practised in the West Bank and Gaza is subject only to (various forms of) resistance. To the contrary, much resistant activity involves some adaptation and accommodation to the global governance agenda: the power of financial institutions like the World Bank is such, for instance, that they cannot be purely and simply resisted. While focusing here on (various forms of) resistance, therefore, it should not be thought that I mean to deny the extent of accommodation and adaptation, or to operationalise a straightforward binary opposition between the clashing forces of global governance and resistance. Moreover, it should not be thought that the distinction between 'governance' and 'resistance' is necessarily clear and distinct. To the contrary, and as I hope to illustrate in the cases to follow, while the project of global governance is typically met with various forms of resistance, these very forms of resistance are often in another sense forms of governance, albeit ones that are antithetical to the global governance agenda. Global governance is often met with resistance, but such resistance is often simultaneously governance by different means and with a very different agenda.

Simulations

Right from their inception, the Madrid and Oslo peace processes have involved a 'simulated' adherence to internationally accepted norms and principles about the ways in which states, societies and economies should be governed. Much of this seeming commitment to norms of global governance has been wholly insubstantial, typically more discursive than real. Many instances of such dissimulation are too obvious to merit lengthy discussion: Israel, for instance, has long claimed to support Resolution 242, calling for 'withdrawal of Israel from territories occupied' in the 1967 war, but has accompanied this formalistic deference to the international community with an ongoing military occupation and ever-expanding settlement programme. Other cases of simulated adherence to global governance norms have been less commented upon, however. Here we consider three such examples, two regarding the Oslo process in general, the other relating more specifically to the water sector.

While the Oslo process did not grant Palestinians sovereignty over any part of the West Bank and Gaza (questions of sovereignty having been deferred to permanent status negotiations), the process did nonetheless involve a minimal formal commitment to a Westphalian model of the state. The 1648 Treaty of Westphalia, to recall, was pivotal to the development of the modern idea of 'absolute sovereignty', this being exercised by the sovereign state over discrete territorial jurisdictions corresponding to distinct blocks of colour on the world map (Wight, 1977). In line with the principle that power (if not sovereignty) should be exercised over distinct blocks of territory, the Oslo process saw Israel transferring such blocks to the newly established Palestinian Authority (PA). Transfers occurred first in the Gaza Strip and the Jericho area of the West Bank following the 'Gaza–Jericho Agreement' (Israel and the PLO, 1994b), and thereafter, as a result of the 'Interim Agreement' (Israel and the PLO, 1995), across large swathes of the rest of the West Bank. Since then the West Bank has been formally carved up into three categories of territory: Area A, consisting of areas under PA civil and security control; Area B, under Palestinian civil control, though with joint Israeli-Palestinian security patrols; and Area C, which has remained under Israeli military, security and administrative control. My purpose in detailing all this is that the Oslo agreements did, formally speaking, grant the PA certain powers within certain territories. In reality, however, the PA's powers never lay primarily in relation to territory, but in relation to a population – the Palestinian population of the West

Bank and Gaza. At no point has the PA held any rights over Israelis, even within Areas A and B (Israel and the PLO, 1995: Article 10). Conversely, the PA exercises powers or at least responsibilities over Palestinians right across the West Bank, even over those that live within the formally Israeli-controlled Area C. Under the terms of the 1994 Rome Agreement – which does not formally exist, but was nonetheless operative at least until the onset of the *intifada* in September 2000 – Israel granted the PA license to undertake *de facto* policing over the Palestinian population of the West Bank as a whole, this in return for ongoing intelligence on the Palestinian and especially Islamist opposition. Significantly, this agreement was reached and became operational long before the PA was granted *de jure* control over its autonomous territories (Usher, 1996: 27–8). In short, the Oslo process's A-B-C division of the West Bank merely simulated adherence to a Westphalian model of the state (this model being an essential premise of the modern global governance blueprint). In reality, the Oslo process has been premised all along more on a 'tribal' than a 'territorial' mode of organisation.

If we turn now to the economic relations between Israel and the PA, we find a similar degree of dissembling. Under the terms of the Paris Economic Protocol between Israel and the PLO (1994a), Israel forwarded 75 per cent of the income tax of those Palestinians employed within Israel to the PA, along with 100 per cent of the income tax of those employed within Israeli settlements – the importance of this lying in the fact that the Palestinian economies of the West Bank and Gaza are largely dependant on day labour in Israel and its illegal settlements (Benvenisti, 1984; Sayigh, 1986; Abed, 1988; Roy, 1995, 1999; Samara, 2000). Israel and the PLO have repeatedly committed themselves not only to economic 'co-operation' and 'co-ordination', but also to principles of 'transparency' and 'accountability' in matters of economic governance (see e.g. the closing declarations of the Casablanca and Amman economic summits, in Peters, 1996: app. 6, 7). The reality, however, is that, for most of the Oslo period, the remittances from Palestinian labourers in Israel and its settlements were forwarded by Israel into a personal Bank Leumi account held by Yasser Arafat, not into an official PA bank account. This arrangement only changed in 1999 following IMF pressure, no doubt to Arafat's disappointment (Bergman, 1999a,b; Haas, 1999). Neither Israel nor the PLO Chairman has in truth betrayed much interest during the course of the Oslo process in abiding by accepted principles of good economic governance.

Within the water sector we find a similar level of disconnect between appearance and actuality. Israel and the PLO have repeatedly emphasised in their agreements the importance of 'co-operation' over water resources and supplies; the importance of satisfying basic 'domestic water needs'; their shared commitment to the 'sustainable use' of water resources; and their equally shared commitment to principles of 'reciprocity, equity and fairness'. In 1995, Israel and the PLO formally established an egalitarian-sounding 'Joint Water Committee' (JWC) for the 'co-ordinated' management of the West Bank's water resources, systems and supplies (Israel and the PLO, 1995: Annex III, Appendix 1, Article 40). Much of what was agreed upon in this 1995 Accord, however, in truth did little more to formalise and legitimate management structures and relations that had existed throughout the course of the occupation. For instance, the accord stipulated that 'in the case of purchase of water by one side from the other, the purchaser shall pay the full real cost incurred by the supplier, including cost of production at the source and the conveyance all the way to the point of delivery'. At first glance this would appear fair and reasonable, and clearly in tune with the neo-liberal commitment to the full cost-pricing of water. Cleverly hidden between the lines of the accord, however, was the fact that these terms would apply only to purchases of water by Palestinians from the Israeli authorities (and not vice versa), and would place no constraints on purchases of water from the Israeli authorities by Israeli settlers in the West Bank. These illegal settlers have always received their water at highly subsidised rates. Thus under the egalitarian-sounding terms of this water accord, Palestinians would have no option but to pay the 'full real cost' of production and supply to the Israeli authorities, while these same authorities would be free to continue supplying Israeli settlers at rates well below the real cost of production and supply. Likewise concealed between the lines of the accord was the fact that the infrastructures and supplies administered by the Palestinian water authorities as part of this 'co-ordinated' management structure would be the very same ones that had been administered by them throughout the occupation. As with the policing system discussed earlier, the Palestinian water authorities would exercise a 'tribal' form of control, having powers across Areas A, B and C, but only in relation to systems and supplies feeding Palestinians. In consequence, Israel would continue to control all of the West Bank's underground water resources, and would be able to continue with its discriminatory water policies, these ensuring not only that Israeli settlers paid less for their water supplies, but also that they received far greater and more regular supplies of water than their Palestinian counterparts – 12 times as much water per capita according to one Israeli estimate (Schiff and Ya'ari, 1989: 97).

In these and various other respects, the 1995 water accords did little more than to dress up domination as 'co-operation', presenting a feigned simulation of commitment to 'co-operation', 'equality', 'full-cost pricing', 'sustainable use', satisfaction of 'domestic needs' and other such principles of good governance in the water arena (Selby, 2003a).

The reasons behind these various dissimulations are not hard to discern. The Oslo process was driven all along (1) by Israel's desire to sub-contract many of the more onerous burdens of occupation, particularly in relation to policing and security; (2) by Israel's desire to achieve this without making too many territorial sacrifices, and without divesting overall control of the economies of the West Bank and Gaza, or of its natural resources, most importantly water; and (3) by the political desperation of the Tunis-based PLO, and of Yasser Arafat in particular. For Yitzhak Rabin, the security considerations were paramount: 'Palestinians will be better at it [imposing order] than we are', he observed with brutal candour, 'because they will allow no appeals to the Supreme Court and will prevent the Israeli Association of Civil Rights from criticising the conditions there by denying it access to the area. They will rule by their own methods, freeing, and this is most important, the Israeli army soldiers from having to do what they will do' (*Ha'aretz*, 7 September 1993). In line with this fundamental principle, Israel raised few objections to the proliferation of Arafat's security agencies, or to the growing numbers of police and security officers employed by him – both in contravention of signed agreements (Usher, 1996; Rubinstein, 1999). Instead it sought to deepen his powers over the Palestinian population, both by allowing him to enforce order in areas formally outside his control, and by topping up his personal finances and hence also his powers of patronage. For his part, Arafat faced strong challenges from opposition forces and local political elites within the West Bank and Gaza, and was therefore more than willing to accept those extra security responsibilities and powers of patronage granted him by Israel. At the heart of the Oslo process, in sum, lay a convergence of interests between the Israeli state and Yasser Arafat, which involved the establishment of a system of governance across the West Bank and Gaza that was thoroughly at odds with accepted norms and principles of good governance. The 'Israel–Arafat agreements' (Chomsky, 1993, 1999: ch. 10) were dressed up in the apparel of global governance in order to persuade various parties (especially the international donor community) of their fairness, legitimacy and credibility. In reality, though, the Oslo process was structured from the beginning not by norms and principles of global governance, but by the blunt mechanics of power and the covert operations of political interest and strategy.

It is within this context that the breakdown of the Oslo process since autumn 2000 must also be understood: as the result of a simulated peace process which was structured in accordance with Israeli power and interests, and that showed little sign of bringing Palestinian dispossession and statelessness to a just or meaningful end. Unable to fulfil the security functions for which it had been established by Rabin, the PA under Yasser Arafat has been declared 'irrelevant', first by Ariel Sharon and later by the Bush administration. Unable to rely upon its client police force in Gaza and the West Bank, Israel has since March 2002 largely destroyed the PA's policing capacity and re-established direct occupation. The idea of the PA has been preserved, though, primarily because it continues to serve 'as a rhetorical buffer obfuscating the true relations of forces on the ground' (Haddad, 2002), and because its continued existence grants Israel's occupation a degree of legitimacy and helps it defer the costs of administering the Territories to the international community. Both Israel and Arafat's administration maintain a simulated adherence to good governance, of course, with Sharon insisting that 'reform' of the PA must come first before further negotiations. But in no way does this represent a conversion to the global governance agenda: all that has changed is that where previously the language of good governance served as a cover for the restructuring of occupation, now this very same language is used to legitimise its brutal continuation.

Confrontations

When we think of 'resistance' in the Palestinian context we no doubt think first not of elite political subversions of global norms, however, but rather of Palestinian youths throwing stones, and sometimes more, at Israeli soldiers and their barricades. Resistances in this sense are something quite different from those forms of political simulation and connivance discussed earlier: they are open and overt (though often hidden behind a mask or *kafiyeh*); they seek to confront a given order either so as to overthrow it, or so as simply to give vent to impotent rage (or both); and they commonly involve mass and collective forms of action, reliant and founded upon at least some degree of group solidarity and organisation. Often they involve resort to violence, at other times merely a refusal of co-operation. In their most well known forms, these are resistances to the Israeli occupation and to the failings of the Oslo peace process – to simulations of global governance, rather than to global governance *per se.* In other cases, however – and the Palestinian water arena provides some particularly clear examples of this – institutions and mechanisms of global governance can themselves become a focus of defiance and dissent.

As considered earlier in relation to 'simulations', global governance was a set of broadly accepted 'norms' and 'principles' about the ways in which states, societies and economies should be organised. But global governance is not simply this; it is also in the present context a web of powerful aid and development institutions, and an ensemble of techniques, mechanisms and procedures through which governance is put into practice, by international institutions as well as by local institutions informed and empowered by them. Many of the core terms of the Oslo Accords simulated a commitment to norms and principles of good governance. One of the effects of these simulations, however, was that the international community became persuaded of – or persuaded itself of – the existence of a peace process, and started devoting its considerable financial resources to the reconstruction and development of the Palestinian territories (with the World Bank in the lead, as we have already seen). In the water sector, international donor organisations started supporting the formation and development of Palestinian water institutions, endeavouring to inculcate them at the same time in the ways of good governance, and they also started funding supply enhancement and demand management projects. Many of these development efforts have to some extent been subverted and dissimulated by the PA: these institutions have typically used development funds for political as well as developmental purposes, using them to employ as many people as possible, or to employ Fatah supporters of Arafat and the peace process, for instance. Beyond this, though, attempts to govern the Palestinian water sector in accordance with principles and procedures of good governance have often been met with open obstructionism and opposition.

Much of this confrontational activity has revolved around questions of control of water supply infrastructures. Ever since its establishment in 1995, the Palestinian Water Authority (PWA) has been busy attempting to consolidate control of the Palestinian water sectors of the West Bank and Gaza. In this, it has been keenly supported by the World Bank and other development agencies, it being a central plank of the good governance agenda in relation to water that all such resources should be, if not 'publicly owned', then at least 'centrally controlled' by 'effective' governmental institutions (Multilateral Working Group on Water Resources, 1996: Article 2). Not all have been keen to acquiesce to this agenda, however, with many local municipalities and village councils being determined to maintain and if possible extend control of their own valuable resources, and to administer them as they see fit. Hebron municipality, for one, has a long track record of non-co-operation with the PA over water issues (international contractors working on water projects in the southern West Bank have been known to refer to Hebron municipality as a 'state within a state'). The municipality controls several wells and also a large network of local pipelines, thus rendering surrounding towns and villages highly dependent on it for their water supplies, and giving it a great deal of political leverage. Equally, Hebron municipality has in recent years managed to attract funding for its own well and infrastructure developments – in some cases developing these in competition with the PWA. In one recent and blatantly defiant case of non-co-operation, the municipality drilled two new wells in an area close to new wells being drilled simultaneously by the PWA, and planned on constructing a pipeline along exactly the same route as the national authority; Hebron refused, however, to allow water from these new wells to be supplied through the same single pipeline, with the end result that two pipelines were laid simultaneously, one on each side of the very same road (Trottier, 1999: 94–7, 2000: 46–7; Selby, 2003b: ch. 7). Other municipalities and village councils resort to still blunter tactics, maintaining control of their infrastructures through use of force. To take the southern West Bank village of Duwarra as an example, in the centre of this village lies an on–off valve connecting the village's internal supply network with a large pipeline passing nearby. This and other such valves are regularly opened and closed by central Palestinian institutions in their effort to ration scarce water supplies, and rotate them between communities. In the case of Duwarra, the central location of the supply valve is an invitation for confrontation. In one incident during summer 1998, Palestinian officials intent on closing the valve were repelled, despite having a police escort, by a third of the village's 1500-strong populace – with the consequence that Duwarra got to keep its water supply, and several PA policemen ended up in hospital with broken limbs (Selby, 2003b: ch. 7). Such incidents – not uncommon in the southern West Bank – amount to clear opposition to and defiance of the project of establishing strong central control of water resources, systems and supplies.

Other confrontational activity has revolved around questions of payment for water supplies. The global governance agenda for water, as noted earlier, places great stock on full-cost pricing of water supplies. In the Palestinian context, however, pricing reforms have proved difficult to impose. Municipalities and village councils are loath to pay for their water supplies, to the extent that between 1995 and 1998, for instance, the central West Bank water authority amassed US$8 million worth of debt from non-payment. Non-payment by individuals and households is also very high, this partly explaining why municipalities have such high levels of non-payment. Faced with these difficulties, though also intent on raising prices so as to make the Palestinian water sector self-financing, the PWA and development agencies have been intent on introducing new tariff and billing mechanisms, on installing new and highly efficient water meters and on enforcing payment and punishing non-payment. The results have been mixed. To give but one example, that of the new water meters – which, after all, represent the 'bio-political' and 'micro-physical' (Foucault, 1977, 1978, 1980) arm of the neo-liberal governance agenda for water, seeking to turn users into 'consumers' who discipline themselves in accordance with their 'willingness to pay' – these have attracted a great deal of suspicion, in large part because they are so efficient, and have led to drastic hikes in water charges. In some areas this has led to mass boycotts and collective non-payment; in others people have responded on a more individual basis by damaging or disconnecting their much-loathed meters (Selby, 2003b: ch. 7).

The patterns of confrontation and refusal across the West Bank and Gaza are far from uniform. While in some areas accommodation to the dictates and financial power of the global governance agenda has been the norm, in other areas the opposite has held true. While Hebron municipality has kept fierce guard over its water supplies, the nearby municipality of Bethlehem has been quite successfully disciplined. While in some areas collective resistance continues, in other areas water users have been successfully individualised as 'consumers' bearing sole and personal responsibility for their payments. Yet despite these regional variations (and there have been developments over time too), it can be said more broadly that in the Palestinian water sector the prevalence of confrontational forms of resistance is principally a consequence of the administrative weaknesses and lack of legitimacy of the central Palestinian institutions relative to Palestinian society at large. There are several factors here. In part, PA institutions are weak because, in the absence of Palestinian national institutions, local Palestinian institutions (principally municipalities and village councils) developed during the course of the occupation their own strong power bases and political-economic interests. In part also, there is a deeply embedded 'culture of resistance' within Palestinian society. Beyond these factors, though, the structure of the Oslo process has rendered it well nigh impossible for the PA to establish control over and good governance within the water sector. Many people question the justice of the agreements reached with Israel, asking why they should have to pay newly high rates for water supplies when the supplies themselves continue to be so haphazard and infrequent, and when Israeli settlers still receive such plentiful supplies at their state-subsidised rates. Furthermore, the PA is not in any position to establish firm administrative control over Palestinian society. The PA was established, we will recall, on the basis of a simulation of good governance, above all to fulfil certain policing and security functions for Israel. In consequence, the PA was established by Oslo as – to adopt Michael Mann's terms (1988, 1993: 59) – 'despotically strong' but 'administratively weak'. It is a neo-patrimonial institution (Eisenstadt, 1973), one in which there do exist formal administrative, juridical and executive structures, but in which there also exist strongly developed informal patronage networks, the latter being generally of the far greater political significance (Brynen, 1995). The rule of law is not strongly developed or applied, governance regulations still less so. Thus however much the World Bank might want to inculcate a particular governance system within the West Bank and Gaza, the PA would and could do so only haphazardly, through a process of informal bargaining with local actors, and through sporadic and piecemeal resort to coercion. Confrontation is in large part the product of a political framework where injustices abound, and where central institutions rely so deeply upon patronage and coercion, standing not above but rather in competition with local actors and institutions.

Sumoud

The Arabic word '*sumoud*', most often translated as 'steadfastness', became one of the emblematic words of the Palestinian national movement during the *intifada* of the late 1980s. It captures much of what the *intifada* was about: not merely direct confrontation of the Israeli occupation, but also a wilful refusal to submit to it, or be humiliated by it; and instead a determination to establish some autonomy in its midst, and to 'get by' in spite of it. While as a mode of resistance *sumoud* has much in common with confrontation, it also differs from the latter in several crucial regards: in the sense used here, it is quiet and often clandestine, relying not upon coercion or even public opposition, but upon practical ingenuity and improvisation; it typically involves not collective solidarity against power, but local and often individual actions under the nose of power; it is ordinary and everyday, not exceptional; in De Certeau's terms (1984), it is that form of 'tactical activity' which is engaged in by the weak in their covert struggles with the strong. In the Palestinian context, *sumoud* is characterised not so much by stone-throwing young men, as by the mundane business of getting past and around Israeli checkpoints without getting caught. *Sumoud* is a specific mode of resistance, but it is also, as we shall see, a specific mode of governance.

In relation to water, *sumoud* is marked by a host of illegal and sub-legal activities. Foremost amongst these is water theft: farmers disconnecting their water meters at night and secretly irrigating their fields; individuals digging into the mains and attaching their own non-metered supply lines; others doing the same, but then filling tankers with the stolen water and selling it at inflated prices on the burgeoning black market in water (Trottier, 1999: 78–80). More generally, *sumoud* in this context is a matter of 'getting by' in the face of water supply cuts, by whatever means possible. It is a matter of finding alternative sources of water (be it a nearby spring or the local garage), of collecting it (whether in pots and pans or canisters), of conveying the water back home (by hand or by car, by donkey or by stolen shopping trolley) and of storing it (typically in rooftop tanks or in underground cisterns). And it is also a matter of using the available water with the utmost care, say by sacrificing cooked meals so as to minimise washing-up, by buying and drinking more cola and other soft drinks, by reusing grey water in toilets and gardens, by letting the laundry pile up until the water returns, by fitting taps with pieces of sponge so that no water is lost, by forbidding children from playing outside in the dusty streets and by taking showers elsewhere at the homes of those fortunate enough to have water. In coping with scarcity, people are continually forced to draw upon their own inventiveness, their own social coping networks and their own tenacity. Such is the quotidian world of 'getting by' in the face of water scarcity (Selby, 2003b: ch. 8).

It would perhaps be stretching the point too far to say that such practices constitute 'resistances' to 'global governance'. They do involve resistances – a general refusal to submit to institutional power, be this an Israeli checkpoint or a water supply regime – but these resistances are generally in relation to the Israeli occupation and its effects, not in relation to norms or principles of good governance (water theft is the one exception here). Perhaps more pertinently, such stubborn everyday forms of practice amount not simply to forms of resistance, but also to forms of governance. Neo-liberal governance has it that there should be a clear divide between experts, administrators and suppliers on the one hand, and docile consumers on the other. Supply and demand management are, in these terms, the sole prerogative of the state and private sector institutions, and not at all the responsibility of consumers. Things work quite differently in the West Bank. Here – where local and national institutions fail in the task of providing regular and predictable supplies through their large-scale technological networks – water users engage in their own alternative forms of 'supply management', finding, collecting and transporting water by whatever means possible. Equally, where institutions have great difficulty in applying and enforcing their neo-liberal governance agenda and thus in regulating consumption (witness the hostility towards new forms of metering), 'ordinary' water users continually carry out their own forms of 'demand management', regulating and rationing their needs through a variety of small-scale practices. Where in Israel and most of the developed North it is the state that administers fluctuations in supply and consumption levels, in the West Bank it is families, individuals and especially women who do the ultimate work of governing domestic water supply and demand. Most West Bank Palestinians are not merely passive 'consumers' of water – conforming to a neo-liberal ideal – but to the contrary are active, inventive and even expert managers of their water supplies. What I have here labelled *sumoud* is not, then, simply a 'mode of resistance', but also a 'mode of governance' – albeit one that is thoroughly out of sync with the international consensus on good governance in the field of water.

How, though, are we to explain *sumoud*? Clearly, such steadfastness is rendered necessary above all by the exigencies of the Israeli occupation, and by the inability of central Palestinian water institutions to fulfil their expected governmental functions. It is rendered possible by no less than the immensely tenacious capacity of people to adapt, to invent, to get around and to get by, if and when necessary. More specifically, though, it arises at the meeting point between institutional and non-institutional power. Where 'confrontation' occurs between competing institutional or collective actors (say the PA and Hebron municipality), '*sumoud*' occurs when there is a ready acceptance that one is weak, that one is on the outside and that one had better just adapt by whatever legal or illegal means appropriate.

Conclusions

My central aim is this chapter has been to characterise three distinct types of resistance – labelled 'simulation', 'confrontation' and '*sumoud*' – which one finds at the intersection of the Oslo process and water management 'global governance complexes'. Resistance, I have argued, is not one monolithic type of practice or activity; to the contrary, it has a multiplicity of different faces, to the extent that the single and over-determined word 'resistance' cannot but do a disservice to the wide variety of phenomena that it is used to encompass. The word 'resistance' serves as a useful umbrella term, and no more. Given this, to make use of a distinction between 'resistance' and 'governance' is not necessarily to fall into a trap of simplistic, essentialist, logocentric or binary thinking. Resistance and governance do not always clash (they do so only in one of my three modes of resistance, confrontation), and neither are they always even distinct phenomena (the Oslo process simulated 'global governance' and through so doing established a Vichy-like system of 'governance' through the sub-contracting of occupation; everyday water users in the southern West Bank have their own practices and techniques of 'resistant governance'). And 'resistance' and 'governance' do not account for everything: even the most recalcitrant actors make compromises, and are forced to accommodate and adapt to the demands of more powerful actors (the PA and Israel have had to submit to IMF pressure over remittances; new water meters, while they have met with some resistance, have in other places generally been accepted). The previous pages have not focused in any great depth on acceptance, adaptation or accommodation, but this has not been out of binary thinking, but because, in the Palestinian context, we simply do not see a great deal of straightforward acceptance of the norms, principles, institutions and procedures of good global governance.

Many of the resistances detailed here are not simply, of course, resistances to the project of global governance; indeed the popular forms of resistance discussed under the labels of 'confrontation' and '*sumoud*' are above all resistances to the Israeli occupation. This does not mean that they are irrelevant to consideration of resistance to global governance, however. To the contrary, most resistances to this thing called 'global governance' – be it a project, a set of norms, an ensemble of institutions, an apparatus of mechanisms and technologies, or whatever – are also resistances to locally developed policies, practices and power relations. It is often not possible to distinguish between those acts motivated by resistance to global governance, and those motivated by resistance to something or someone else (be it occupation forces, a local landlord or municipality, or sheer bloody-mindedness). The Israeli–Palestinian arena illustrates this quite clearly, but so too would other sites of global governance interventions. The local is always a complex arena bearing the traces of power and policy on a range of scales.

These descriptive and hermeneutic aims aside, the chapter has also sought to explain the roots of the various forms of resistance found across the West Bank and Gaza. These various forms all need to be understood in relation to, and as the products of, historically specific social, political and governance frameworks. More particularly, it can be said that 'simulations' are a form of elite political resistance, which emerge at the intersection between global governance norms and principles on the one hand, and the brute facts of power and interest on the other. By contrast, 'confrontations' and '*sumoud*' involve primarily popular forms of action, which arise because of the administrative weakness of central governmental institutions in relation to other actors and sites of power within society. These differences can be considered from the opposite direction, with an eye to the effectiveness and power of global governance. Seen from this perspective, it can be said, first, that the 'norms' and 'principles' of global governance are all too easily simulated, and that they thus place little constraint upon the machinations of state power and interest; and second, that the 'practices' and 'procedures' of good governance can be readily confronted and bypassed when governance institutions lack the power or the legitimacy to inculcate them. In the first of these regards, the Israeli–Palestinian arena is no doubt quite exceptional, since few inter-state or international conflicts involve such stark disparities of financial, political and economic resources. In the second regard, though, the West Bank and Gaza are not as unusual as they may at first appear. As Frisch observes (1998: 134; referring to Jackson, 1990), 'the PA, in transition, is probably more of a state than many "juridical" states in Africa'. Just as the PA has had great difficulty administering and disciplining its society in accordance with accepted ideas of good governance, so precisely the same could be said of many a 'weak' or 'juridical' state across the developing world.

8
Bowling Together within a Divided Community: Civil Society and the Northern Ireland Conflict

Feargal Cochrane

> There is clearly a need to discuss NGOs and civil society in relational terms, in terms of historically specific global, regional, national and local social-relations. Crude functionalist typologies of the roles of NGOs in democracies and in emerging democracies are unhelpful, as is measuring 'civil society' by the numbers of associations registered in a particular country.
>
> (Deacon *et al.*, 1997: 156)

Introduction

Within current literature on global governance and conflict management, it is assumed that a functioning civil society is a prerequisite for a functioning and healthy democratic polity.[1] The very phrase *civil society*, has become absorbed into the lexicon of academic discourse and has accompanied the rise of that other great mantra of the post-Cold War era, global governance. Despite the terminological vagueness of such phrases, those working and writing in the fields of conflict management are intrigued by the potential of civil society, and increasingly view it as a useful item in the tool-box for reducing, or even preventing, the outbreak or escalation of violent conflict.

This chapter will look at the nature of civil society and argue that within a divided region such as Northern Ireland, the normal gravitational forces that underpin the concept within more stable polities (a sense of community, desire for associational life and sense of civic duty) are sharpened to a degree that they can just as easily mutate into *uncivil* norms and values. In other words, while some envisage a decline of American democracy with an increasing trend towards 'Bowling Alone' and a drop-off in associational life, (Putnam, 2000) within a divided society like Northern Ireland, joining *the group* or having a strong sense of *community* can have a wholly different, (and violent) set of outcomes. Thus, within the political infrastructure of a divided society, where, by definition, there is more than one set of politico-cultural values, people may be so interested in *their* community, that they become willing to kill those within the *other*, whom they perceive to be a threat to their political, social or economic position. In such circumstances, bowling alone would seem to be a reasonable conflict management strategy, notwithstanding Putnam's observations on participative democracy within more stable societies.

The focus of this chapter, therefore, is to examine the dynamics of civil society within the context of Northern Ireland over the course of the last 30 years of political conflict, to illustrate that concepts such as community spirit and civic duty are far from neutral values, but exist within a wider political and cultural context. The notion of social capital (an alleged asset of civil society), will be examined to illustrate that within a divided society such as Northern Ireland, global norms function in specific and particular ways. The chapter will argue that to encourage 'bowling together' for the sake of it, without contextualising the nature of the society concerned, will do little to further the liberal goals of global governance or conflict management.

As Maloney *et al.* (2000) have observed when discussing the concept of social capital:

> Knowledge of civic organisations and a generic understanding of their civic vibrancy expressed through their numbers, their access to information and networks does not enable us to make immediate comment on the quality of governance in a given locality. Nor does the identification of a certain set of values and attitudes held by individuals in a community provide a sufficient basis for ascertaining the performance of governance arrangements. It is behaviour that matters. ...social capital is a relational concept. It is specific to and is made manifest in particular relations. ...In short social capital is context specific. Only by being sensitive to the different locations in which social capital is created or inhibited

is it possible to judge its impact on governance. (Maloney *et al.*, 2000: 803–4)

Locating civil society

The phrase civil society has become *de rigeur* in recent years for Western governments eager to combat declining levels of trust and participation in the democratic process, and international organisations anxious to find some means of tackling protracted social conflicts and ethnic violence. However, whilst it may have become more fashionable after the democratic changes in Eastern Europe at the beginning of the 1990s, the concept of civil society has been a strong undercurrent in Western political thought throughout the twentieth century. From Italian Marxist Antonio Gramsci to New Labour leader Tony Blair, the concept of civil society has been deployed (for vastly different ideological objectives) in pursuit of progressive political change. Of course as Robson has tartly observed, 'the fact that the concept of "civil society" had passed through Hegel to Marx and thereon to Lenin and the Italian Gramsci, probably never occurred to any of those who cheered the success in 1997 of the "new" party of the working class' (Robson, 2000: 15). The fact that Gramsci and Blair can both embrace and utilise civil society as an agent of progressive social and political change, illustrates the concept's strength, and its weakness. On the one hand, it captures an important reality. Namely, that politics and power go beyond the narrow level of the state, and are woven into the other sinews of society and community (associations, churches, trade unions, business groups, NGOs and even the family itself). On the other hand, the breadth of such a definition (and confusion over its limits), risks diluting the phrase to the point that it becomes meaningless. As Scholte has observed, 'seventy years ago Gramsci regarded civil society as an arena where class hegemony forges consent, whereas much contemporary discussion treats civil society as a site of disruption and dissent' (Scholte, 2000: 4).

This chapter contends that it is important to define the limits of civil society within a given political context and to acknowledge that civil society is a relational concept, rather than a static phenomenon with a universal meaning. Gramsci understood this, and used it to breathe life into revolutionary socialism in his *Prison Notebooks* written in the 1930s. Gramsci refers to civil society in terms of private organisations and associations such as trade unions, churches, schools, political parties and cultural associations 'which are distinct from the processes of production *and* from the coercive apparatuses of the state. ... Civil society is the sphere where capitalists, workers and others engage in political and ideological struggles and where political parties, trade unions, religious bodies and a great variety of other organisations come into existence' (Gramsci, in Simon, 1982: 69). For Gramsci then, civil society was central to the creation and operation of hegemonic power. It was through access to (and manipulation of) civil society that hegemonic relations would be changed and socialist goals would be achieved. Thus the social relationships within civil society, for example, within the family unit, between the teacher and student, or between priest and worshipper, provide an interwoven fabric of power relationships where the hegemonic classes (parent, professor, priest) exercise power and control over the subordinate classes (child, student, worshipper). In this sense, power is diffused throughout civil society as well as being embodied in the coercive agencies of the state. It was this realisation that brought Gramsci to emphasise the centrality of civil society to his dialectic and his conception of the nature and role of civil society is central to his refinement of classical Marxist understandings of power. For Gramsci therefore, civil society was the catalyst for revolution, with the capacity to transform hegemonic power relationships within the state and achieve the socialist ideal.

This (to put it mildly) is not what Tony Blair is after when he promotes the Third Way, or seeks to work with the other social partners to tackle Britain's current social, political and economic problems. Yet he too advocates civil society and its constituent elements as integral to the development of social capital, democratic renewal and progressive political change. Lowndes and Wilson (2001) capture the limits of the Blair vision with regard to civil society's role in contemporary British politics and quote the words of the Prime Minister himself: '... if communities are to deal with difficult cross-cutting issues like youth justice, drug abuse and social exclusion, we have to harness the contribution of businesses, public agencies, voluntary organisations and community groups and get them working to a common agenda' (Blair, T. in Lowndes and Wilson, 2001: 635). However, the New Labour agenda could not be further removed from that of Gramsci in regard to the role of civil society as an agent of political change. Lowndes and Wilson (2001) contend that far from seeing it as the midwife of revolutionary socialism, New Labour are co-opting civil society groups as statutory agencies and service-providers, weakening rather than strengthening its capacity to provide a voice to a mobilised citizenry. 'While citizen involvement in local governance is championed by New Labour, new institutional arrangements tend to prioritize individual over collective forms of public participation, and to focus upon the service delivery role of local voluntary bodies. Despite the stated intention to foster "a new brand of involved and responsible citizenship", new institutions may be in danger of suppressing, rather than exploiting, the full potential of local associations to nurture social capital' (Lowndes and Wilson, 2001: 641). Robson (2000) puts the case more starkly: 'The community activist is as likely nowadays to read the *Financial Times* as the *Socialist Worker'* (Robson, 2000: 72). In this sense, then, when Blair, Giddens *et al.* use the phrase *civil society* (or aspects of it) they do so to enshrine the prevailing capitalist hegemony, rather than to undermine it and replace it.

The point here is not to argue that Gramsci's version of the phrase is superior to its current articulation within New Labour press releases, or friendly agencies such as the Institute for Public Policy Research (IPPR), but simply that the concept of civil society can be used to justify and defend a multiplicity of political values and objectives. This brings us back to the point. The concept of civil society is contextual and relational. As such, its parameters require definition.

This chapter prefers an inclusive definition of civil society to reflect the positive and negative aspects of the society itself and to reflect the fact that the line between what is deemed positive and negative within a society, is itself a value judgement that may change over time (this will become apparent in the examination of the evolution of civil society in Northern Ireland). Civil society is understood here to refer to the groups, associations and individuals, from trade unions, churches, business communities, educational sectors, cultural organisations, NGOs, media groups, the arts, peace groups and other pressure groups, that mediate between the individual and the state. Whilst this focuses upon those non-governmental individuals and groups that make a positive engagement with the liberal-democratic polity, it does not exclude those people and organisations that might be perceived as exerting a *negative* and destructive influence upon the society. To take the case of Northern Ireland as an example, paramilitary organisations such as the Provisional IRA and Ulster Defence Association (UDA) and ethno-centric cultural/religious organisations such as the Orange Order and the Gaelic Athletic Association (GAA), are some of the most powerful and important constituents of civil society within Northern Ireland, and thus are impossible to exclude from any definition if the political and social dynamics of that society are to be properly understood. As Wilson

(1998) has remarked, 'civil society will of its diverse nature contain a much broader spectrum of concerns (including many unsavoury ones) and throw up more creative talents (as well as many destructive elements)' (Wilson, 1998: 103).[2]

Civil society as a global norm

> Transnational advocacy networks have been instrumental in shaping global decision-making, persuading and pressuring governments to ban landmines, endorse international environmental agreements and denounce female genital mutilation. These and countless other citizen initiatives, campaigns and movements are ushering in an era in which governing is no longer left only to governments. The operative word now is 'governance' – a process that is more inclusive, participatory and democratic than in the past. Governance focuses less on the institutions of government and more on solving problems and making and implementing decisions that are of direct interest to the public. Governance reflects the growing capacity and will of citizens to control their own lives and to transform their societies. (*Civicus World*, 1999)

The concept of civil society found a renewed currency during the 1990s. This was accompanied by two other features of the decade; first, the ending of the Cold War and democratic movements in Eastern Europe, and second, the increase of ethno-nationalist violence and civil wars within state boundaries (Kaldor, 1999; Ryan 2000: 157–8). The increased opportunities facilitated by the end of the Cold War provided the international community (in the shape of the United Nations and its agencies) with the opportunity to intervene as a third party in such conflicts. The changing nature of war in the 1990s, the rise of ethno-nationalist conflicts and the concomitant impact on civilian populations required it to do so. This set off renewed thinking within international organisations, the academic community and NGO practitioners themselves, as to what role civil society could usefully play in preventing, reducing or resolving such conflict. It is clear that civil society activism played an important role in political change in places such as South Africa during the early 1990s. Taylor (2001) argues that such activity played a major role in destroying the apartheid system of government and in the creation of a democracy based on non-racial lines. 'Among the social forces that made for peace, for creating the "new" South Africa, were the innovative actions of an ever increasing network of progressive movements, institutions, non-governmental organisations and associations (which included churches, trade unions, civics, and women's groups) engaged in a "war of opposition" against apartheid rule' (Taylor, 2001: 41). The renewal of interest in the role of civil society during the 1990s also reflects a growing emphasis on conflict prevention, given the failure of international efforts to intervene successfully in conflicts that had already broken out (Ryan, 2000: 114). Miall (2000) has illustrated the way in which latent conflict has been prevented by civil society actors in conjunction with international agencies. Commenting on conflict prevention efforts in Macedonia in the late 1990s, Miall observes that 'at grass-roots level the various initiatives and projects for inter-ethnic relations sponsored by Search for Common Ground, the Soros Foundation and other NGOs ... undoubtedly contributed to fostering a moderate constituency on both sides, and to maintaining a dialogue, although their impact on inter-ethnic co-operation at the highest level is difficult to assess' (Miall, in Lund and Rasamoelina, 2000: 41). Academic commentators and international agencies alike have attempted to deal with the underachievement of interventions within ethnically divided or imploded states by turning to conflict prevention rather than conflict management initiatives. This trend has opened up a space for the more proactive involvement of civil society actors within such societies as a bridge between the conflict parties and external agencies with the capacity to intervene. Thus, efforts to prevent conflict that focus on *deep* conflict prevention (removing underlying political or economic grievances, building trust between protagonists etc.) or *light* conflict prevention (maintaining cease-fires, providing early warning systems of latent tensions, or rapid response facilities once hostilities have begun) have tended to advocate an expanded role for civil society actors.

It is undeniable that the well known alphabet soup of international organisations (UN, OSCE, WTO etc.) have determined a need, and are eager to support a role for civil society organisations in preventing the outbreak or escalation of violent conflicts. A foray into the search engines of such international bodies will produce a plethora of online articles and speeches on the subject.[3] The World Bank advocates civil society groups as legitimate actors within the political process and sees a role for such groups in the processes of democratisation and development. The Secretary-General of the United Nations, Kofi Annan, remarked that civil society organisations were one of the crucial building blocks in maintaining international peace and security in the modern world. 'The United Nations once dealt only with Governments.

But now we know that peace and prosperity cannot be achieved without partnerships involving Governments, international organisations, the business community and civil society. In today's world, we depend on each other.'[4] The International Committee of the Red Cross suggests that new global dangers in the areas of environmental decay, famine, poverty, terrorism and conflict (many of which of course are interconnected), have forced the policy-making community at national and supranational levels to think beyond the confines of the nation-state, and involve a wider array of actors in efforts to tackle such problems.

While there is much that can be done by civil society actors to prevent either the outbreak or escalation of violent conflict, it would be inaccurate and foolhardy to decontextualise such groups and individuals from the societies within which they are located. In other words, civil society is not intrinsically virtuous or peaceful, though under the right circumstances it may be the vehicle for conflict prevention or conflict transformation to occur. The following comparison of the media within Burundi and Rwanda illustrates the point. In Burundi, an NGO launched a radio station aimed at transforming negative stereotypes between conflict parties in the region. *Studio Ijiambo* was staffed by members of Burundi's two main ethnic groups, Hutus and Tutsis. The station produced current affairs and drama programmes (including a soap opera) that emphasised commonalities as well as ethnic difficulties between the two communities, with the stress being on the interdependence of both. The story lines of these programmes were underpinned with the values of reconciliation, tolerance and peacemaking. In Rwanda, on the other hand, Hutus and Tutsis experienced a rather different media experience. In 1998, a radio station calling itself *Voice of the Patriot* began broadcasting scare stories that Tutsi soldiers from Rwanda and Burundi were coming to massacre local residents. More famously perhaps, in Rwanda during the 1994 genocide, a radio station calling itself *Radio Television Libre des Mille Collines* became notorious as a consequence of its broadcasts inciting Hutus to kill Tutsis. The privately owned radio station, established in 1993, played a role in organising militias, broadcast lists of people to be killed and, above all, incited hatred. Clearly, therefore, the media, like religious organisations, NGOs and other civil society actors, can be a source of conflict as well as being a mechanism for its prevention.

In their haste to grasp a practicable strategy for combating violent conflict, the academic, national and international policy-making communities must avoid viewing civil society and its constituent groups as a wonder pill that will cure all ills. As the following section dealing with Northern Ireland will illustrate, community cohesion, civic activism and the desire for associational life, which are the building blocks of civil society, can lead to very uncivil outcomes.

Civil society in Northern Ireland

So far this chapter has focused on the theoretical underpinnings of the concept of civil society and its current usage within global discourse on conflict prevention. The final part of this chapter will look at how it is to be understood within a specific region, and in particular, within the divided society of Northern Ireland. The argument here, is that while many of the actions and activities of this hydra-headed beast called civil society have contributed positively to conflict management and conflict transformation in the region, this is only one side of the coin, and many others have had the opposite effect. The purpose of focusing on Northern Ireland is to illustrate the central argument in this chapter, namely, that civil society is not an intrinsic force for good, but must combine with other factors to achieve what its academic and policy-making champions expect of it.

Northern Ireland is a small, though highly complex region, with a sophisticated, politically literate and vibrant civil society. Many of its constituent elements, educators, religious organisations, media, business leaders and trade unions have all played their part in encouraging the peace process that resulted in paramilitary ceasefires in 1994 and the Good Friday Agreement (GFA) in 1998. In a society with just over 1.5 million people, NGOs abound, with a recent estimate putting their number in excess of 5000 with an annual turnover of £400 million (NICVA, 1997: 6). These NGOs range from overt peace and reconciliation organisations to more economically focused community development groups. Many of these NGOs are supported financially by the British government and by funding from the European Union, though not without some controversy. 'The EU peace money in the 1990s arrived with a call to get the money "on the ground" quickly. The result was that funders soon found that they had more money than they could spend in time. Many (most)? of the projects funded have been ill-thought out, poor in quality, and in some cases, just plain silly (Ulster Scots and Gaelic classes to improve the job prospects of ex-prisoners)' (Martin, 2000: 16).

It is argued here that the role of civil society groups in contributing to progressive social and political change in Northern Ireland has been an important (if indirect) one over the last 30 years of low intensity conflict in the region. While often unacknowledged by the political class, these groups have had a slow-burning positive impact on the political debate, were integral to the 1998 negotiations that resulted in the GFA and saw this influence reflected in post-GFA political structures such as the establishment of a Civic Forum. Thus, they have played, and continue to play, an intrinsic role in the governance of the region (Cochrane, 2001; Cochrane and Dunn, 2002).

After the GFA was agreed by the main political parties, several key elements within civil society came together to advocate a 'Yes' vote in the subsequent referendum of May 1998. This culminated in the establishment of a non-party political 'Yes' Campaign, populated in the main by trade unionists, voluntary and community activists and academics. A nucleus of activists drew together the various strands of civil society, mobilising support from Church leaders, educators, journalists, actors local sporting heroes and business leaders. The Director of the 'Yes' campaign, was aware of the risks that were being taken by a coalition of individuals normally expected to remain outside of the political fray. 'But who were we – other than a group of friends and colleagues, some drawn from the voluntary sector and others from the business sector – and what was our legitimacy? We knew we had none, in electoral terms, but we felt we had rights as citizens and as inhabitants of Northern Ireland – and, indeed, a duty to help the political process along' (Oliver, 1998: 9). It would be fair to say that without the efforts made by civil society initiatives and specifically by the independent 'Yes' campaign, the result of the referendum[5] would have been significantly closer and the GFA would have received a significantly smaller mandate, imperilling its existence.

More recently, the murder of Catholic postal worker Daniel McColgan in January 2002 by loyalist paramilitary group the Red Hand Defenders[6] saw the Irish Congress of Trade Unions (ICTU) call on all public sector workers to stage a half day strike action and mass rally in Belfast on 18 January. It was partly in response to the solidarity shown by the constituents of civil society (the trade unions, church leaders, peace groups and community workers) that the Red Hand Defenders were 'stood down' by their parent body, the UFF, shortly after these threats were made against public sector workers in Northern Ireland.[7]

This is exactly the sort of activity that global institutions such as the UN see as being part of civil society's contribution to governance aimed at conflict prevention. However, at the local level, the benefits of civil society activism are often contested and resisted. Those working for peace and reconciliation in Northern Ireland are sometimes denigrated by the people who live there as being part of a community relations 'industry', a middle-class sector of professionalised quangocrats, or simply as 'toffs against terrorism' who use the political conflict as a site for philanthropic projects to occupy their leisure hours. Government attempts to fund cross-community activities between Catholics and Protestants, or provide core-funding for NGOs engaged in reconciliation work, are often seen as a façade within urban working-class areas, or as unrealistic given the sectarian bitterness that exists. At times, new NGOs have been formed to resist what is seen as a hegemonic and ephemeral governance project from the outside, based on the idea of the 'contact hypothesis'.[8] One example of this trend is the Springfield Inter-Community Development Project (SICDP) which was formed out of failed cross-community initiatives of the past that had been imposed on the area. This NGO emerged in 1990 when a group of community activists on a sectarian fault line on Belfast's Springfield Road, came together to build their own initiative from the ground up, motivated by the failure of more traditional community relations activity. The SICDP attempted to build a community based NGO from the ground up, rather than from the top down. It did so in response to community need, developing a range of activities incrementally and pragmatically, based upon the priorities of the local area, rather than parachuting in from the outside. Controversially perhaps, the organisation was led by Billy Hutchinson, a former member of the loyalist paramilitary group the Ulster Volunteer Force (UVF) and now a leading figure within the Progressive Unionist Party (PUP). Rather than pursue the traditional strategy of campaigning against, condemning and confronting sectarian violence, the SICDP sought to employ and recruit from among those who may have been ambivalent to (or even supportive of) some paramilitary violence. They took this approach in order to gain access to communities that 'outsiders' had been unsuccessful in influencing in the past. '…what you really needed to be doing was involving those people who were involved in the conflict, and using ex-prisoners as a type of local hero…[people] with street cred' (Hutchinson, in Cochrane and Dunn, 2002: 29). At one stage during its formation, the SICDP successfully resisted pressure from a funding agency to appoint well-known unionist and nationalist political figures to its management committee. It believed that this would send the wrong messages to the people within the communities it was seeking to work with and influence.

This NGO, and others like it, illustrate the ways in which local initiatives at the community level have emerged in Northern Ireland in response to the perceived failure of an externally driven hegemonic project concerning what civil society consists of, and what its role in governance should be. Many of the individuals and groups within Northern Ireland's civil society have worked tirelessly to promote peace and reconciliation (either directly through trade-union sponsored public rallies and vigils, or indirectly through cross-community anti-sectarian workshops), often against a backdrop of vicious and violent conflict within those same communities (Sutton, 1994). Indeed, it has often been this sense of *community* which has motivated both the positive *and* negative components of civil society in Northern Ireland. Ironically perhaps, the motivations for the establishment of human rights organisations, reconciliation groups, church-based peace groups and community development organisations were similar to those of the main paramilitary factions in Northern Ireland. The sense of *community values* and desire to defend, protect or augment that community's position has led to a strong (but dichotomous) community cohesion in Northern Ireland. Returning to Putnam's (2000) metaphor for the decline of associational life in the United States, people in Northern Ireland are clearly bowling *together* as the sense of community is thriving. In a society of 1.5 million people with over 5000 active NGOs and numerous interventions by other civil society actors such as Church leaders, trade unionists and business leaders, people are seemingly falling over one another to do something for their community. However, in a divided society like Northern Ireland, *the community* is a contested concept. Put simply, there is more than one community, and those who are overly concerned about which community they belong to have sometimes been prepared to kill those they have determined to be in another community. While a plethora of civil society groups have been working for peace and reconciliation over the last 30 years, perhaps just as many groups and individuals have engaged in uncivil activities. Their motives have often been articulated as being in pursuit of civil rights, defence of community cultural heritage/identity, or the protection of human rights. Unfortunately, definitions of political, legal and cultural rights and identities have frequently been defined in oppositional terms by the unionist and nationalist communities. The Grand Orange Lodge of Ireland, for instance, makes a claim to a human rights agenda and defines this in terms of the 'right' to parade. 'The Grand Orange Lodge of Ireland is committed to the principle of Human Rights. We are convinced that fundamental rights in Northern Ireland have been violated. ... We need to uphold the right of people to be able to walk peaceably down a public road without hindrance. We need to uphold the right of people to peaceably express their culture and traditions.'[9] The Garvaghy Road Resident's Coalition, one of the NGOs in the forefront of protests against Orange parades, has a radically different view of rights and liberties. 'For two years, the community has been under constant siege by the Orange Order and its supporters. The residents continue to stand strong and struggle for their right to equality, freedom from sectarian discrimination and harassment.'[10] The point therefore, is that while both of these NGOs are fundamental elements of civil society in Northern Ireland, their articulation of concepts such as civil rights is contested and subjective, as the communities are themselves contested and defined in an oppositional relationship. Whatever about their relative merits, these NGOs, and many others like them, are anything but apathetic. They are populated by the type of energy and commitment so admired by proponents of social capital and civil society.

There has been a near obsessive desire to *bowl together* along a fractured and dichotomous community divide.[11] The existence of two separate communities competing for space and power within the region has produced a desire to bowl together separately! This was just as apparent in 1969 at the beginning of the 'troubles' as it is today. One of the first observable forms of community organisation during this period was the formation of the main paramilitary groupings within nationalist and unionist urban areas. The Provisional IRA characterised itself as *defending* Catholics who were being burnt out of their homes and intimidated by loyalists in parts of Belfast. On the unionist side, the Ulster Volunteer Force (UVF) had formed in 1966, while the Ulster Defence Association (UDA) emerged in September 1971. This acted as an umbrella organisation bringing together a range of Protestant vigilante groupings such as the Loyalist Association of Workers (LAW) and the Shankill Defence Association in response to a desire for more co-ordinated action against the Provisional IRA and its attacks on the Protestant community.

These groupings were all motivated by Putnam's desire for participation in their community and for associational life. They wanted to make a contribution to their community and support it. The organisations they joined in their effort to do this, however, were violent ones. Many of those within the voluntary and community sector in Northern Ireland are veterans of this period, and some became involved in paramilitary activity in the 1970s and 1980s. It may seem anomalous that people who are today engaged in conflict resolution and community development activity were themselves once direct actors in that conflict. This is explained by the fact that the types of people who are now attracted to re-building their communities in 2002 were also anxious to defend those same communities in the early 1970s. In this sense, the formation of both sets of paramilitary groups in Northern Ireland was an act of community self-organisation identical in motivation, though differing significantly in ideology, activities and impacts, to the civil society initiatives that exist today and focus on community development and reconciliation.

The argument here is that we need to understand civil society for what it is, namely, a subjective reflection of community(ies) values and not an intrinsic force for peace. As argued earlier in this chapter, this has not been sufficiently articulated by international institutions, policy-makers, or academics such as Putnam (2000), who place the emphasis upon the universality of the concept rather than the specificity of the context. The positive spin that is put on the *civil* aspect of civil society is very much in the eye of the beholder, as the motivations and mindsets of the paramilitaries in Northern Ireland and their supporters illustrated in the 1970s. To carve up the phrase civil society, allowing entry only to those groups and individuals perceived to be working for the community or public *good*, is to misrepresent and misunderstand the nature of that society. This error is compounded when dealing with a divided society, as it fails to comprehend the dynamics of the conflict incubated within that society. To allow one NGO into the civil society club, but not another, is to place one's own value system upon that society and obscure the reality of its dynamic forces. To stretch Putnam's metaphor, the argument in this chapter is that a healthy and vibrant democratic polity will not be created simply by encouraging bowling together *per se*. Though this may provide valuable socio-political glue for an energised and educated citizenry within a stable society, it will only be useful within a divided society such as that in Northern Ireland if an equal amount of effort is put into managing, healing or transcending the divisions between the bowlers.

Governance and resistance in Northern Ireland

The nature of civil society in Northern Ireland illustrates that governance is subject to multiple sites of conformity, resistance and adaptation. There are numerous instances of this, though the focus here will be on one specific area, namely, the funding of NGOs within Northern Ireland.

One of the anomalies of the NGO sector within the region, particularly the peace/conflict resolution organisations (P/CROs) that are a central component of civil society there, is the extent to which they are supported financially by institutional backers, particularly the British government, the European Union and various funding agencies within the United States. Since the early 1990s, successive British Governments have been eager to fund community development and community relations groups. They had two reasons for doing this, both of which linked into a top-down conception of governance. First, it suited the developing ideology of contracting the state and privatising the provision of services. Thus, statutory agencies were encouraged to shuffle-off responsibilities to the NGO community, funding and co-opting community groups to fulfil what used to be the responsibility of statutory agencies. Some have claimed that another motive for doing this was to emasculate the radicalism of NGOs and force them into the position of service-deliverers rather than advocates of radical social change (Robson, 2000). This trend was common within the NGO community within Northern Ireland in the 1980s and 1990s. Whilst many groups were formed to resist state hegemonies, in practice many found themselves sucked into existing political and economic power structures and conforming to this aspect of governance, sometimes without even realising that they were doing so.

The second reason why the government has funded community relations NGOs and peace groups throughout Northern Ireland, is that (in common with the prevailing orthodoxy within the international agencies outlined earlier) they see these organisations as one of the building blocks that will encourage peace and stability in Northern Ireland. The paradox of this attempt to translate what is perceived to be good governance from an international (or national) level to the local level is epitomised by many NGOs that take a pragmatic view of available funding, accepting the resources that are available from national and international sources, while discarding much (if not all) of the political agenda that inevitably accompanies such funding.

The following example provides a good illustration of the dissonance that has been present within Northern Ireland between the agenda of the NGO on the one hand, and that of the external funder on the other. A representative from the radical loyalist Ulster Community Action Network (UCAN) – a mainly Protestant community development organisation with its roots in the UDA – was asked if they would accept money from the International Fund for Ireland (IFI). In the past, many loyalist groups saw this funding as being part of the Anglo-Irish Agreement (AIA), and thus as a bribe from the American government to encourage acceptance of a policy that they disagreed with politically. In the wake of the signing of the AIA in November 1985, the general unionist community was encouraged to shun the IFI by unionist politicians. However, despite these efforts, the focus for UCAN (Londonderry) was on the practical benefits that funding could bring to their community. 'To tell you the honest truth, the job is more important. ... If there is a need and there is money, take it' (UCAN, in Cochrane and Dunn, 2002: 141).

The typical pattern for many of these NGOs within Northern Ireland was to soak-up whatever funding they could lay their hands on, whilst ignoring the ideological agenda of the agency providing it. At a surface level this often looked like a conformity to the macro-funding environment. Thus NGOs within republican and loyalist communities would submit grant applications that emphasised the cross-community education and conflict resolution work that was being done. Given that this was often a prerequisite for obtaining the funding from British government and European Union sources, it is no surprise to find this highlighted in the funding applications of both republican and loyalist NGO organisations. In practice, however, this often functioned as a resistance to such funding agendas. There were instances, for example, where community groups that were primarily based within one ethnic background would make 'paper links' with partner organisations from the opposite side of the community. Thus, they may have had members of their management committee, patrons, or trustees who would be perceived as coming from both Protestant and Catholic backgrounds. There might even be reciprocal arrangements where individuals would serve on the boards of other NGOs to provide a semblance of cross-community contact. In reality, however, each group might remain largely separate from the other in practice. Whilst such chicanery may have been the exception rather than the rule, it serves as an extreme example of the pragmatic relationship between some NGOs and the funding community. It also illustrates that global norms, and attempts at governance, can, in practice, be adapted and subverted at the local level. As with many acts of resistance, the most effective means of doing so for NGOs within Northern Ireland has been to give the impression of conforming to hegemonic controls whilst quietly subverting, avoiding and getting around them. While funding agencies are aware of the abuses that have taken place within the voluntary and community sector in Northern Ireland, tackling them effectively has proven to be a difficult task. To withdraw the funding of an NGO involved in community development work or human rights activity in Northern Ireland (whatever the reason) is a highly political thing to do. It will often be accompanied by allegations of political bias, discrimination and favouritism to the other side. However, the issue of NGO funding illustrates the difficulty of imposing a global agenda onto a locality.

This particular example embodies the theme of this chapter and the general theme within this collection. First, civil society is not a universally consistent force for public good, but it may function to contribute to a particular political and social agenda – that is perceived to be one of progressive peaceful change – within certain circumstances. Second, governance is not a linear phenomenon, delivered by one small powerful group (government) onto a larger but weaker group (the governed). Governance in Northern Ireland, as in the other regions covered in this collection, is a two-way street. Ironically perhaps, as Gramsci and others have observed, ultimately power (and the power to govern) resides not within national governments, or the rules and regulations of the European Union and its many agencies, but in the collective will of the governed. When civil society networks (whether in the form of the voluntary and community sector or the paramilitary groups) collectively aim to resist these rules and regulations, it can be extremely difficult for national and international governing agencies to enforce their will, or implement any preconceived notions of governance.

Notes

1. Throughout the 1990s, the literature on conflict management has been replete with references to the role of civil or civic society organisations in reducing violent conflict. See for instance practitioner reports such as the Aspen Institute's *Conflict Prevention: Strategies to Sustain Peace in the Post-Cold War World* (Washington: Aspen Institute, 1997). The UNESCO report *From a Culture of Violence to a Culture of Peace* (UNESCO, 1996). The Carnegie Commission on Preventing Deadly Conflict, *Preventing Deadly Conflict: final report with executive summary*.
2. Wilson, R. 'Placing Northern Ireland' in, New Order? International models of peace and reconciliation (Belfast: Democratic Dialogue, 1998, p. 103).
3. An internet search whilst writing this chapter produced 2840 hits for the phrase 'civil society' on the UN's web site.
4. Annan, K. from United Nations web site. (URL: http://www.un.org/partners/civil_society/home.htm)
5. The referendum in Northern Ireland was held on 22 May 1998. Seventy-one per cent voted in favour of the GFA while 29 per cent voted against it.
6. The Red Hand Defenders is a cover name for the Ulster Freedom Fighters (UFF) the nom de plume used by the Ulster Defence Association (UDA) for its paramilitary activities. Thus, the UDA could continue its violent campaign under an assumed name and avoid having those released on license as part of the terms of the GFA, being returned to prison.
7. A statement that the Red Hand Defenders were 'stood down' by the Ulster Freedom Fighters (UFF) was announced on 17 January 2002. This did little to reassure people in Northern Ireland, given the fact that the UFF was itself believed to have been responsible for the attacks.

8. The 'contact hypothesis' sees community sectarianism as a product of dysfunctional inter-communal relationships and believes that by increasing the amount of contact between the conflict parties (either explicitly or implicitly) these negative stereotypes will be broken down.
9. Grand Orange Lodge of Ireland website (http://www.grandorange.org.uk/covenant1.htm).
10. Garvaghy Road Residents' Coalition website (http://www.garvaghyroad.org/).
11. There is no sign of voter apathy in elections, for example, to the extent that the proponents of civil society have identified in regions such as Great Britain and the United States. At the last Westminster general election in June 2001, the turnout in Northern Ireland was 68 per cent and in some constituencies went as high as 80 per cent. These figures were significantly above the UK average of 59 per cent.

Part III

Resistance to Global Regimes

9
Global Environmental Governance and Local Resistance: The Global Trade in Ivory

Rosaleen Duffy

Introduction

The increasing importance of environmental issues in global politics has generated new and powerful interest groups keen to manage natural resources in particular ways. The transboundary nature of global environmental change has meant that it has become a key site for global governance. Oceans, forests, wildlife, the atmosphere and so on all cross human constructed national boundaries; good environmental management has largely been defined in terms of supranational conventions, policies and agreements. The environment has clearly become a key area for governance of local resources from the global level because numerous international regimes are deemed to operate for the 'global good'. However, an examination of these global environmental regimes reveals that they embody multiple and competing interest groups rather than representing a common global view that can be effectively implemented at the local level. In this chapter the case of the Convention on the International Trade in Endangered Species (CITES) is taken as an example of how global environmental governance operates and what kinds of resistances it generates.

The global trade bans under the CITES regime have been strongly resisted by ivory producing states, most notably in southern Africa. It is in this gap between the global regime and the local management practices that resistances to global governance can be found. Those resistances manifest themselves in two forms, the legal and public resistance to the imposition of global norms, and the illegal and less visible activities that ignore, subvert and adapt those norms. The mismatch between global environmental regimes and local ideas about good conservation practice has created a site of dysgovernance, where global regimes have failed to establish a high degree of control. This chapter first examines the conceptual framework centred on global governance versus local dysgovernance. Second, it investigates the ways in which the global environmental movement has ensured that its version of good conservation practice has been globalised and extended through international environmental regimes, such as CITES. It then analyses the local response to that governance, in the form of consistent pro-trade campaigns. Finally, it examines sites of 'dysgovernance', notably illegal activities that subvert global environmental governance

Global governance versus local dysgovernance

The Commission on Global Governance suggested that governance includes formal institutions and regimes empowered to enforce compliance, as well as the informal arrangements that people or institutions have agreed or perceive to be in their interest (Commission on Global Governance, 1995: 4). Global governance highlights a shift in the location of authority in the political, economic and social realms. In the context of global integration with fragmentation, concepts of global governance indicate a shift away from the state-centric view of global politics (Hewson and Sinclair, 1999: 5–11). The turbulent global arena means that the state-centric system now co-exists within an equally powerful, decentralised multicentric form of organisation. This change has given rise to a new set of complex and dynamic global arrangements (Rosenau, 1990: 10–12; and McGrew, 1992: 13).

The multiple forms of resistance to global governance create spaces that challenge attempts at global control and indicate the contours of and limits to global governance. The various forms of global governance clearly generate their own forms and sites of resistance. The idea of global governance is very open, or fuzzy, and rather than viewing global governance as an effective and efficient hegemonic project, we need to rethink the extent of its reach. In many ways global governance theorists are so preoccupied with governance itself that the forces that might challenge or undermine order are ignored or treated as undesirable disruptions. These are the forces that strain and stress the global order, thereby threatening to produce instability. These forces are essentially ungovernable, and they are not recognised by the discourse on global governance, which assumes an ability to extend and enforce global control over all people and things. Since the logic of global governance does not allow anything to roam outside the governance grid, resistances to it are re-conceptualised as dysgovernance (Latham, 1999: 31–9). In a sense dysgovernance is where attempts to govern have gone wrong or failed completely, and so it can be redefined as 'dysfunctional governance'.

Global environmental regimes encounter essentially ungovernable forces that seek to resist, adapt and ignore their attempts to enforce compliance with global norms. Turning to Africa, the internal dynamics of African societies have presented significant barriers to any attempt to impose global norms. Since Africa is at the heart of western imaginings of the barbarous 'other', the explanations of the complexity of Africa have been congruent with western notions of development. Africa has often seemed to represent the initial stages of western notions of progress or the dark opposite of civilisation, and as such it is constructed and presented as the backward, primitive and barbarous continent (Chabal and Daloz, 1999).

An important area for analysis for this book is whether the resistances examined here are specifically responses to new forms of global governance, or if they are older pre-existing processes that just happen to stand in contravention to attempts to impose global controls. Bayart suggests that the externally defined periodisation of Africa's past reflects a misunderstanding where the determining dynamics of the continent are presented as external. This fails to acknowledge the importance of Africa's historicity, which underestimates the internal processes, and the lengthy African history of living without organising European style state systems (Bayart, 1993). The importation of a state system by European colonisers was resisted in various ways by African societies, and this has resulted in a complex mix, which means the African state is a rhizome rather than a root system. As a rhizome, the state is horizontally organised along patrimonial lines, and has reappropriated the institutions that originated under colonial rule. The civic arena is affected through factional struggles, the rhizomatic nature of the state and patronage politics (Bayart, 1993). Bayart suggests that the salient feature of African politics over the last 300 years is not the growing integration of Africa into a western dominated global economy, but the contrary; it is the latter's inability to pull the continent into its magnetic field. This is not to suggest that African societies are holistic with a poorly developed sense of individualism so that some kind of traditional or pre-modern culture cannot be overcome (Bayart, 1993; also see Reno, 1998). The political, economic and social logic of the contemporary Africa creates a specific form of modernity that does not fit with western experiences of modernisation or development (Chabal and Daloz, 1999: 141–4).

These resistances to earlier imperial projects and to more recent forms of externally imposed governance have taken particular forms because they essentially represent the resistances of less powerful groups (in global terms). In this way global governance as a hegemonic project produces new varieties of resistance as well as highlighting the pre-existing forms of passive and active, visible and invisible, silent and vocal resistance. There are dominant public transcripts and private subordinate discourses, as such variable discourses can be carried out at the same time (Scott, 1985, 1990; Twyman, 1998: 759). These overlapping voices create sites of passive and active resistance to global governance. They also indicate the power relations between the local and the global, since they assist in defining the precise reach of global governance when faced with the local context. A study of the interface between local practices and global conventions provides an ideal vantage point from which to analyse the nature of global governance.

Since national borders do not bound the environment, global environmental management has proven to be central to the creation and extension of global governance. Global conventions have been established in response to transboundary activities and problems where domestic legislation has proved inadequate, and so they are especially significant in the area of environmental management. One form of global governance can be found in international agreements that are intended to govern a variety of local, national, regional and global processes. In the case of global environmental regimes, the interaction between global social movements and the member states of those organisations has been critical. The interaction between global regimes and social movements has to be understood in terms of the global discourse about environmental issues. Environmental NGOs have had an increasing impact on global regimes through pressure group politics, including sophisticated relationships with the media and campaigning activities. Their ability to disseminate environmental information through the media and mass mobilisation has been used to embarrass governments and international organisations, as well as heightening awareness about key issues (O'Brien *et al.*, 2000: 109–23). In many ways global regimes have transformed their ways of governing in response to their encounter with the environmental movement (Princen and Finger, 1994; O'Brien *et al.*, 2000: 206–33). This is clear in the case of environmental regimes, where NGO campaigns have directly informed the creation and enforcement of norms to govern resource management at the local, regional and global scales. This complex multilateralism has indicated a shift away from a state-based system in global politics, which has not challenged the fundamentals of the existing world order but has incrementally pluralised governing structures (Commission on Global Governance, 1995: 1–4; O'Brien *et al.*, 2000: 3–12). Young (1989) argues that international regimes have, in general, been formed by states seeking to control transboundary activities in order to guarantee benefits to dominant parties. In the case of international environmental agreements it is clear that certain norms, usually based in western political ideologies, also have a critical role to play. Nadelman (1990: 479) suggests that these norms strictly control the conditions under which states and other actors can participate in and authorise certain activities.

Global environmental regimes have also raised questions about the contested nature and status of scientific knowledge. In particular, global regimes rely on ideas of positivist and uncontested science that can be used to draw up universally applicable forms of environmental management. These are then used to justify and legitimate highly political global interventions at the local level. The ability of knowledge brokers to frame and interpret scientific knowledge is a substantial source of political power. Such knowledge brokers are influential under conditions of scientific uncertainty that characterise environmental problems. In international environmental regimes, global NGOs have claimed that they have access to the most relevant and up to date scientific knowledge that should be used to set norms and guide local policy (Wynne, 1992; Litfin, 1994).

The resistances to global norms have arisen particularly in response to the ways that such scientific knowledge and global norms are created. Litfin suggests that scientific information, like all forms of knowledge, is embedded in structures of power, including disciplinary power, national power and socio-economic power. Due to its unrivalled status as a universal legitimator, science may facilitate international co-operation. However, as scientific knowledge becomes incorporated into stories and discourses, it is framed, interpreted and rhetorically communicated. As such, this politically embedded scientific knowledge is vital in revealing, shaping and revising the ways that varied actors perceive their interests (Litfin, 1994: 51; Sivaramakrishnan, 1999; Neumann, 2000). It is in the spaces between competing scientific discourses that resistant actors have an opportunity to challenge global environmental norms, and argue that their local scientific knowledge takes account of micro level specificities.

This idea of neutral scientific management translates into the use of prohibition, or the threat of prohibition, as a norm – that is, a standard rule to regulate the behaviour of parties. The international trade in wildlife products operates under a global legislative framework that has been created as part of a broader landscape of conservation ideologies, which are presented as politically neutral environmental science. The formation of global regimes to govern the behaviour of state and non-state actors is often at odds with local norms that govern everyday activities and behaviours. One area where this is apparent is in the disputes over the global trade ban on ivory sales, which has pitted southern African producing states and East Asian trading states against a more preservationist international environmental movement and allied European and North American states. In the view of wildlife policymakers in Zimbabwe, CITES has evolved from a regulatory regime to a prohibition regime with regard to certain wild species. The tensions over the decision to ban trade in ivory highlight the deep divisions between Zimbabwe and the international community over the operation of a global norm. This is especially significant in light of successful campaigns for a qualified lifting of the ivory ban for Zimbabwe, Botswana and Namibia. In many ways the success of pro-ivory trade campaigns by the southern African ivory producing states has indicated the limits to imposing global governance as a political project.

Global governance and CITES

The wildlife trade is a global business that encompasses legal and illegal trade in animals and plants. Trade Records Analysis of Flora and Fauna in International Commerce (Traffic) estimates that the value of the wildlife trade is second only to the drugs trade among illegally traded goods, but recognises that accurate figures are impossible to obtain since much of the wildlife trade is illegal and unrecorded. Current estimates of the value of the trade in plants, animals and their derivatives stand at around US$14 billion per annum, with the illegal trade in wildlife products accounting for approximately US$3.5 billion of that total.[1]

The function of CITES is to regulate this global trade. The basic regulatory tools and principles of CITES are set out in a system of appendices where an Appendix I listing constitutes a trade ban, Appendix II allows controlled and monitored trading and an Appendix III listing requires the trading state to notify CITES in order to prevent over-exploitation. CITES does have provisions for species to be transferred between the appendices: for instance, to include, delete or transfer a species requires a two-thirds majority vote of the parties at the biennial conferences. In addition, the convention has provisions for a split listing of a species which allows certain local populations of a single species to be listed on a different appendix (Wijnstekers, 1994: 14–16). These appendices are the centrepiece of CITES' claims to be engaged in scientifically determined environmental management that is politically neutral. The CITES appendices are an excellent example of the ways that global environmental regimes elevate scientific knowledge and the opinions of epistemic communities justify highly political environmental interventions from the global level at the local level.

Although the criteria for a CITES appendix listing are presented as scientifically determined, they are subject to disagreement because, in effect, an appendix listing operates as a highly politicised global norm. In general, all populations of a single species are treated equally under an appendix listing, regardless of its local, national or regional status. The system of appendices has proved the most contentious issue for Zimbabwe because policy-makers in government institutions, local NGOs and community organisations argue that the basic norm that underlies most of the operation of CITES is the precautionary principle. This principle requires parties to demonstrate that trade is non-detrimental to the survival of the species being traded, and if there is any doubt states are asked to cease all trade until non-detriment findings are proven (EIA, 1994: 5; O'Riordan and Jordan, 1995).

The status of scientific knowledge within global regimes has been enhanced in the case of CITES by its peculiar relationship with international environmental NGOs. These organisations have proved keen to appeal to notions of pure and uncorrupted science of the non-governmental sector. For example, moral proselytism about what constitutes good environmental management is a key element in global prohibition regimes (Nadelman, 1990: 481–3; O'Brien *et al.*, 2000: 109–23). In the case of CITES the role of moral entrepreneur has been played by NGOs, such as IUCN and WWF-International, which were critical actors in lobbying for the creation of CITES. Consequently, NGOs have retained a unique and powerful position in a convention that is essentially an organisation patronised by states. For example, biennial meetings are held to evaluate progress and consider new proposals, and NGOs and trade organisations are allowed to take part in the discussions, but are not allowed to vote on policy decisions (WWF, undated; Princen and Finger, 1994: 135–8).[2] NGOs have been central in arguing for trade bans as a moral issue to save certain species, such as elephants, whales, rhinos and tigers. Clearly, CITES is not simply an organisation that is based around inter-state diplomacy, since it involves multiple actors and complex bargaining between different interest groups that operate on the local, national and global levels.

The institution and implementation of the ban on the global ivory trade in 1989 is an excellent example of global environmental governance and of local level resistances to it. Until 1988 the idea of an ivory ban did not hold much currency and CITES regulations were informed by the idea that a controlled trade was sufficient to ensure that trade did not threaten the survival of the species (cf. Parker, 1979: 207). The ivory ban was instituted in 1989, and has been strongly resisted through campaigns to reopen a legal ivory trade.

Resisting global governance: public protest

From the perspective of southern African ivory producing states, the division between local norms and global norms can be characterised as a clash between preservation and utilisation. At the global level, CITES is informed by preservationist ideas about how to manage wildlife, while Zimbabwe's policy is determined by local priorities, which are thought of as best served through sustainable utilisation. Sustainable utilisation can be briefly defined as use of wildlife without jeopardising the continued survival of species. The policy of the Zimbabwe Department of National Parks and Wildlife Management (DNPWLM), or 'the Parks Department', is that wildlife cannot survive in a developing country unless it is economically self-supporting. In effect wildlife use has become another form of land use that is able to compete with crops and livestock. The policy objective is to persuade commercial and subsistence farmers to define wildlife as an economic resource, and in turn this will mean a greater area of land is made available for wildlife to allow wild populations to increase. In this way sustainable use aims to satisfy the demands for humane treatment of animals and concerns for human rights and development rights.

Since a global trade ban operates as a blunt policy instrument, it fails to take account of the complexities of local situations. As a result, as with many aspects of global governance, the ivory ban has been the focal point of resistances to global environmental norms. The ivory trade ban has been consistently resisted by southern African nations, and in turn their lobbying has been challenged by various actors who support the international regimes and view global governance as beneficial. One of the problems with the debates over the ivory ban in the 1980s was that the African elephant was globally defined as a single population that covered most of the continent. In the post-ban period Zimbabwe has been keen to point out that different populations of African elephants require different management policies.

Over the 1990s southern African range states consistently argued that the ban was not working and was in fact in contravention of their interests. In 1997, the tenth CITES conference, held in the heated atmosphere of Harare, proved to be the arena where all the main interest groups converged to battle it out over a partial reopening the ivory trade. The first proposal, to downlist the African elephant to Appendix II, was the most ambitious and politically contentious, but it was agreed amongst pro-trade interest groups that if the downlisting proposal failed, the second choice was to allow Namibia, Botswana and Zimbabwe only to trade with Japan (as the largest ivory consumer) as long as the four states involved could prove that they had adequate controls to prevent illegal ivory trading. This was the first time that southern Africa had a real chance of overturning the ivory ban since 1989.[3] The concerns of southern African states had to be taken seriously because of the real possibility that Zimbabwe (in particular) would go it alone and declare a reopening of the ivory trade. Consequently, the same tactics of media hype, blackmail with threats of withdrawal of aid, rumour and counter-rumour were used by alliances formed from the ever more entrenched interest groups seen in 1989. This meant that the conference was about *for* versus *against*, with little political space for uncertainty.

The attempts to extend and consolidate global environmental governance over wildlife in Africa have been strongly resisted by Zimbabwe, in conjunction with its allies in the Far East and the southern African region. A major political bargaining chip at CITES was that Zimbabwe held one of the largest and most secure elephant populations on the continent. The delegates at CITES have always been aware of the importance of keeping such important elephant range states within the boundaries of the convention. The pro-trade alliance argued that the ban had not shut down markets for ivory as effectively as its supporters suggested. Zimbabwean delegates argued that since there was a continuing demand for ivory across the world, Zimbabwe had the right to utilise its resources to take advantage of such markets (see Dublin and Jachmann, 1991: 62–3). The pro-trade alliance also formed the Southern African Centre for Wildlife Management (SACWM) to lobby for a qualified lifting of the ivory ban (DNPWLM, 1992a; SACWM, 1994). Consequently, during the conference it was inferred that if CITES members did not take account of southern African interests then Zimbabwe would break the international trade ban. The then Minister of Environment and Tourism, Chen Chimutengwende, suggested that if CITES did not act in favour of Zimbabwe's interests then it would have made itself irrelevant to Zimbabwe.[4] The fact that Zimbabwe has such a large elephant population meant that this was a threat that all the parties at CITES could not ignore, even though it was a risky position for Zimbabwe to take. Developing states also tried to link the debt and aid question to public protests against the ivory ban. The southern African nations put forward a proposal for a debt-for-ivory buy-out. Zimbabwe's position has always been that the ivory stockpiles (produced through culling, natural death, problem animal control and seizures of illegal ivory) constitute an unacceptable waste of a natural and renewable resource. It was suggested that the World Bank Global Environmental Facility could provide funding to environmental organisations to buy ivory stockpiles from African governments.[5] The newly purchased stockpiles could then be burnt to prevent it from entering a legal or illegal international trade.

The ways that local communities claimed rights to use wildlife were also used to resist the imposition of globally determined conservation policies. The presence of Zimbabwean rural community groups at the conference was used to re-emphasise that ivory trading was as much about rural development as about revenue generation. Zimbabwe has one of the most high profile and successful schemes for integrating conservation and rural development. The Communal Areas Management Programme for Indigenous Resources (Campfire) has been used as a model scheme by other African states such as Zambia, Mozambique, Namibia and Botswana. It allows rural communities to extend ownership rights over wildlife in their area and to retain the revenues that are generated from using that wildlife in activities such as sport hunting, tourism and meat production. The community then decides how to spend those revenues to enhance local development.[6] The then-director of the Campfire Association, Taparendava Maveneke, stated that holding the 1997 CITES conference in Harare was important because it was the first time that rural communities had come face to face with key policy-makers in the field of international wildlife trading, and that this was significant because it meant parties at CITES would be made to understand the problems being faced by the various parties to the convention.[7] Global environmental NGOs that adhere to a preservationist philosophy have found the argument that wildlife is a resource to be used to benefit rural communities one of the hardest to reject. Indeed, there were accusations at CITES that environmental NGOs and preservationist western states were frustrating developing countries by imposing a new form of imperialism through global environmental governance. Such governance, critics argued, implied that African states, organisations and communities should not be in control of environmental decision-making, but that global institutions should be. Opposers of wildlife utilisation have generally been characterised as misanthropes who seek to deny the rural poor a chance of earning a living from animals that are otherwise at best a nuisance and at worst crop destroyers and a threat to human life. This dispute essentially grew from competing definitions of wildlife as a national resource to be used for domestic benefits, and the view of western states and global environmental NGOs that elephants were a world resource to be protected at all costs for the global good.

The continuing public protests from Zimbabwe and other southern African nations was met with attempts to extend and consolidate global control. The creation of a need for certainty provided an opportunity for sections of the global environmental movement to attempt to extend global governance. The animal welfare lobby organised into a global network to promote their particular definition of good conservation practice. It played a major role in the 1997 CITES meeting, and in particular the International Fund for Animal Welfare (IFAW) openly opposed Zimbabwe's position on the ivory trade. It was part of the Species Survival Network, a coalition of 50 NGOs that included high profile global NGOs such as Greenpeace, formed in 1992 and dedicated to strict enforcement of CITES regulations. IFAW and its allies argued that Zimbabwe and other southern African states would not be capable of preventing illegal exports if CITES allowed a partial or total lifting of the ivory ban.[8] The management problems and the power struggle in Zimbabwe's Parks Department were also used to full effect as part of the discussions about the ivory ban. A confidential report by a panel of CITES experts noted that illegal ivory trading had continued unchecked in Zimbabwe, citing, for example, a consignment of carving made from 70 tusks that had been shipped to Japan. In addition, critics of the Parks Department's capacity to manage a legal ivory trade pointed out that since the Department had been systematically starved of funds by the central government, it needed every source of revenue available, including the sale of ivory and that its lack of management capability made it unlikely that the money would be used effectively for elephant conservation.[9]

The anti-ban alliance also used the debt and aid question to try to force pro-trading states into withdrawing their proposal for a partial lifting of the ivory ban. The southern African states accused the animal rights lobby of engaging in international blackmail and spreading misinformation. It was reported that some observers at the CITES conference believed that members of the pro-ban alliance had paid some

African countries to vote against southern Africa, thereby exploiting the historical split between east and southern Africa on the ivory trade. Indeed, it was also reported in the local press at the time of the conference that animal rights lobbyists and Northern states opposed to the trade had threatened to withdraw development aid from states that supported Zimbabwe, Namibia and Botswana, and that Northern delegates at CITES had stated they would only vote if there was a common African policy on the ivory trade.[10] In this way the debt relief question was captured by animal rights NGOs and other anti-trade interest groups to force African states to promise never to engage in ivory trading.

Finally, the legal and public forms of resistance from southern Africa were successful, and at the 1997 meeting Zimbabwe, Namibia and Botswana had their elephant populations downlisted to Appendix II. This decision came with the proviso that trading was only to be allowed in 1999 if adequate measures were introduced to ensure that trading can be sustainable and free from illegally hunted ivory.[11] The decision meant that in 1999 Namibia, Zimbabwe and Botswana could reopen a restricted trade with Japan. The 1997 decisions paved the way for further relaxation of the ivory ban at the CITES conference in Chile in November 2002.[12] Of course the decision was immediately met with the concern that this would provide a signal to poachers to go ahead and restart the levels of commercial poaching witnessed in east Africa in the 1980s.[13] It remains to be seen if the partial lifting of the ivory ban does result in a renewed round of poaching, but the anti-trade interest groups immediately started to regroup to argue in favour of a renewed ban on ivory trading. This in turn is indicative of the ways that global regimes respond to the sites of resistance to global governance. Since southern African countries have persistently remained resistant spaces that challenge global controls, their legal forms of lobbying have become the focus of counter-lobbying by organisations that favour global governance in the realm of environmental management.

Resisting global governance: evasion and subversion

The attempts to extend global governance have also encountered a less visible set of challenges. Numerous local, regional and global interest groups engage in multiple forms of illegal activities that have proved highly resistant to any kind of control. These illegal activities, specifically illicit ivory hunting and trading, have a long history in southern Africa, stretching over the pre-colonial to the post-colonial period. These criminalised spaces are characterised by their fluidity and adaptability. It is this ability to respond rapidly to changes that means they are capable of subverting, adapting, ignoring and actively resisting global governance. The limits of global governance are clearly indicated through an analysis of the illegal methods used by various interest groups in southern Africa to resist attempts to control their ivory activities.

The involvement of criminal global networks coupled with corrupt local agents and interest groups have created spaces that are essentially ungovernable. The continuance of ivory poaching and trafficking is highly dependent on globalised networks of international trade. It is the illegal trade in ivory that has caused greatest concern, but its extent is impossible to quantify. The illegal trade has long been dependent on well-organised and long established smuggling routes that stretched from Africa to Europe, the Middle East and the Far East. One of the most striking features of the illegal trade in ivory is its fluidity, as it manages to avoid most regulations, and if one entry point is shut down another quickly opens. The involvement of triads and the Mafia in the ivory trade has also made it difficult to regulate. In debates about reopening the ivory trade this factor is often ignored, yet the interest that ivory attracts from criminal elements is a significant issue for global and local law enforcement (Currey and Moore, 1994: 3; EIA, 1994: 4).

The involvement of officials in the illegal ivory trade has made the extension of global governance especially difficult. Such involvement neutralised the enforcement capacity of wildlife departments and of global attempts to stamp out the trade. Diplomatic immunity is widely used to protect movements of ivory. The use of privileges associated with the diplomatic bag means that diplomats, with relative impunity, can export wildlife products. The involvement of diplomats continued in the post-ban period. For example, in 1995 Kenya requested that the UN lift diplomatic immunity on two UN officials (an American and a Sri Lankan) involved in the UN Operation in Somalia (UNOSOM) who were accused of smuggling ivory from Somalia to Kenya.[14]

The extent of the illegal ivory trade and the poaching it fuelled were real causes for concern for conservationists from the late 1980s. The persistence of the illegal ivory trade and the ways that officials were engaged in it have presented real challenges to global control, thereby turning global governance into global dysgovernance. Ivory poaching in Zimbabwe reveals that commercial poaching is a highly organised international business that is reliant on structures within a state or society, rather like any other business. It is clear that militaries and rebel groups in southern Africa were the organisations with the necessary capacity to hunt with relative impunity and with the internal structures and criminal links to poach and ship ivory to the consuming states of the Far East. The case of ivory poaching indicates that illegal users of wildlife constitute a significant challenge to global governance. The coercive capacities of the Parks Department proved to be no match for well-armed and funded militaries in neighbouring countries that were exploiting opportunities for commercial poaching. In addition, the norms favoured by CITES had little impact on the ways that poaching and smuggling networks operated.

Although the Parks Department has been largely concerned with rhino poaching, illegal hunting of elephants is a closely related issue. It is an issue that is often ignored, and has even been subject to cover-up and denial by conservation authorities. Ivory poaching has been a problem since the early 1980s, yet its extent was left uninvestigated until a decade later, since an official definition of who these ivory poachers were has not been forthcoming. However, elephant poaching was more openly discussed as a result of the ban on international ivory trading in 1989. Before and after the ban the Parks Department consistently argued that an ivory ban would cause an increase in poaching. The reported rise in ivory poaching was deployed as a politically important legitimating argument for Zimbabwe's policy stance on the ivory trade. A number of interviewees cited the ivory ban as the main reason for the increase in poaching, suggesting that as a result of the ban ivory prices had at first collapsed but have steadily grown since 1989.[15] Usually the price paid to poachers was a fraction of the value of the ivory or rhino horn obtained by smugglers and dealers. However, it is very difficult to obtain accurate prices for ivory in the post-ban period because all trade is illegal. Nevertheless, in the immediate post-ban period prices initially slumped, but then the trend for black market ivory prices was upwards (Dublin *et al.*, 1995), despite the fact that the ivory ban was supposed to have effectively shut down such black markets. Parks Department reports demonstrate that Zimbabwe has definitely witnessed a rise in illegal hunting of elephants for ivory. From 1989 to 1992 there was an increase in ivory recovered from poachers by Parks staff and in elephant poaching activity (Murphree, 1992). There were a number of explanations for this rise. One explanation was that ivory poaching was linked to increase in rhino horn poaching. As rhino numbers declined poachers increasingly turned to ivory to finance their expeditions, because if they could not return with rhino horn they could at least recoup some of the cost with ivory. Another explanation was that the amount of money available for law enforcement had sharply declined due to the belief amongst donors and global environmental NGOs that the ban had solved the problem (Dublin *et al.*, 1995: 84–7).

The attempts to extend global governance in the realm of environmental management were strongly challenged by the networks of official complicity and corruption. The involvement of officials in poaching and smuggling is significant because it neutralises the enforcement capacity of national, regional and global institutions. It is clear that the levels of poaching experienced across the continent could not have occurred without a degree of official complicity. At worst there was direct and personal involvement in sponsoring poachers and conducting smuggling, while at best there was official complacency about poaching and turning a blind eye to illegal activities. As a result of this complicity, traders and dealers bought off officials to ensure that their operations were left unhindered. Although there is very little written evidence of official and military involvement in poaching and smuggling, a number of interviewees from the conservation sector stated what they perceived to be the case (see Duffy, 1999).

What is clear is that poaching is part of a vast industry with a number of different types of poachers, ranging from local subsistence poachers to ruthless commercial poachers allied to governments and illegal smuggling rings (Iain Douglas-Hamilton, cited in Wildlife Society of Zimbabwe, 1993). Illegal trading routes and groups are crucial factors in the survival of the black market trade supplied by poachers. Smuggling routes for ivory through South Africa, Mozambique and Zambia were almost an open secret amongst conservationists in Zimbabwe. Smugglers are the link in the chain which transports ivory from the field to markets. Available information showed that an illegal trade in ivory was flourishing in one of the neighbouring countries in the post-ban period.[16] Zambia has a busy and lucrative black market in ivory and Lusaka was a major conduit for rhino horn, which was mostly poached in northern Zimbabwe (Cumming *et al.*, 1990: 56). Ivory poached in Zimbabwe made its way to Zambian carving houses and from there to South Africa (EIA, 1992: 14). Poaching and smuggling are organised by the same gangs involved in drugs, arms and gems and these gangs operated an international network that supplied poachers and sold ivory (Thornton and Currey, 1991: 119).

The implication of Parks staff and the Zimbabwe National Army (ZNA) in poaching and smuggling is also a highly controversial topic. Anti-poaching initiatives on local, national and global scales are rendered ineffective if the poachers are assisted by the very body responsible for preventing access to wildlife. Illegal hunting by poaching networks has had a long history in the south east lowveld, and especially in Gonarezhou. The strategy of 'freezing' national parks was employed during the liberation war, and afforded Rhodesian security services the opportunity to poach with impunity. One source suggested that the poaching was also linked to an ex-Rhodesian Army syndicate.[17] Renamo were blamed for poaching in the park during the mid-1980s, but EIA research suggested that it was the ZNA with the complicity of wildlife officials (EIA, 1992: 20).

Conservationists outside Zimbabwe, and a few individuals within Zimbabwe, were convinced that members of ZNA had an extensive poaching and smuggling operation in Mozambique and Gonarezhou. A military officer whose nickname was Rex Nango was reported to be at the centre of poaching and selling of ivory for personal gain in the 1980s.[18] As a frozen zone there was little communication between the northern and southern portions of the park, and once the ZNA moved in to deal with Renamo incursions in the north of the park it became a poaching free-for-all. In addition, since the railway to Zimbabwe from Mozambique crossed the border at Sango, when the military declared Sango unsafe, trains carried on to Rutenga 150 km inside Zimbabwe where there were no customs controls (Currey and Moore, 1994). The ZNA stated that this decision was based solely on security, but anecdotal evidence suggests that ivory was transported from Rutenga, a place well serviced by roads, and so ivory and rhino horn were quickly distributed from there.

It is clear that since the ivory trade ban poaching has subsided in the south eastern lowveld, but the main organisers of the poaching ring that operated in the 1980s have not disappeared and consistently try to find new ways to reopen poaching rings in the area.[19] Complicity from Parks officials was essential to commercial poachers and there were persistent rumours of a poaching faction in the Parks Department whose alliances in the ruling party were related to the power struggle in the Department.[20] In Gonarezhou, a former warden and game scout was implicated in poaching. However, rather than being investigated, they were merely moved to other posts in Gokwe and Matetsi safari areas and Chizarira national park where poaching suddenly increased after their arrival (EIA, 1992: 20; Duffy, 1999: 115). Corruption is often cited as the central factor in the continuance of poaching in Zimbabwe. Without corrupt officials within the Parks Department, poachers would not have been able to hunt at such levels and sell on their trophies. Official and military corruption is particularly problematic because in effect it neutralises the enforcement capabilities of global regimes. In terms of global governance, it is clear that illicit hunting and trading of ivory present a significant challenge to attempts to construct and enforce universal notions of good conservation practice. The multiplicity of illegal activities can be characterised as a rational and organised form of disorder that stretches and reshapes the boundaries of global governance.

Conclusion

The successes and failures of CITES in the realm of controlling the international ivory trade indicates the capabilities and limitations of global governance. The case of continued ivory trading in line with CITES regulations and in contravention of them highlights the different forms of resistances that global governance encounters at the local level. There are legal means of resisting global conventions through lobbying and mobilising support from various global and local interests. In addition, there are illegal means of subverting or adapting global regulations. In a sense these essentially ungovernable processes provide an alternative form of governance that is more appropriate and enforceable at the local level. The political interplay between different factions and interest groups involved in the ivory issue illustrates how global norms are resisted and adapted by local communities, national government agencies, regional organisations and NGOs. A study of the interface between the global and the local highlights the complex interactions involved in debates about what constitutes best conservation theory and practice. The ungovernable activities that CITES encounters challenge and reshape the boundaries of global governance. While much of the literature assumes global governance to be a hegemonic project which is able to extend its reach across the globe and down to the local level, it is clear that a study of the ivory trade reveals that various actors are successful at resisting, subverting and adapting global controls. Legal and illegal methods of subverting, resisting, adapting and even ignoring global environmental norms indicate that global governance encounters sites of ungovernability. From the point of view of relevant actors and interest groups in Africa and the global system, continued ivory trading is an example of dysgovernance, because ivory trading continues to roam outside the governance grid.

Examining global governance in relation to the ivory trade demonstrates that environmental management regimes claim to secure the long-term interests of the global environment. In so doing, global regimes elevate the status of scientific knowledge to justify highly political interventions at the national and local levels. In particular, global regimes claim to secure the long-term interests of the environment in the face of what they define as the short-termism of interest groups that are involved in damaging the environment. CITES, and the problems associated with global environmental management, indicate some of the broader challenges to global governance. Any attempt to create universally applicable ideas of conservation, conflict resolution or statehood encounters challenges at the local level. The ways that global norms may be enforced at the local level create and sustain resistances to them. In turn these resistances stress and strain the capacities of global governance. As such, these resistances highlight a need to rethink and reconfigure how global governance is defined. Rather than being a hegemonic project, able to create and enforce universal norms and practices, it is clear that some activities at the local level create ungovernable spaces.

Notes

1. http://www.wwf.org.uk/wildlifetrade/law. (Accessed 3.5.02); also see http://www.traffic.org; http://www.cites.org; http://www.wcmc.org.uk/ CITES (Accessed 3.5.02) for further discussion.
2. Also see http://www.cites.org (Accessed 3.5.02).
3. See http://www.traffic.org; http://www.cites.org; http://www.wcmc.org.uk/ CITES for further discussion (Accessed 3.5.02).
4. Herald 16.6.97 *CITES or No CITES, We'll Go it Alone*; Pretoria News (South Africa) 17.6.97 *Zimbabwe Backs Off Threat to Break Ivory Ban*; Guardian 17.6.97 *Harare Resists the Ivory Sale Ban*; and Guardian 18.6.97 *Ivory Trade States to Try Again After Near Miss*.
5. Interview with John Gripper, Sebakwe Black Rhino Trust, 14.10.94, Ascott-Under-Wychwood; Pretoria News 17.6.97 CITES *Proposal to Buy Some of Africa's Ivory Stocks*; and Herald 13.6.97 *Maveneke Rejects Debt Relief on Ivory*.
6. Herald 16.12.94 *Allow Trade in Legally Obtained Ivory and Rhino Horns: Campfire*.
7. Herald 13.6.97 *Maveneke Rejects Debt Relief on Ivory Trade*.
8. Star (South Africa) 11.6.97 *Reopening of Trade Slated as Danger to the Big Three*; Star 13.6.97 *Massive Illegal Wildlife Trade Revealed*; and Herald 11.6.97 *Downlisting of Jumbo: IFAW Still Opposed*.
9. Mail and Guardian 6.12.96 *Zim's Illicit Ivory Trade Exposed*; Mail and Guardian 31.6.97 *Zim Parks in Trouble*.
10. Herald 12.6.97 *African States Divided on the Ivory Issue*; and Herald 13.6.97 *Maveneke Rejects Debt Relief on Ivory*.
11. Milliken, T. (1999), *African elephants and the 11th Meeting of the Conference of the Parties to CITES*, http:// www.traffic.org/briefings/elephants-11thmeeting. html (Accessed 3.5.02).
12. http://www.cites.org (Accessed 3.12.02).

13. Herald 18.6.97 *CITES: Three States Down But Not Out*; Herald 20.6.97 *At Last, the Ivory Trade War is Won!*; and Mail and Guardian 27.6.97 *All Clear for Ivory Trade.*
14. Herald 28.3.95 *Kenya Asks UN to Lift Smuggling Suspects' Immunity.*
15. For example, interview with Jon Hutton, Director of Projects, Africa Resources Trust, 13.3.95, Harare; interview with Steven Kasere, Deputy Director of the Campfire Association, 14.3.95, Harare; and interview with Charl Grobbelaar, Chief Executive of the Zimbabwe Hunters Association, 12.2.95, Harare.
16. Glenn Tatham quoted in Herald 18.6.95 *4 People Killed During Battles with Poachers*; and also see Herald 6.5.95 *Poachers Slaughter Hundreds of Jumbos.*
17. Mail and Guardian 4.10.96 *Palme's Murder Still a Mystery*; and Daly (1982) for further discussion of Rhodesian involvement; anonymous interviewee; and also see EIA (1992: 20) and Pearce (1991: 70).
18. Interview with Stephen T. Bracken, Second Secretary, US Embassy, 21.3.95, Harare.
19. Interview with Clive Stockil, Chair of the Save Valley Conservancy, 13.5.96, Chiredzi.
20. Anonymous interviewee. Also see Financial Gazette 9.2.95 *Parks Grant Notorious Poacher a Hunters Licence.*

10
Global Economic Governance in the Information Age: Counter-Hegemonic Challenges and Sub-Hegemonic Adaptations in East Asia

Ngai-Ling Sum

Introduction

This chapter adopts a neo-Gramscian international political economy approach to global governance (Cox, 1987; Gill and Law, 1988; O'Brien *et al.*, 2000). Thus it highlights the contested future of global governance as a key stake in struggles to legitimise and consolidate the dominant, neo-liberal form of globalisation. Neo-Gramscians argue that the rise of global neo-liberalism, which is most strongly and powerfully advanced by the arch neo-liberal United States, inevitably provokes new forms of opposition even as older forms of struggle and resistance are marginalised. But they also interpret projects for global governance in its neo-liberal guise as attempts to mobilise broad social support for transnational neo-liberalism and to absorb or domesticate new oppositional movements. One such project was proposed in the United Nations Commission report, *Our Global Neighbourhood* (1995), which offered a vision of 'global governance' as the benign – and democratically accountable – management of a single, harmonisable 'global' world. It invoked values and norms such as democracy, human rights, and environmental justice, and advocated institutional mechanisms to integrate key individuals and civil society organisations into the work of neo-liberal institutions such as the IMF, WTO, World Bank and G8. For neo-Gramscians, then, global governance involves a series of mechanisms to institutionalise, channel and regularise the many and varied social conflicts created or reinforced by (neo-liberal) globalisation. As such it can be interpreted as a form of passive revolution that is intended to neutralise the disruptive potential of global capitalism by building a coherent global politics rooted in civil society as well as in market forces and states.

Given this, it is no surprise that the diverse objects of global governance (e.g. global economy, peace, human rights, democracy, civil society) are deeply and hotly contested. Thus global governance can be defined as a site of ideational/discursive and institutional struggles between hegemonic and counter-hegemonic social forces over the reconstitution of global–regional–national social relations in an era of neo-liberal globalisation. This invites us to: (a) study the discursive as well as material constitution of various objects of governance and the correlative remaking of economic, political, and social identities; (b) consider the attempts on a range of scales to conform these objects and subjects/subjectivities to the perceived regulatory needs of the emerging neo-liberal global order; and (c) highlight the continuing struggles over agency and institutional design and over their respective roles in establishing different objects of governance.

This chapter does not proceed from the *political* objects proposed in the UN report but from some novel global *economic* objects of governance, especially those rooted in the widely acknowledged transition to a globalising knowledge-based economy. In particular, it focuses on the development of a Global Information Infrastructure (GII) and the attempts to flank and support this with an expanded intellectual property rights (IPR) regime and basic information infrastructures at the regional and national levels. These issues are interesting for different reasons. Efforts to enforce IPR are highly contested through counter-hegemonic strategies (such as civil and state support for the *Linux* open source movement) and the tactics of everyday life (such as software piracy). Conversely, the call to build a regional and national information infrastructure offers opportunities for regional–national forces to adapt to the GII project and join the transnational class alliance that is actively promoting it. The chapter ends with some remarks on the heuristic value of cultural international political economy (Jessop and Sum, 2000).

New governance objects of the information age and the emergence of the GII–IPR–TRIPs complex

One of the earliest US-inspired projects to create key material conditions for the emerging global knowledge-based economy was Al Gore's 1995 call to build a 'global information marketplace' via the construction of a 'GII'. This proposal can be seen as an extension to the global scale of his 1993 'National Information Infrastructure' (NII) initiative to create and access digital information.

Al Gore's hegemonic construction of a global information infrastructure

In his capacity as US Vice-President, Gore called for the creation of a GII in the International Telecommunication Union (ITU) Conference in Buenos Aires in March 1994. His intention was to promote the development of the global arena as an information marketplace in ways favourable to US and related informational interests. His project won substantial backing in Brussels at the 1995 G7 meeting between the United States, United Kingdom, Canada, France, Germany, Italy and Japan and was endorsed by an industry coalition formed by the (US) Information Technology Industry Council (ITI), the European Association of Manufacturers of Business Machines and Information Technology (EUROBIT), and the Japan Electronics Industry Development Association (JEIDA). This coalition identified five essential means of governing global information: (1) promoting market access and stimulating the free movement of products and services; (2) relying on private-sector voluntary international standards process and proprietary technologies in standards rather than state regulation; (3) implementing the Trade Related Intellectual Property Rights (TRIPs) Agreement under GATT and its later incarnation under the WTO to enable content providers to use the GII with full protection of their intellectual property rights; (4) ensuring universal access to informational service; and (5) creating a flexible regulatory environment that can keep pace with rapid technological and market changes.

These industry-sponsored recommendations were underscored in Gore's own G7 speech. He highlighted the link between GII and IPRs in the following way:

> (L)et's develop and enforce effective intellectual property rights for the GII. If our content providers are not protected, there will not be content to fill the networks and give value to services. (Gore, 1995)

This link between GII and IPRs reinforced an emerging policy agenda with two interrelated objectives: (1) broadening and deepening rights in industrial and intellectual property, including digitalised information goods and services, and (2) facilitating the extension of the property regime through technical (especially GII) means as well as juridical (especially TRIPs–WTO) measures. This new digital agenda, which was supported by transnational IT interests and the Clinton administration, required a reorientation of US foreign economic policy around global IPRs (Drahos, 1995: 12). Before discussing some of its technical aspects, we should briefly examine the US approach to IPRs and their global consolidation.

The articulation/deepening of intellectual property rights and the TRIPs complex

Drawing on critical theories of the discursive construction of reality, Halbert (1999) offers a national case study of IPR that is also relevant to the global level. She examines how the US White Paper on NII extended the traditional defence of copyright to control intellectual property in the information age. This copyright 'story' acquired some material credibility with the NII Copyright Protection Act of 1995, which outlaws unwanted behaviour, such as piracy. The United States has translated this story globally through a series of general international treaties, bilateral agreements and unilateral actions using trade instruments (1999: 77). The IPR narrative goes like this:

> The hard-working intellectual property company spends money and time creating product. The company's hard work and ingenuity should be rewarded so it gets to own the product exclusively. Anyone caught with unauthorised copies is a pirate. These pirates are engaged in illegal and immoral activities, which deprive the rightful owners of their profits. Pirates are lazy because they steal instead of create. They should be punished for their actions. (Halbert, 1999: 78)

This IPR/piracy discourse has developed stepwise as the United States began in 1891 its slow transition from self-interested poacher to game-keeper on behalf of all commercial producers of intellectual property. By 1967, the legal and institutional foundations (e.g. the World Intellectual Property Organisation, see next paragraph) to protect IPRs were in place. With Gore's echoing calls for the NII and then the GII, IPRs were not only linked more directly with the information age but also moved up their policy agenda for global economic governance.

Historically, IPR as an object of global governance dates back at least as far as the Paris and Berne Conventions in 1883 and 1886. Responding to the rise of industrial technology, these conventions reinforced the legal protection of patents, trademarks, industrial designs and copyrights. In 1967, the World Intellectual Property Organisation (WIPO), a UNESCO agency, was created to monitor adherence to these conventions. It was criticised by firms from developed countries for its failure to set adequate minimum standards to protect IPRs and to enforce dispute resolution mechanisms. These firms doubt whether the WIPO would provide enough protection, believing that the policies and agenda of UN agencies are controlled by developing countries opposed to IPR protection. To address these worries, the International Intellectual Property Alliance (IIPA) and the Intellectual Property Committee (IPC) were established in 1984 and 1986 respectively. The former body lobbies on behalf of a coalition of seven trade associations representing US copyright-based industries such as film, publishing, motion pictures and music. The latter is an *ad hoc* coalition of 12 major US corporations from various industries. These coalitions argued that the US economy's profitability, innovation and competitiveness are tied to IPR protection. Narrating copyright-based industries as the United States' 'most prized trade assets' and 'largest source of exports', they claimed that failure to protect IPR would 'threaten' American profit levels and competitiveness. Whereas large firms are depicted as real or potential victims, pirates, especially those from developing countries, are portrayed as immoral actors.

Promoting this line to the Clinton administration, especially to the Office of the US Trade Representative (USTR), the IPC significantly shaped US proposals and negotiating positions on the TRIPs Agreement. With technical support from intellectual property experts, the USTR pushed aggressively for the globalisation of American-style intellectual property protection via the GATT–TRIPs regime. The Agreement – concluded in 1993 under the Uruguay Round of the GATT – aims to update the Berne Convention for the information era by specifying copyright norms for information-based goods and services traded through the GII (Hamilton, 1997: 244–6). The WTO, which succeeded GATT in 1995, has a key role in enforcing these norms.

Overall, these pressures and development have consolidated a well-entrenched GII–IPR–TRIPs complex (see Figure 10.1) that reinforces US economic hegemony through material and discursive powers and resources. For example, new narratives such as the copyright story and new data compilations such as piracy statistics lead to redefinitions of self and others. While countries classified as copyright partners may then join the most-favoured nations, those regarded as copyright enemies (i.e. pirates) are placed on the US Watch List. Depending on their

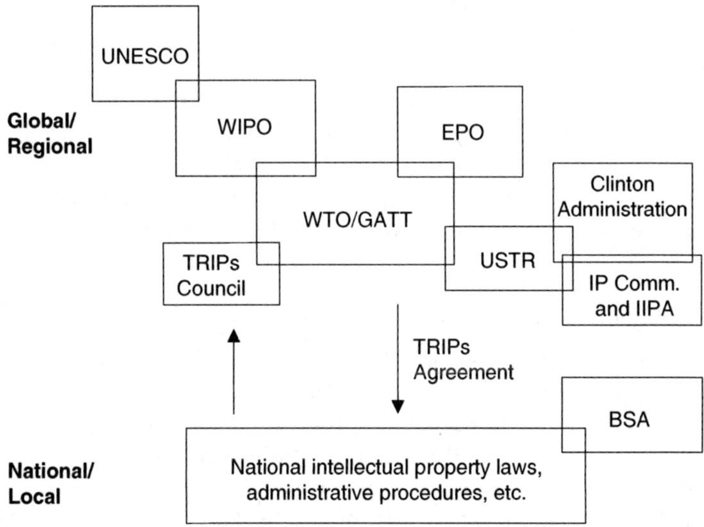

Figure 10.1   The GII–IPR–TRIPs complex

discursively constructed degree of delinquency, the latter countries are subjected to various juridical-material penalties. These include diplomatic pressures (e.g. in bilateral negotiations), surveillance mechanisms (e.g. TRIPs Council),[1] and sanctions (e.g. the Special 301).[2] This mix of discursive and material powers enables the WTO to force changes in national IPR regimes in line with the interests of leading transnational companies and to protect their quasi-monopolistic profits in over 100 countries (Comor, 1997: 361; Singleton, 2000: 217).

Complementing these global activities to promote a GII–IPR–TRIPs complex, the European Patent Office (EPO), which was established by the European Union, also runs technical cooperation projects to promote a modern patent system. For example, it set up an International Academy in 1997 to train patent examiners, patent judges and patent attorneys from member and candidate states.

Two configurations of glocality: counter-hegemonic challenges and pro-hegemonic adaptations in East Asia

A wide range of actors operating on different scales in the Americas, Europe and East Asia have reacted to the GII–IPR–TRIPs, its ideas and institutional practices. This has produced a complex set of multiscalar interactions that cannot be adequately interpreted in terms of a simple global–local dichotomy, let alone a dichotomy that posits a necessary antagonism between these two scales. The concept of glocal is useful here because it highlights the inherently tangled, co-constitutive and mutually implicated nature of interscalar relations. Referring specifically to East Asia, I now explore two types of glocal response to the GII–IPR–TRIPs complex: the first illustrates counter-hegemonic tactics and strategies, the second pro-hegemonic accommodation.

Counter-hegemonic challenges: strategies and tactics

The glocal transfer of the GII–IPR–TRIPs complex to East Asia has produced different modes of counter-hegemonic resistance. I deploy resistance here as an analytical rather than descriptive category by drawing on de Certeau's distinction between strategy and tactics (1985). For him, strategy is the weapon of the strong. The latter maintain their advantages by establishing well-defined, defensible institutional and/or spatial positions that can be controlled effectively in conducting 'wars of position' against outsiders. In contrast, tactics are the weapon of the weak and are mobile and furtive (Cresswell, 2001: 16). Tactics are used by those who lack these solid bases of operation but cannot escape the milieu that marginalises or oppresses them. So they must defend or promote their interests opportunistically by engaging in a permanent 'war of manoeuvre'. This turns everyday life into a continuing battle of wits in which the weak are always 'on the watch for opportunities that must be seized "on the wing"' (de Certeau, 1985: 35). They must seize the moment, engage in short-term, decisive actions and use speed to throw entrenched powers off balance, in the hope of gaining what may often prove transient victories and temporary advantages. Whereas de Certeau's distinction refers primarily to the practices of the strong and the weak respectively, there can be strategies as well as tactics of resistance. Thus strategies are pursued by the strong in East Asia who seek to counter the hegemony of the GII–IPR–TRIPs complex through measures such as backing Linux as an alternative to the dominant Microsoft standard. Complementing this are the counter-hegemonic tactics of the weak evident in everyday practices such as piracy.

Counter-hegemonic strategies to resist Wintelism: support for Linux

Wintelism is a neologism coined to refer to the global structural dominance of those who provide architectural and operating standards symbolised by the 'Microsoft Windows installed' and 'Intel Inside' labels on so many personal computers (see Zysman and Borrus, 1997; Hart, and Kim, 2002). The GII–IPR–TRIPs complex reinforces these structurally embedded competitive advantages and makes it harder to circumvent them. Unsurprisingly, Wintelism is increasingly provoking counter-hegemonic strategies from other key players – official, commercial and non-commercial – who feel disadvantaged or threatened by this dominance. I now explore some state strategies to resist the continuing dominance of Microsoft in East Asia.

Microsoft's open but proprietary standard maintains its dominance in three ways. First, because it owns the right to develop and alter its software, other software developers can only use its codes to develop Microsoft compatible products. Second, given its market dominance, programmes that cannot run on Windows operating systems will find relatively few buyers. And third, Microsoft is large and rich enough to purchase its competitors' products (to incorporate or stifle them) and/or develop and integrate alternatives into later rounds of its own products in order to kill off competition. Indeed, without losing control of its source code, Microsoft has established a dominant position in a wide range of interdependent software products (e.g., operating systems, word processing, spreadsheets, internet browsing, e-mail and PowerPoint) that operate as a suite of programmes. Its bundling strategy locks users into the full Microsoft range at high prices and, in addition, Asian users must wait for Microsoft to release Windows in their own languages.

This has prompted various attempts at the international and regional levels to move away from Microsoft and its related IPR regime. In particular, from the late 1990s onwards, there has been growing transnational support for the open source movement. Among many other open source products (such as the Apache system), Linux[3] is seen as a particularly viable alternative to Windows. Its open source nature means that: (1) software is created by a loose-knit group of programmers based on hacker ethics of shared information; (2) no single group/company owns the codes; and (3) piracy and IPR are almost non-issues because there are no proprietary rights. Linux operates under a General Public Licence so that any code written for the system and distributed beyond the developer must be made available to all at no cost. This means that users can download, adopt, improve and modify Linux without having to pay licensing fees or play by Microsoft and IPR rules. There is already a worldwide Linux community that is backed by a loose network of programmers, an anti-property rights academic community and some firms. This community provides Linux with information, tools, applications and regional content in local language versions including French,

German, Italian, Japanese, Chinese, Korean, Portuguese, Russian, Spanish, Swedish and English. In addition to commercial and non-commercial players with interests in contesting the Microsoft's quasi-monopoly, official backers of Linux include the Department of Energy in the United States, the German Parliament and the Post Office in China (Associated Press, 2002). Taken together, we can see these private and public forces as engaged in forms of transnational collective resistance based on a long-term 'war of position' to undermine Wintelism and, possibly, the neo-liberal IPR–TRIPs regime that links creativity and innovation to profit and legal instruments.

Support for free software is also found in East Asia. Apart from regional techno-academic communities, the governments of South Korea and China have given especially strong backing to the open source movement. This not only enables them to challenge the cultural hegemony of Microsoft, but in a neo-mercantilist manner facilitates the building of their own post-PC[4] software industries outside the GII–IPR–TRIPs complex.

The South Korean government announced in 1999 that it would support hardware and software industries based on Linux. It established a Linux consultative body of experts from the government, academic and industry sectors to standardise Korean versions of Linux and develop programs based on its operating system. In September 2000, the Minister of Information and Communication announced a new Linux policy at the 'Global Linux Year 2000' Expo in Seoul. He claimed that 'Linux is the epicentre of change in the communication world' and Linux Year 'is going to be a great terminal and investment bridge for Korean Linux companies and foreign companies' (Cunliffe, 2000).

The Chinese government is promoting similar schemes on national security as well as economic grounds. Regarding external security, it fears that Microsoft's control of Windows code could give the company (and possibly other US companies and even the US government) a hidden backdoor into Chinese computer systems, thus posing a security risk. Likewise, regarding internal security, it believes that Linux, as a server technology, could provide a simple means of social control by monitoring Chinese users computer activity. Thus, Linux's open source could enable China to control its national security and engage in domestic surveillance of its own netizens. Economically, China sees Linux as an opportunity to participate in the global software industry at a lower entry cost. Following its WTO entry, China could exploit the techno-economic space opened by Linux to develop its own post-PC software and escape Microsoft's dominance in foreign markets as well as at home. Given these security and economic concerns, both the China Academy of Science and the Ministry of Information Industry have supported the development of a localised version of Linux (Red Flag Linux). It was reported in March 2001, for example, that the Chinese government had ordered the Beijing bureaucracy and some state-owned companies to use Chinese-language Linux to run computer servers and to operate programs that access the internet. Likewise, to compete with Microsoft Windows and Office, in early 2001, Red Flag Linux released Chinese 2000, a software program that combines applications such as a spreadsheet, a Chinese-language word processor, graphics and business programmes aimed at small companies.

Microsoft has counter-attacked these challenges in three ways. First, it narrates open-source as 'a cancer', 'an intellectual property right destroyer' and even as 'un-American' (Festa, 2001: 2). Second, it has promoted shared source as an alternative to open source. This strategy would enable other large software companies to develop and debug applications without allowing them to modify its code or distribute it further. Microsoft calculates that revealing Windows source code might satisfy larger customers and reduce their interest in Linux.[5] Nonetheless Hewlett-Packard and IBM are now selling Linux-based products and working on open-source projects. IBM announced in 2001 that it would invest USD 200 million in the Asia-Pacific region over the next four years on seven Linux centres. Two of these would be located in China (Beijing and Shanghai) and one in South Korea (Seoul). Third, to undermine the growing market share of Linux, it has begun to sell Microsoft software at discounted rates to the public sector in a growing number of countries.

Counter-hegemonic tactics towards GII–IPR–TRIPs complex: the cultural politics of piracy

The counter-hegemonic strategies of the strong coexist with broadly equivalent tactics that have become part of the everyday politics of the weak. This section concentrates on piracy of software and media products (e.g. VCDs and DVDs) in East Asia. In China, Vietnam, Pakistan, Thailand, and other countries, software piracy is now a way of life. It is practised by consumers (businesses, non-profit organisations, high school and college students, etc.) and by producers (especially petty capitalists). Their activities are justified by counter-truths that subvert the hegemonic GII–IPR–TRIPs order. These range from the ethical stance that property rights should only apply to tangible goods and not intangibles, such as information, to the more commercial argument that multinationals ask consumers in developing countries too much for their software. The ethical justification rests on the claim that information- and knowledge-based products are part of a global intellectual commons that depends on sharing, common access, or cooperative production. It is further argued that the rhetoric of protecting rights of creators is hypocritical because ownership benefits accrue to corporations rather than true creators (e.g. programmers and artists), who are just employees. The commercial justification sees IPR protection as unfair/ unaffordable for low-income consumers in some Asian countries (e.g. China) who cannot pay the full price for the software – especially as the latter is often priced around 20 per cent higher than the same or equivalent software in the United States. As for the producers, there is 'a feeling among some people that the pirate software dealers are simply engaged in competitive business practices against companies who are charging too much for their products' (Cohen, 1997). Some even accord them Robin Hood status (Swartze, 2001). In between these extremes, there are others who are puzzled by the concept of IPR and see its infringement as at most a victimless crime. They argue that the success of the East Asian economy is based on flexible imitation, regard IPR as an alien concept that originates from a rights-based society, or claim that much of western IPR is itself based on past or present acts of piracy (e.g. biopiracy of food crops). This wide range of counter-IPR narratives and practices has generated a battleground over piracy in East Asia, especially China, Vietnam, India and Thailand, with endless cat-and-mouse raids, seizures and prosecutions intended to stop the challenges from the pirates.

The strategies of the cat to defend the discourses and institutions of GII–IPR–TRIPs include routine local surveillance of pirates to supplement its global systems of control. A key role is played here by the US-based Business Software Alliance (BSA). It has branches in 65 countries to promote and protect the interests of the US software industry (and, more recently, software firms based elsewhere). Members include Adobe, Apple, CNC Software/Mastercam, Macromedia and Microsoft. Some hardware suppliers, such as Compaq, Dell, IBM, Intel and Sybase, are also represented on its Policy Council. BSA branches regularly receive tip-offs from commercial intelligence and whistle blowers via hotlines and the internet about unlicensed use of software by individuals, companies or organisations. It investigates these cases before deciding whether to bring complaints against the companies/individuals on behalf of its members. It can also ask the relevant national government to investigate and assist it with expert witnesses and tests to prove suspected software is illegal. As a result of this mix of strategies, the piracy rate in the Asia/Pacific region fell from 64 per cent in 1995 to 47 per cent in 1999 but rose again to 51 per cent in 2000 (see Table 10.1). Nonetheless it was the only region that increased its piracy in 2000, with the piracy rate in China, India, Korea, Malaysia, Pakistan, Thailand and Vietnam being over 70 per cent. It was also claimed that the regionally incurred loss for global software multinationals was nearly USD 4.1 billion in 2000.

The tactics and activities of the mouse are pervasive. Despite the national imposition of IPR laws, piracy is a widespread way of life. Piracy, especially when pursued by non-commercial players, involves a 'war of manoeuvre' in which consumers seize time and space whenever and wherever possible to resist the increasing wealth and power of the information industry. Their resistance tactics, which may be linked to their freeware or socialist identities, include: (1) passing onto friends or colleagues copies of licensed software; (2) swapping master disks among friends and colleagues; (3) exchanging information on access to new unlicensed software; (4) uploading and downloading unlicensed software from bulletin boards or the internet; (5) frequent switching of third party storage sites for illicit software (e.g. college students putting them on campus servers); (6) copying a handful of licensed software products to the rest of the computers in an organisation; (7) transferring licensed software from office computers to domestic use; and (8) obtaining

Table 10.1   Piracy rates in newly industrializing countries in Asia in 1995 and 2000 (%)

	1995	2000
Asia-Pacific	64	51
China	96	94
Hong Kong	62	57
India	78	63
Korea	76	56
Malaysia	77	66
Pakistan	92	83
Singapore	53	50
Taiwan	70	53
Thailand	82	79
Vietnam	99	97

Source: Sixth Annual BSA Global Software Piracy Study 2000.

unlicensed software from shopping malls, night markets and mobile hawker stalls at fair and affordable prices.

Consumer resistance coexists with the tactics of producers. Petty capitalists, who undertake piracy for profit, operate on three levels: production, distribution and retail. In China, for example, a substantial amount of pirated goods is produced in the coastal areas of Guangdong and Fujian Provinces, sometimes with finance from Hong Kong and Taiwan. Production occurs in scattered, unorganised, and small-scale operations with workers from other provinces. State-owned factories in China have also been involved, especially during times of poor domestic demand for legal products. While manufacturing tends to be scattered, distribution of pirated goods is more organised. From production sites in China's coastal provinces, they are distributed along three main routes: (1) trucked to central distribution centres in China (such as Yiwu); (2) smuggled across China's borders into Hong Kong, Russia, Pakistan, Vietnam and Burma; and (3) loaded onto cargo ships bound for the United States, with shipments organised and financed by crime syndicates using traditional drug-smuggling routes (Chow, 2000: 16–18).

Petty capitalists sell the goods openly in certain sites such as shopping malls, which are well known as markets for pirated software. Such traders expect occasional raids and treat fines as a calculable business cost. There are also more covert sales practices. These involve the sale of coupons/software covers that enable buyers to pick up the pirated software at another time or in less centrally located areas. Others sell their pirated software from temporary outlets (such as shops on short leases), mobile sales points (e.g. hawker stalls, car boots, suitcases), and over the ether (such as pagers and the internet). This makes it very hard for the authorities to track sellers down and gather hard evidence. More recently, pirates have begun to employ juveniles and illegal immigrants to sell software. The former cannot be imprisoned and the latter can only be deported.

The consumer's resort to counter-hegemonic tactics is important from the viewpoint of the cultural politics of everyday life. It enables the 'mouse' to gain temporary and tactical advantages over the hegemonic information industry; and it also warns the latter that control and surveillance can never be complete. Yet the endless cat and mouse raids around piracy can hardly form the basis of a counter-hegemonic project similar to Linux. On the supply side, petty capitalist producers and instrumental consumers are often no more than neo-liberal opportunists in disguise. And, ironically, on the demand side, piracy may even perpetuate the dominance of the Wintel standard because pirated

Microsoft software is sold at an affordable price. This locks users in at the expense of cheap and legitimate alternatives such as Linux. In turn, this may slow the development of Linux, prompting consumers to remark that it is less user-friendly due to the lack of support through training classes, handbooks and help discs. The Linux community also worries that some neo-mercantilist users in the region are breaking the terms of the General Public License by modifying the code and keeping the results to themselves.

Sub-hegemonic adaptations: the making of global–regional–national information infrastructure

Compared with the counter-hegemonic Linux movement and piracy tactics, the hegemonic call to 'build regional and national information infrastructures' as an integral part of the GII has encountered limited challenges. Gore's proposals for the GII in the Brussels G7 meeting in February 1995 were reinforced in a later G7 summit meeting in Halifax in June 1995. To quote:

> Governments around the globe have come to recognise that the telecommunications, information services, and information technology sectors are not only dynamic growth sectors themselves, but are also engines of development and economic growth throughout the economy. By interconnecting local, national, regional, and global networks, the GII can increase economic growth, create jobs, and improve infrastructures. Taken as a whole, this worldwide 'network of networks' will create a global information marketplace, encouraging broad-based social discourse within and among all countries. By interconnecting local, national, regional, and global networks, the GII can increase economic growth, create jobs, and improve infrastructures. (1995)

Successful realisation of this US-led call to build a 'network of networks' depends on extant and new institutional support. Because the GII is conditional on technological compatibility, a key role falls to the ITU in defining telecommunications standards, policy and regulation. Similarly, the WTO plays a major role, especially through its International Investment Promotion Network, in shaping regional and national information infrastructure projects and encouraging their liberalisation. A new GII Commission (GIIC) was also set up, initially for three years, to foster the leadership of international capital in these areas and transmit their roadmap to various information-infrastructure stakeholders. Its commissioners are drawn from private- and public-sector organisations around the world and include representatives from Siemens, Fujitsu, Cisco, USB, Deutsche Telekom, Ford, INTELSAT, Hitachi, Oracle, Nokia, Harvard University and the United Nations. All three groups communicate with other stakeholders at regular meetings on the importance of neo-liberalism as the organising and disciplining principle for information infrastructure on global level.

At the GIIC inaugural meeting in Brussels in February 1995, participants from transnational telecommunications/computer corporations (e.g. Apple Computers, EUROBIT, Mitsubishi) and international organisations (e.g. ITU, World Bank) stressed the key role of private–public co-operation in developing information networks. One of the participants, World Bank Vice-President Jean Francois Rischard, even praised Gore's emphasis in his 1995 speech on the 'global information marketplace' and neo-liberalism. Such backing can be seen as part of a linked series of discourses that constitute a new hegemonic regime of truth that is thought to be universally applicable because it is interpreted as the natural way of doing things in the information age. In this regard, the Clinton administration, the GIIC and the World Bank can be seen as global centres of persuasion promoting neo-liberal common sense in the information marketplace.

The alleged global validity of the new neo-liberal regime of truth may well gain further credence through the activities of regional forces in adapting neo-liberal principles to local circumstances. They produce discourses and practices that operate in sub-hegemonic ways to complement, extend and embed neo-liberal hegemony in regional and national frameworks. On the regional scale, South Korean President Kim Dae-Jung called for the construction of an Asia-Pacific Information Infrastructure (APII) in 1995. The First APEC Ministerial Meeting on Telecommunications and Information Industry was held six months later in Seoul and the APEC members assembled there formulated the Seoul Declaration. This mainly reinforced the neo-liberal outlook of the Clinton administration, the GIIC and the World Bank. Discourses such as competition, private sector investment, open and nondiscriminatory access and protection of intellectual property rights were repeated on the regional scale (Charles, 1995: 84–5). In this regard, the APII can be seen as a regional relay of neo-liberalism insofar as it converts universal hegemonic discourse into sub-hegemonic objectives that are more functional in character, as well as technically feasible. This can be seen in the adoption of regional goals such as interconnected and interoperable information infrastructure and human resource development – goals that are couched in technical terms and relatively easy to implement by functional agencies of APII, such as the APII Cooperation Centre (see Figure 10.2).

Adaptations of the neo-liberal hegemonic project have occurred nationally as well as regionally; but national adaptations are more diverse in their glocal re-imaginations. Initial efforts in this direction occurred at the First Asian NII Meeting in November 1995 in Bangkok, held under the sponsorship of the GIIC and the World Bank. National participants from China, Thailand, Australia and Indonesia presented their own versions of this project for an integrated information infrastructure. China, which is moving from a planned to a socialist market economy, presented its information infrastructure development in terms of 'reasonable' and 'appropriate competition' under 'comprehensive planning' (Xu, 1995: 18). In contrast, Indonesia affirmed its commitment to 'the principles of competition, liberalisation and deregulation in the tele-communication market' and its support for a 'fully liberalised economy' as its 'future goal' (Parapak and Sulistyo, 1995: 32). These contrasting discursive stances on issues of competition and liberalisation highlight the different ways in which countries and economies in the region seek to transfer neo-liberal principles to their own national circumstances (see Table 10.2).

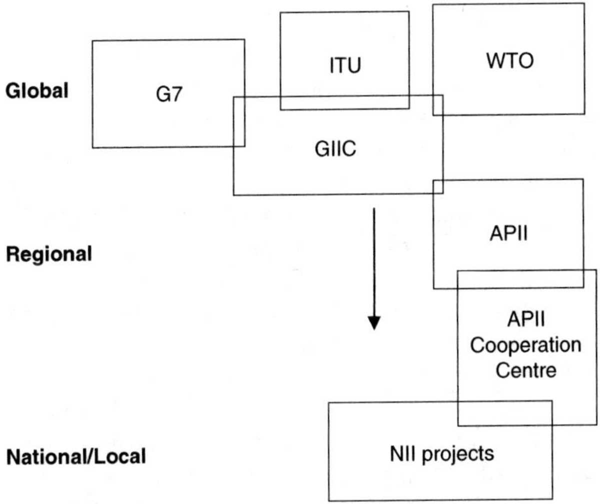

Figure 10.2   The GII–APII–NII complex

Table 10.2   Asian NII projects for national competitiveness

Country	NII programme	Time frame	Cost USD bn
Japan	Japan NII	National broadband infrastructure by 2010	330–50
South Korea	Korea II	Broadband infrastructure installed by 2010	57.9
Singapore	IT 2000	Fibre to building; full-service by 2000	2.65
Taiwan	NII 2005	Broadband infrastructure by 2005	10
Malaysia	Malaysian Information Highway	Fibre to home by 2020	30
Thailand	IT 2000	Broadband access by 2002	18
Indonesia	Indonesian NII (INFONAS)	Broadband infrastructure by 2010	n.a.
China	China NII	Broadband net delivering over a million telephone lines and 10k TV channels by 2020	200

Source: Adapted and updated from Lovelock, 1997: 3.

The two main post-socialist economies in the region, China and Vietnam, have so far adopted a strong public-dominated approach. Because their state-owned firms are still important, and private companies are still developing, calls for private-sector leadership with strong private finance and investment are not so relevant. A mix of public–private partnerships occurs in Taiwan, South Korea, Singapore and Malaysia. Here, the global push for competition policy comes into conflict with industrial policies that give their governments important catch-up roles in building national information infrastructures. And, at the other end of the spectrum from China and Vietnam, we can find Hong Kong. Private participation has predominated here, subject to some public guidance. These different sub-hegemonic translations have clearly been shaped by political ideologies, public policy styles, government–industry relations, levels of economic and technological development, market size and the changing balance of local political and economic forces. Although this chapter cannot discuss these adaptations individually, the range of approaches shows that attempts to establish the GII–APII–NII complex (see Figure 10.2) are being more or less skillfully translated and adapted through specific material practices to national situations. But this does not mean that individual NIIs have escaped the grip of the neo-liberal hegemonic regime of truth. On the contrary, the global–regional–national interface involves a two-way interaction that has both material and discursive aspects. On the one hand, the economic identities and practices promoted by the global neo-liberal project are translated and adapted into regional and national sub-hegemonic projects; on the other hand, these sub-hegemonic modifications are limited enough that they can still be subsumed within the overall consensus around the neo-liberal project.

National and regional adaptations reflect the rise of a transnational class of public and private actors in the region as well as national preferences in competitiveness policies. The nature of this emerging class is not structurally pre-given nor discursively pre-scripted, but emerges from the interaction of different forces as they pursue their own regional–local rationalities and identities and develop shared interests in the course of pursuing interlocking national–regional projects. One of the distinguishing features of this emerging transnational regional class of public and private actors is its greater commitment to a range of public–private partnership policy solutions, compared to the market-oriented approach favoured by the transnational neo-liberal class alliance (on the latter, see van der Pijl, 1998). This does not mean that the regional–national projects are totally opposed to the global neo-liberal project – indeed I have already indicated the range of tactics and strategies to accommodate as well as challenge it. Indeed, alternative national projects (e.g. catch-up industrial policies) are framed primarily within discursive and institutional limits set by the hegemonic neo-liberal project. In this sense, by providing scope for regional and national manoeuvre, these alternatives may well help to consolidate the overall hegemony of the GIIC–World Bank complexes.

Conclusion

This chapter has applied a cultural international political economy approach to two topics: first, US attempts since the 1990s to rebuild its hegemony by promoting a GII–NII–IPR nexus; and, second, attempts to resist or adapt to these initiatives. This approach highlights how new discourses/narratives have shaped the forms, objectives and objects of global economic governance and how economic symbols and everyday practices both mediate and challenge attempts to govern the global economy. This can be seen in the articulation between GII and IPR and the role of TRIPs in shaping the international IPR complex in ways that generalise a changing American IPR regime to become the dominant global norm. Leading players in the globalizing knowledge-based economy (including the culture industries and advanced producer services) have been deploying a range of hegemonic strategies and disciplinary practices to build a global IPR regime that favours their interests and maintains developing countries as subordinate players. Those who seek to resist are condemned as pirates and subject to a range of sanctions. Although the United States has thereby succeeded in restoring its hegemony and mobilising a transnational bloc behind its strategy to consolidate informational capitalism, it has not stopped resistance through various counter-hegemonic strategies and tactics. On the contrary, the latter have also shaped the global development of the new informational capitalism and its local, national and regional instantiations. In short, hegemony and counter-hegemony are always linked dialectically and mediated through discourses and material practices.

In showing the multiscalar or glocal nature of the re-making of social relations in informational capitalism, this chapter also reveals the limits of one-sided emphasis on the global. Although my case material derives primarily from the national and regional scales, it is sufficient to reveal the complexity of the interconnections and relays between local particularities and global construction. Thus the emerging intellectual property rights regime involves interaction between conflicting interests on different scales. These conflicts are rooted in contrasting positions in the circuits of capital, the general tension between intellectual property and intellectual commons (e.g. proprietary versus open source code), and with regard to national security/development. This can be seen in the counter-hegemonic strategy to promote Linux against Microsoft and to challenge, if possible, the emerging IPR–TRIPs regime. It is also evident in the unequal cat-and-mouse game between consumers and petty capitalists and international capital and its associates. Nonetheless, as my second case shows, glocal interactions are not always conflict-ridden or polarised. Thus, while actors in East Asia have embraced the idea of the GII, they have also rescaled it to the regional and national levels and adopted a public–private partnership rather than neo-liberal approach to building the NII. We could interpret this as a regional–national adaptation to the overall GII hegemony. Future research on the glocal configurations of informational capitalism should examine other scales too (Dirlik, 2001).

Finally, I have noted the dialectic of counter-hegemonic challenges and pro-hegemonic adaptation in the re-making of US hegemony in the information age. As my case studies illustrate, new objects of global governance and new global practices are never just transplanted in a frictionless manner from some free-floating global level. They are as contested as the global level itself, and are challenged or adapted as they get disseminated or adopted on sub-global levels. How this occurs depends on pre-existing social relations and interests rooted in different regional, national and local terrains, as well as the current balance between resistance by the strong and the weak and efforts to engage in local adaptations. Moreover, if actors' interests and calculations change, they may switch between resistance and adaptation and/or pursue different strategies and tactics as circumstances change. This is quite clear from attempts to develop appropriate forms of governance for the globalising knowledge-based economy in East Asia.

Notes

1. The GATT established the TRIPs Council to monitor the operation of TRIPs. The Council collects data on progress in pro-TRIPS changes in national IPR laws and their enforcement.
2. The Special 301 provision of the Omnibus Trade and Competitiveness Act of 1988 enables the United States to sanction developing countries and other trading partners that it identifies as engaging in unfair trade practices, such as infringing US intellectual property rights.
3. Linux was developed by Linus Torvalds, a Finnish undergraduate computer scientist, in 1989–90. Linus began turning the MINIX kernel into a kernel for Unix on the Intel x86 processors, which ran the world's commodity process at that time. He named the resulting kernel Linux and released it on the net in 1991 under the Free Software Foundation's General Public License. This ensured that the results of work by countless programmers who devoted time and energy to its refinement would always remain public and free.
4. The post-PC computer era requires software that is cheaper and demands smaller memory capacity and this makes Linux ideal for mobile phones, MP3 players, personal digital assistants and so on.
5. Microsoft announced on 14 January 2003 that it will provide the underlying code of its Windows operating system to governments for the first time.

11
A Provocative Dependence?
The Global Financial System and Small Island Tax Havens

Mark P. Hampton and John Christensen

Introduction

The global financial system may be seen as an arena within which global governance is regularly contested. This chapter examines one particular aspect of global finance, offshore finance, and its global level regulation, and considers small island tax havens and their resistance to forms of global governance. Over the last 40 years many small island economies (SIEs) – defined as having under 1.5 million populations (Commonwealth Secretariat, 1997) – have come to host offshore finance centres (OFCs). OFCs are located around the European periphery (for example, the Channel Islands, Isle of Man, Malta, Cyprus); in the Caribbean (Cayman Islands, British Virgin Islands (BVI), The Bahamas); the Pacific (Vanuatu, Cook Islands) and Indian Ocean (Mauritius, Seychelles). Many SIEs have become highly dependent upon hosting OFC activities with extreme examples such as the British Channel Island of Jersey having over 90 per cent of its government revenues from such activities, and the OFC directly employs up to 20 per cent of the local labour force.[1]

The value of the wealth held offshore has been estimated at over US\$6 trillion (The Edwards Report, 1998), and is apparently still growing. The two main user categories of offshore are trans-national corporations (TNCs) and the world's wealthiest individuals. Since the 1960s a range of services have been created including global asset management for wealthy individuals using asset holding trusts and offshore companies; specialist offshore corporate vehicles such as International Business Corporations (IBCs); captive insurance and offshore funds.

Some OFCs now specialise in captive insurance (Bermuda), offshore company registration (the BVI) or trust management and securitisation (Jersey).

Since the late 1990s, however, an unprecedented sequence of international initiatives have been taken which have the potential to significantly re-configure the global finance industry and offshore finance in particular. This process may have been further accelerated by the terrorist attacks on the United States on 11 September 2001. This chapter begins with an examination of the key initiatives concerning harmful tax competition and tax harmonisation; money laundering; and offshore financial regulation. Given the political power of the onshore interests ranged against offshore finance we argue that island hosts of OFCs face a volatile and increasingly unpredictable international context over which they have neither influence nor control. Their destinies therefore often depend upon decisions taken by international fora at which they are not directly represented, and the welfare of SIEs dependent upon their tax haven activities will only be one amongst a number of arguably more important strategic concerns about global financial stability, money laundering, fiscal degradation, and moves to define international tax policy in the context of globalisation. In the light of rising uncertainty about the structure (maybe the future) of offshore finance, we examine the economic dependence of many SIEs upon such activities, and argue that this dependence has been exacerbated by the structural problems of smallness and the unique political economies of islands. We also consider how offshore finance crowds-out SIEs by acting as a 'cuckoo in the nest' and identify barriers that restrict diversification in the post-OFC period.

Key initiatives against offshore finance

Until recently tax havens have only attracted intermittent attention which is surprising given the rapid growth of transactions routed through the offshore circuits, the stock of wealth held offshore and the rising number of jurisdictions that host OFCs.

Data on offshore finance is sparse and collating statistics presents methodological problems arising from the secrecy that surrounds offshore finance and the potential for double-counting (even when jurisdictions publish offshore bank deposits). Nonetheless the available data illustrates the rapid growth of offshore finance. In 1968 an estimated US$11 billion was held in OFC bank deposits. By 1978 this had increased to US$385 billion (OECD, 1987). At the end of the 1980s

Table 11.1 Indicative data for selected island OFCs, 2000

OFC	Offshore banks	Number employed in OFC	Assets (A) or liabilities (L) US$ billions	Offshore companies	Captive insurance companies
Bahrain	37	n.a.	85.7 A	n.a.	n.a.
British Virgin Islands	9	n.a.	n.a.	400 000	190
Cayman Islands	464	2 100 (1996)	648 A (1998)	59 922	522 (2001)
Cyprus	30	2 140 (1996)	8.5 L (1999)	24 000 (1996)	9 (1993)
Guernsey	77	5 000	95.7 L	15 453 (1999)	369 (2001)
Jersey	70	8 000	164.1 L	33 000	167 (2001)
Labuan	60	n.a.	19.5 A	2 721	68
Netherlands Antilles	45	n.a.	36.4 A	30 000 (1988)	21

Notes: Bahrain data for June 2001, BVI data for 1999.

Sources: Bahrain Monetary Authority; BVI Financial Services Department; Cayman Islands Monetary Authority; Central Bank of Cyprus; Guernsey Financial Services Commission; States of Guernsey Economics and Statistics Unit; Jersey Financial Services Commission; Labuan Offshore Financial Services Authority; Central Bank of the Netherlands Antilles.

deposits in the Caribbean alone amounted to over US$400 billion (Peagam, 1989), and in the early 1990s Kochen (1991) put the total value of offshore deposits at approximately US$1 trillion. This figure rose sharply during the 1990s. The most recent estimate values the stock of wealth held offshore at around US$6 trillion (The Edwards Report, 1998). The scale of the flow of funds offshore is large and significant, and appears to be increasing. Table 11.1 illustrates key data for selected island OFCs.

In the academic sphere offshore finance was relatively unexplored until Johns (1983) applied a neo-classical analysis to the economics of offshore finance, and Gorostiaga (1984) examined finance centres located in less developed countries (LDCs).[2]

During the 1990s the subject attracted further research, including neo-classical analyses of the role of offshore finance in the global economy (Johns and Le Marchant, 1993; Hines and Rice, 1994); analyses of how offshore finance functions (Roberts, 1994; Hampton, 1994, 1996b); the regulation of OFC activity (Sikka, 1996; Le Marchant, 1999); the political and economic geography of 'offshore' (Cobb, 1998; Hudson, 1998); the role of OFCs within the discourse of the state, sovereignty and jurisdiction (Roberts, 1995, 1999; Palan, 1999; Picciotto, 1999); the role of OFCs in developing countries (Marshall, 1996; Possekel, 1996; Abbott, 2000) and the social anthropology of OFCs (Maurer, 1995).

Recently the discussion in the growing offshore literature has considered the re-configuration of the 'regulatory landscape' (Picciotto and Haines, 1999; Christensen and Hampton, 2000); and discussion over the fluidity of the nation state, its boundaries, legitimacy and new forms of global capital and sovereignty (Smith, 2000). The chapter now considers the relationship between OFCs and:

- the onshore policy-makers
- the OECD and tax escape
- the European Union
- the FATF and money laundering
- global financial regulation
- civil society

OFCs and the policy-makers

Until the late 1990s, government interest in offshore was largely restricted to the concerns of revenue departments of larger nations. The US Internal Revenue Service has periodically acted against certain Caribbean havens (*Los Angeles Times*, 1977; The Gordon Report, 1981), and the revenue departments of many European states have also pursued tax evasion schemes such as the Rossminster case in the 1970s (Clarke, 1986). Past media coverage of tax havens has also tended to focus on blatant tax evasion, money laundering or bank failures such as the BCCI case, and has seldom shifted attention from the scandal to the broader political economic picture.

In the United Kingdom, successive governments encouraged the overseas territories and dependencies[3] to establish themselves as tax havens to reduce their dependence upon UK grants. An example of this official support for tax havens was the Gallagher Report (1990) commissioned by the Foreign and Commonwealth Office. The wider issue of the role played by tax havens and OFCs in re-configuring the global political economy was not, until recently, on the mainstream political agenda,[4] largely because states such as France and Germany recognised that effective action against tax havens would be ineffective other than on a multilateral basis.

Since the late 1990s, however, major international initiatives have been launched against tax havens and OFCs by the Organisation for Economic Cooperation and Development (OECD), the Group of Seven (G7), the United Nations Office for Drug Control and Crime Prevention, and the European Union. This is a new phenomenon and tax havens have been caught off-guard and somewhat defenceless against international institutions with which they have no direct dealings. This lack of direct representation arises from the fact that a significant proportion of tax havens and OFCs are located in UK Overseas Territories and Crown Dependencies and are therefore represented on international fora – such as the OECD and the EU – by the UK government. The UK government finds itself under pressure, particularly from the United States and from the EU, to improve financial regulation in its overseas territories and to strengthen cross-border information exchange agreements[5] and Chancellor Gordon Brown recently reinforced his commitment to financial transparency (*The Financial Times*, 2002).

At the 2000 Feira summit, EU members agreed to introduce unrestricted information exchanges between national tax authorities as an alternative to implementing an EU withholding tax on non-resident's savings. The UK government had a major part in negotiating this agreement and is therefore under pressure to extend information exchanges to its overseas territories and dependencies. For its part, the French government is applying pressure on the government of Monaco to cooperate more fully with information exchanges, and on the government of Luxembourg (an EU member) which agreed in November 2000 to cooperate with information exchanges with the US Internal Revenue Service.

The confluence of these powerful initiatives against offshore has created a situation in which the future of tax havens is in doubt. A variety of factors have motivated the initiatives of the different agencies involved. For example the OECD has focused on harmful tax competition, whereas the G7's Financial Action Task Force (FATF) is concerned with money laundering. There is, however, a significant degree of overlap of interest between these groupings embodied in the general recognition of the role that secrecy plays in sustaining money laundering and in enabling individuals and TNCs to engage in harmful tax practices.

The OECD, tax escape and tax havens

The OECD's Fiscal Affairs Committee published its report on harmful tax competition in 1998 and subsequently published a second report in June 2000 which identified 35 'tax havens' as being involved in harmful tax practices (OECD, 1998, 2000). The OECD list included a number of high profile OFCs such as the Isle of Man and both main Channel Islands (CI) of Jersey and Guernsey (Table 11.2).

Despite extensive lobbying, only six offshore jurisdictions persuaded the OECD to remove their names from the list in the period

Table 11.2   OECD tax havens list

Andorra	Maldives
Anguilla	Marshall Islands
Antigua and Barbuda	Monaco
Aruba	Montserrat
The Bahamas	Nauru
Bahrain	Netherlands Antilles
Barbados	Niue
Belize	Panama
British Virgin Islands	Samoa
Cook Islands	Seychelles
Dominica	St Kitts and Nevis
Gibraltar	St Lucia
Grenada	St Vincent and the Grenadines
Guernsey	Tonga
Isle of Man	Turks and Caicos Islands
Jersey	US Virgin Islands
Liberia	Vanuatu
Liechtenstein	

Source: OECD, 1998.

immediately prior to its publication. Bermuda, the Cayman Islands, Cyprus, Malta, Mauritius and San Marino applied to be considered as Advanced Commitment Jurisdictions and gave high-level political undertakings to follow OECD guidelines towards making significant improvements by mid-2001.

The 35 havens identified by the OECD were given one year to commit themselves to fundamental fiscal reform and to agree to broaden information exchange with national tax authorities. Those choosing non-compliance faced economic sanctions including the abrogation of existing tax treaties relating to double taxation between the OFCs and OECD members. The OECD threat was potent. John Cashen, the Isle of Man's Chief Finance Officer, acknowledged the island's vulnerability by asking 'What would we do instead? If the OECD closed us down, we would become depopulated and derelict' (quoted in *The Financial Times*, 2000). The Isle of Man provides an interesting example of adaptation to governance. In response to the OECD threat it broke ranks with the other Crown Dependencies and began reforming its fiscal system, including information exchanges through double taxation agreements with other tax authorities, and ending the tax advantages offered to non-residents that are ring-fenced to prevent Isle of Man's own residents from also enjoying similar nominal tax rates.[6] The Isle of Man's commitment to ending harmful tax practices resulted in its transfer to the OECD list of 'committed jurisdictions'. Between mid-2000 and early 2002 a further seven OFCs followed the Isle of Man's example: Antigua, Aruba, Bahrain, Barbados, Netherlands Antilles, Seychelles, Tonga (OECD, 2001; Peel, 2002).

The other two Crown Dependency OFCs – Jersey and Guernsey – had taken the most belligerent stance towards the OECD. They increased their expenditure upon political lobbyists and public relations, and publicly appeared to want to tough it out. Their hostility towards the OECD initiative appeared to have little support from the UK government especially given that the Chancellor of the Exchequer, Gordon Brown, was known to be concerned about tax escape and supportive of measures to curtail tax havens: 'The chancellor's view has always been that all citizens should pay their fair share of tax. ... The government's plan is to convince its own "tax havens" in the Channel Islands to provide it with details of interest on bank accounts held by UK firms and citizens and shepherd other financial centres into similar agreements' (an unnamed Treasury official quoted in Ungoed-Thomas and Jay, 2000).

However, despite their belligerent public stance, the CI finally agreed to comply with the OECD on the day before the final deadline in

February 2002. It appears that they came under significant pressure from the UK government to comply to new governance structures with threats of possible UK sanctions (Bennett and Peel, 2002). Even then, the CI still argued that it was 'unfair and immoral' for the OECD to list them without also including Switzerland and Luxembourg, saying publicly that they reserved the right to withdraw from any agreement with the OECD unless countries with similar tax arrangements were also forced to revise their fiscal arrangements (Bennett and Peel, 2002). After the passing of the OECD's February 2002 deadline, around 20 tax havens remained on the OECD blacklist including Anguilla, The Bahamas, the BVI, Gibraltar, the Turks and Caicos Islands, Panama and Vanuatu. However, the pressure to comply with new governance structures appeared to have forced a change of attitude in most of these jurisdictions and within weeks of the deadline most had made public pronouncements agreeing to cooperate with the OECD. By April 2002 only seven jurisdictions remained on the OECD blacklist of un-cooperative tax havens (Andorra, Liechtenstein, Liberia, Monaco, the Marshall Islands, Nauru and Vanuatu) and they are expected to face economic sanctions.

EU offshore initiatives

Two main areas of EU concern are tax harmonisation and information exchange. The proposal in the late 1990s for an EU-wide withholding tax charged on dividends was strenuously resisted by the UK government who argued that it would seriously damage the lucrative London-based Eurobond market. After a prolonged series of proposals and counter-proposals – and, we can assume, intense behind-the-scenes lobbying of the UK government by the financial institutions – it was eventually agreed in 2000 that the withholding tax would not be applied to the UK Eurobond market. As noted earlier, however, withholding taxes will be gradually phased out across the EU and replaced by direct information exchange between national tax authorities.[7] Not surprisingly, reactions to this policy change varied between member states. For some EU members with significant 'offshore' finance such as Austria and Luxembourg, these moves provoked heated reactions: 'It's absolutely unacceptable for us to apply [the UK-proposed system]. For us the exchange of information is incompatible with banking confidentiality' (Luc Freiden, Treasury Minister of Luxembourg, quoted in Ungoed-Thomas and Jay, 2000).

For non-EU members, particularly Switzerland, Liechtenstein and the CI, global governance in the form of the EU's proposed directive posed a serious challenge to bank secrecy law and the effective secrecy space created by current banking practices. The EU's moves towards increased information exchange are highly significant since banking secrecy is one of the fundamental requirements of offshore finance.[8] Despite protestations to the contrary, banking secrecy remains in high demand by offshore customers engaged in hiding transactions from their governments, tax authorities, family members or courts.

Money laundering initiatives

The FATF was established by G7 in 1989 as a result of heightened concern over money-laundering, especially regarding the proceeds of the illegal drugs trade and fiscal crime. In April 2000 the FATF published a Report on Non Co-operative Countries and Territories (FATF, 2000a) which listed the criteria to identify detrimental practices that restrict cooperative measures to combat money laundering and also stated that counter-measures would be developed against non cooperating jurisdictions. A second report published in June 2000 listed 15 'non co-operative' jurisdictions (FATF, 2000b).[9]

Interestingly, by October 2000 – only four months after the second FATF report – seven of the 'named and shamed' jurisdictions had rushed legislation through in an attempt to be removed from the list (FATF, 2000c). Since then several jurisdictions including St Kitts and Nevis have passed anti-money laundering legislation. It remains unclear, however, whether the new legislation will be effective in removing obstacles to international cooperation against money laundering. In addition, in the aftermath of the 9/11 terrorist attacks, the FATF was given a new remit to counter money laundering of terrorist funds placing further pressure on OFCs (*The Economist*, 2001).

The rush to legislation might be a window dressing exercise, rather than a genuine attempt to cooperate with the international community, particularly concerning fiscal crime. Switzerland, for example, still does not recognise tax evasion as a crime and refuses to remove statutory obstacles posed by banking secrecy provisions in cases of tax authorities' legitimate inquiries. Despite claiming to have state-of-the-art anti-money laundering legislation (Fleck, 2000: 2) Swiss money laundering investigations remain concentrated at cantonal level, and lack coopera-tion between cantons. Successful prosecutions are rare, and Geneva prosecutors have yet to achieve a successful prosecution in several cases involving Russian money laundering.

There are also global level regimes and initiatives aimed at controlling money laundering. One major initiative originates from the United

Nations Global Program against Money Laundering. Following its 1998 report (Blum *et al.*, 1998), the UN Office for Drug Control and Crime Prevention held a plenary meeting in the Cayman Islands in 2000, which resulted in a communiqué signed by 31 OFCs agreeing to a high level political commitment to support the UN programme against money laundering. Signatories agreed to the formation and support of local Financial Intelligence Units (FIUs) to help combat money laundering in the OFCs (UN Information Service, 2000). However, as with other grand-sounding declarations, it remains to be seen whether this amounts to anything more than a familiar form of resistance to global governance, with OFCs only paying lip service to increasing international pressures to reform. Much depends on whether the new FIUs in the offshore centres will be effective, adequately resourced and staffed, and sufficiently distanced from interference by local political elites to function unimpeded by vested interests that would rather not see their OFC business leave.

Offshore financial regulation

In the wake of the 1997 East Asian financial crisis the G7 Financial Stability Forum (FSF) formed a Working Group to examine the role of OFCs within the global financial system. The Working Group's report (FSF, 2000a) noted the role of OFCs during periods of financial crisis and commented that poorly regulated OFCs 'allow financial market participants to engage in regulatory arbitrage and constitute weak links in the supervision of an increasingly integrated financial system. The *"loopholes" presented by some OFCs hinder efforts to improve the global supervisory financial system … frustrating collective efforts to reduce overall exposures to global financial instability, and creating a potential systemic threat* to the financial system' (FSF, 2000a: 1, emphasis added).

The FSF recommended that the IMF become responsible for coordinating the assessment of OFCs. In May 2000, the FSF released an international listing of OFCs grouped into three categories ranging from the well regulated (Group I) through to the least regulated (Group III) (FSF, 2000b). Interestingly, FSF Group I jurisdictions only included three microstate OFCs, that is three British Isle centres (Jersey, Guernsey and the Isle of Man). The other Group I jurisdictions were Hong Kong, Singapore, Luxembourg, Switzerland and the Dublin city IFSC.[10] No Caribbean OFC achieved Group I, and only Barbados was categorised in Group II.[11] OFCs with larger supervisory authorities such as the Cayman Islands were placed in the same category as the (widely perceived) poorly regulated OFCs such as Antigua.

OFCs and civil society

Alongside the multilateral governmental initiatives, concern about tax havens has been mounting within wider civil society including non-governmental organisations (NGOs) and the media. In 2000 the UK development NGO Oxfam published a briefing paper on tax havens and their effect on global poverty (Oxfam, 2000). The Oxfam paper included an estimate of TNC tax avoidance in developing countries of US$50 billion annually, equivalent to the entire flow of global aid programmes. Other NGOs with an interest include Transparency International which has been drawing up voluntary guidelines for private banks to combat money laundering; and the Association for Accountancy and Business Affairs established an Offshore Watch web site to monitor tax havens.[12] Most recently the World Social Forum in Porto Alegre, Brasil in January 2003 saw the establishment of a global campaign against tax havens.

There has also been an increasing volume of media analysis of offshore finance both from the United Kingdom and the international media including *The Wall Street Journal* (Sesit, 1996a,b); *The Economist* (2000, 2001); *BBC News 24* (BBC, 1999); *France 3* (2001); *The Financial Times* (2000; Groom, 2000; Bennett and Peel, 2002; Peel, 2002); *The Guardian* (Denny, 2000a,b; Webster, 2000); and *The Observer* (Sweeney, 2000; Walsh, 2002). Significantly, present media coverage now attempts to report offshore tax scandals within a wider context and the role of offshore in the interplay between the nation state and big business (e.g. *The Economist*, 2000).

The collapse of US energy company Enron in 2002 has been linked to the extensive use of offshore companies registered in the Cayman Islands, Barbados, Bermuda, the Turks and Caicos and Aruba. These companies were used for various purposes including tax avoidance and the hiding of off-balance sheet liabilities (James, 2002; Mitchell and Sikka *et al.*, 2002).

Microstates and Economic Dependence on Offshore Finance

Confronted with the combined political power of the international initiatives ranged against offshore finance, the SIEs that host OFCs have ample grounds for fear. Like the majority of remote and peripheral areas, most SIEs are characterised by profound economic disadvantages including restricted comparative advantages, diseconomies of scale, dysfunctional market structures, high transport costs, high level of openness to international trade, tendencies to be price-takers not price-makers, limited natural resources, small labour markets and deficiencies in professional/institutional knowledge and experience (Briguglio, 1995; Armstrong *et al.*, 1998; Royle, 2001). On the other hand, the global growth of offshore finance played to their geo-political advantages, such as fiscal autonomy, independence from mainstream regulatory authorities, judicial independence and secrecy in the banking and political spheres. Perhaps not surprisingly, many SIE governments greatly encouraged the growth of OFC activity, often without considering the adverse impacts of such growth upon pre-existing industries. It is reasonable to ask, however, why so many SIE governments allowed themselves to become dependent upon an activity that common sense suggests would sooner or later become the focus of international intervention. Was it merely a failure of prudential risk management on their parts, or were other forces at play that prevented them from managing their dependency upon external factors? In other words how did tax haven governments lose control of their destinies?

In a provocative paper Baldacchino (1993) considered the relatively few economically successful microstates and argued that unlike their low income counterparts, the winners were those that overcame their disadvantages of small size and small scale, and had actively managed their dependency on large countries. Neatly reversing Gunder Frank's classic dependency theory (Gunder Frank, 1967), Baldacchino argued that successful microstate economies were those who were able to manipulate the larger countries (or regional blocs) to create a local advantage for themselves. Pursuing this theme, Baldacchino argued that this exemplified an 'opportunist pragmatism' with microstate governments seizing passing opportunities in a similar manner to which islanders have historically been pirates and privateers in many parts of the world.

We argue, however, that this notion of 'managed dependency', whilst elegantly describing past events, has been overtaken by the recent initiatives launched against microstate hosts of OFCs. The uncomfortable situation in which many microstate governments now find themselves is more accurately described as 'mis-managed dependency', because of the extent to which their destinies are inextricably linked to the future of tax haven activity. As a result of this mis-managed dependency, the interests of these small states have been subsumed to the needs of global capital, in a way analogous to the experience of many LDCs being penetrated by trans-national capital with resultant issues of loss of control and over-dependence upon one firm or sector.

In the 1960s at the outset of the period of booming OFC growth, the emergence of offshore finance was regarded by many SIE governments as a welcome opportunity for diversification into an industry that would complement existing activities such as tourism and light manufacturing. Small island cultures appear well suited to the successful development of tax havens because media independence is frequently partial or absent; there is a general lack of higher education institutions or an intellectual community to critique policy; and the insularity and inward-looking focus common to small island communities suppresses whistle blowing (Mitchell and Sikka, 1999; Mitchell and Sikka *et al.*, 2002). Small polities have few democratic checks and balances upon the executive power wielded by key individuals and the parliament may not have an effective formal opposition as in the case of the CI which have never held a general election.[13]

It could be argued that due to their size and insularity small island societies will exhibit relatively strong social cohesion and that their particular forms of social capital – that is community attitudes and values, social norms, networks, culture, language and the role of trust – might be a precondition for successfully hosting offshore finance. The concept of social capital and its effects upon economic growth is particularly associated with Coleman (1990) and Putnam (1993). It 'measures the degree to which a community can co-operate towards achieving desired results' (Nel *et al.*, 2001: 4). Further, networks of linkages have been suggested, combining both horizontal relationships within communities, with vertical relationships between communities and institutions such as government bodies.

Anderson *et al.* (2002) observe that although social capital (especially local horizontal linkages) may be broadly positive, some forms of social capital might improve the positions of some individuals whilst leading to worsening positions for others within society. It is possible that existing forms of social capital might result in an overall 'buying-in' to the idea of the tax haven within a community, that is, a general acceptance of the legitimacy of the OFC's activities. Over time, however, this could be seen to act in combination with the control of dissent noted earlier, so that individuals who go against the norm, that is who critique the legitimacy of the OFC are in a sense, going beyond the community's shared values. It could thus be argued that at this high level of abstraction the island's form of social capital helps create the benign milieu that is attractive to international financial institutions. Nevertheless, the complex relationships between the state, offshore financial institutions, the local community(ies) and the role of social capital in islands requires further research developing from Maurer's (1995) initial work on the social anthropology of offshore finance.

The political economy and culture of smallness feeds the element of secrecy that is a prerequisite for offshore financial activity, and any move to prise open that 'secrecy space' (Hampton, 1996a), for example, through the introduction of information exchange, is likely to reduce if not entirely negate the benefits of holding assets offshore.

Governmental advisers to many SIEs – both those of local origin, and those from external institutions including the IMF (McCarthy, 1979) – continue to argue that a symbiotic relationship exists between the financial services sector and pre-existing sectors, particularly tourism. Tourism and offshore finance both required rapid air transport links (Powell, 1971). Both also needed hotels, restaurants, shops and attractive climates.[14] The links appeared straightforward and self-evident. Likewise the benefits. The assertion ran that wealthy tourists would visit the islands, enjoy the lifestyle and subsequently establish residence and invest. At the same time bankers and accountants would be attracted by the climate and lifestyle and would bring with them their knowledge and experience, adding to the virtuous circle. How could such a favourable situation for a small economy go wrong?

Park (1982) argued that hosting an OFC would promote the internationalisation of the local economy by attracting foreign direct investment and generating specialist knowledge and experience thereby 'helping local industry become internationally competitive' (Park, 1982: 34). What he ignored was the 'crowding out' effect of a booming sector in a resource constrained economy, which would inevitably lead to a situation of over-dependence.

Like many OFCs, the CI are in monetary union with a large currency, in this case, Sterling. Arguably a linkage to a major global currency is crucial to the interests of both the OFC and the host economy. Monetary union with a major trading currency serves the interests of financial capital by creating a relatively risk free financial space, particularly since an independent local currency would have little trading attraction. In the medium term it also serves the interests of the host SIE by slowing the process of crowding-out of other industries, thus enabling the OFC to gradually expand into the local economy without precipitating uncontainable social and political resistance.

In the absence of monetary links with a major currency, an independent currency operated by an SIE would inevitably appreciate in relation to the currencies of its trading partners as a result of the rapid growth of OFC activity. The impact of such currency appreciation on those industries not engaged in, or reliant upon, the financial services sector, would be 'significant and severe' (Powell, 1997: 14). In effect this would be similar to the 'Dutch disease' (Struthers, 1990) or the 'booming sector model', in which traditional trading sectors rapidly lose competitiveness in the world markets as a result of currency appreciation. This phenomenon was noted in the Netherlands during the 1960s when the exploitation of hydrocarbon reserves adversely affected manufactured export competitiveness, but other relatively small economies have experienced similar impacts. Heeks' (1997) work on Brunei confirmed such observations noting the 'spending effect' where additional income from the booming sector is spent within the small economy on imported goods and non-traded services such as education, health or construction. Although OFCs tend to be located in service-based rather than mineral-based economies these economic insights are nonetheless applicable.

Although the huge volume of funds either on deposit with or managed by them, most OFCs are not directly linked to the local economy. The hosting of OFCs has tended to crowd-out other industrial sectors, particularly agriculture, tourism and light manufacturing. Crowding out occurs as a result of price inflation caused by the demand pressures exerted by a booming leading sector. If this inflation differs significantly from the rates of its leading trading partner it will undermine the competitiveness of existing local industries, which will lower local and export market share. Key skills and knowledge transfer to non-traded sectors such as construction, distribution and other downstream service providers. The public sector also competes for scarce skills and is forced to import labour on expensive short-term contracts. Jersey and Guernsey[15] illustrate the rapidity and extent of this crowding out effect.

In the 1960s Jersey and Guernsey's principal sources of employment, government revenue and export earnings were tourism, agriculture and light manufacturing (Powell, 1971) but as their finance sectors grew during the 1970s and 1980s, both islands experienced shortages of virtually every type of labour from professional through to unskilled. Inflationary pressures emerged, particularly in the labour and housing markets, and the politically dominant business and rentier classes applied pressure to resist the application of the islands' immigration controls. Both islands experienced rapid influxes of labour. Between 1961 and 1991 Jersey's population increased by over 40 per cent, almost entirely as a result of inwards migration of economically active non-islanders (1991 Census). This rate of population growth further stimulated inflationary pressures, and the islands came under rising pressure to increase office and house construction, to enlarge their infrastructural bases, and at the same time accommodate rising consumer aspirations. The traditional industries and the public sector experienced rising costs and lost skilled labour to the financial services sector. The resultant social, cultural and environmental degradation was considerable (Burgess and Collins, 1998). The process of industrial restructuring was swift. By the end of the 1990s the financial services sector in Jersey directly employed 12 per cent of the island's workforce, but was responsible for virtually all of the island's export earnings and tax revenues. The majority of the remaining service sectors (retail, construction, health, education, and other public sector services) were largely dependent upon the export earnings and tax revenues from the OFC.

Employment in Jersey's hospitality sector represented less than 4 per cent of the 1996 total, (1996 Census) and the profitability of those hotels and restaurants engaged in leisure tourism activity – that is not principally providing for the needs of local residents and business travellers – was negligible. The number of hotel bed-spaces for tourists declined from 25 000 in the 1970s to approximately 17 000 in 2000 (Jersey Tourism, 2000). Over 90 per cent of the island's tax revenues were directly or indirectly derived from the island's OFC and related downstream activities.

Manufactured exports from Jersey had virtually ceased by the late 1990s. The small number of light manufacturing plants fell throughout the 1980s and 1990s, and the last manufacturing plant in Jersey engaged in export activity, Channel Islands Knitwear, transferred production to England in 1997 with a loss of 80 skilled and semi-skilled jobs. High labour costs were cited as the cause of this closure. Nevertheless, the demand for labour is such (registered unemployment has seldom exceeded 0.5 per cent in recent decades) that any redundant labour is rapidly re-absorbed into the labour force. In addition, the buoyancy of labour demand and the large budgetary surpluses enjoyed by the Jersey government are beyond the wildest aspirations of most local authorities elsewhere. And the budgetary surpluses burn holes in the politician's pockets to such an extent that public expenditure over-runs upon prestige projects have become common.

The export contribution of agriculture represented less than 5 per cent of the island's GDP, but once subsidies, repatriated earnings and negative environmental 'externalities' – particularly the pollution of ground water by high dosages of agricultural chemicals – are taken into account, the true contribution of agriculture to Jersey's economy is probably nil or even negative. The strength of Jersey's brand image in its core market appears to have been eroded by poor marketing and high price.

The CI, like many SIEs, have notionally adhered for many years to economic strategies of maintaining a balanced and diversified industrial structure. But in practice the dynamic growth of the OFC exerted irresistible inflationary pressures that rapidly crowded out pre-existing industries. Furthermore, the high cost bases – skilled labour and housing costs are comparable to the more expensive parts of south-east England (Kemeny and Llewellyn-Wilson, 1998) – restricted the development of other sectors apart from those servicing the downstream needs of either the OFC or the public sector, such as information services.

Given the limited comparative advantage of an SIE located on the EU's periphery, a diversification strategy should have focused on protecting traditional sectors from excessive current account expenditure (with its concomitant inflationary pressures) whilst also assisting those industries to improve productivity and output quality. In practice, however, the subsidies paid to tourism and agriculture in Jersey have largely been absorbed into higher cost structures (agricultural land prices and construction costs are amongst the highest in Europe) and investment in training and service quality remains low. Whilst tourism has been strengthened elsewhere in the region – for example, in both Normandy and Brittany – Jersey's tourism figures show a consistent decline trend with low investment levels and falling visitor numbers.

In some SIEs crowding out has been so great that the OFC has emerged as the dominant player in the local political economy. Jersey illustrates how over-dependence upon a single sector runs the risk of that sector becoming a 'cuckoo in the nest', not only crowding out pre-existing sectors but also dominating the state apparatus. Having established themselves in this position the major finance institutions have been able to use their influence over the local polity to secure favourable tax and regulatory advantages. Such was the case with the Jersey Limited Liability Partnership Law[16] the introduction of which led to the States of Jersey being branded 'a legislature for hire' (Sikka, 1996).

So this is the position in which the CI and other island OFCs now find themselves. Their economies are dominated by tax haven activities that are increasingly subject to new forms of global governance. Their cost bases are such that pre-existing industries have generally been displaced, and new start-up businesses in non-financial services related activities are also crowded-out by high costs and by the lack of skilled labour. In addition, the earnings aspirations of the local labour force are geared to the high salaries of the OFC sector, and even the public service providers, including education, health, police and fire services, are obliged to compete with the OFC for the limited supply of local labour. Commercial and residential real estate prices are amongst the highest in Europe. In other words the economies of both islands are dependent upon the sustained presence of their OFCs. This scenario of crowding-out and over dependence on the offshore sector can also be seen in other small island hosts of OFCs such as the Cayman Islands or Bermuda.

It is reasonable to suggest that if the current moves to curtail tax haven and OFC activity are successful there will need to be a dramatic change not only in local property prices but also in terms of earnings aspirations and in the working culture in general. The medium-term prospects for regenerating the CI tourism sector are not encouraging. Both islands have become overcrowded with people, houses and cars with the result that Jersey in particular has lost much of its distinctive character (Jersey Tourism, 2000). High construction and labour costs undermine the potential for profitable investment in new hotels, and high transport costs make the islands relatively unattractive compared with other European locations, including other destinations within the Normandy/Brittany regions. Both CI governments appear to espouse the development of information technology (IT) based sectors, but their ideas are nebulous, and in practice existing IT businesses serve the finance and public sectors. What other prospects remain? And what is to be done with all those tax lawyers and accountants and their tanned and besuited ranks of trust and company administrators?

Conclusion

In terms of offshore finance, attempts at globally governing the sector began with the publication of the OECD's 1998 report on harmful tax practices, which was followed by other initiatives centred on global regulation of tax havens. These reflected rising disquiet over offshore regulation in relation to the global financial system (G7's Financial Stability Forum); money laundering and non-cooperative jurisdictions (G7's FATF, and the UN Global Program on Money Laundering); and information exchange (the EU). The year 2000 saw the publication of reports from the OECD listing 'tax havens'; the FSF grouping OFCs into three categories; and the FATF 'naming and shaming' non-cooperative jurisdictions. The year 2002 then saw an important landmark with the OECD moving towards the introduction of sanctions against non-coop-erative tax havens (Bennett and Peel, 2002). In early 2003 the EU finally agreed to introduce withholding tax.

The fundamental attractions of OFCs – low or no taxation, banking secrecy, minimal financial regulation and political stability – face signif-icant threat of erosion. Until recently political stability has been taken for granted, particularly in places like the CI and Monaco, but the pressures being exerted by the multilateral agencies and by national governments have triggered local resistances. Prince Ranier of Monaco, for example, has spoken about reviewing the relationship between France and Monaco (Webster, 2000). A Jersey politician has proposed to negotiate independence from the United Kingdom in response to the latter's involvement in the OECD initiative (Kelso, 2000). Despite such rhetoric, however, SIEs cannot risk being identified as pariah states and will therefore come under increased pressure, not least from within the financial services community itself, to engage with global governance institutions and to comply with at least some of the proposed measures.

Global governance has its successes in terms of regulating OFCs. For example, the cumulative pressures for reform will significantly re-configure the offshore finance industry. Offshore finance may return onshore to the large, functional financial centres such as London or New York. As noted earlier, OFCs exist because funds tend to move offshore to exploit fiscal advantages, for secrecy reasons, or to avoid regulation. The value-added component of a transaction via, say, the Cayman Islands, is not based on activities performed there. It lies instead in the tax benefits, or in the secrecy space afforded by routing the transaction through the offshore circuits (Roberts, 1995). Without such offshore 'spaces' there is no economic reason to divert a transaction through a tax haven en route to a large capital market.

The likely outcome of the current re-configuration of the global financial architecture will be an erosion of the distinction between offshore and onshore finance, with the former losing many of the advantages that originally attracted finance capital to the 'islands in the sun'. Some OFCs will experience significant reductions of their principal economic activity, with job losses, falling government revenues and lower spending effects from the once-booming OFC sector. It is unlikely that the effects will be uniform across all OFCs, however. For functional OFCs such as Jersey (which has over 90 per cent of its government revenues from offshore activities) it is likely that any reduction of OFC would have serious economic consequences. For other OFCs hosts, especially those less economically dependent upon offshore finance such as the Cayman Islands, the possible economic outcomes may be less bleak. In the Cayman Islands, for example, there is a significant tourism sector, with both staying tourists and cruise ship day visitors, although some tourism arises from visitors combining a vacation with a visit to their offshore bank manager or to buy some real estate.

This chapter has demonstrated some of the structural impediments to diversification of the economies of many tax haven islands. We argue that many of these impediments are not merely a function of their smallness, openness, nor due to diseconomies of scale, but stem from the crowding-out effects of international financial capital. Financial capital has been able to successfully penetrate these small, vulnerable political economies, often capturing their states to promote favourable legislation. Further, we propose that there is an element of path dependence at work here, arising from the fact that SIEs like Jersey, Guernsey and other functional OFCs have become locked into their relationships with the offshore finance industry by their dependence upon the earnings potential of predominantly imported skills and expertise, and their lack of skills and knowledge in alternative sectors. Thus any attempts at diversification would be constrained by the need for wholesale re-skilling and the acquisition of new knowledge bases.

Nevertheless, part of the challenge facing policy-makers, both in the small states themselves, and within larger onshore economies, is how to promote diversification within economies dominated by offshore finance. One UN report (Blum *et al.*, 1998) suggested that if the global community wishes to roll back tax haven activity, then in an analogous manner to coca farming in Latin America, the havens should be offered financial/technical assistance to diversify and to encourage alternative forms of local business. Offering such assistance will also strengthen the moral justification for taking defensive measures against tax havens. In the propaganda battle during negotiations between the OECD and OFCs during 2001 press releases from some of the smaller Caribbean tax havens portrayed the OECD initiative as 'neo-colonialist' and accused the OECD of threatening local livelihoods:

> Attracting sanctions from the world's wealthiest countries is a daunting prospect for small states whose economies will doubtless suffer. So too will civil order and the maintenance of democracy, which cannot be sustained in conditions of economic decline. At the same time jurisdictions cannot simply surrender to OECD demands that will strengthen the financial services sectors of OECD member countries at the expense of their own. To do so would be to cause their death anyway; this time by a thousand cuts.[17]

The majority of the wealthier tax havens, including those on the periphery of Europe, need to recognise their vulnerability to the plethora of global governance initiatives and take serious measures to address the structural impediments to their economic diversification. If they fail to take such measures their futures would appear unsustainable. This in itself indicates the power of global governance in OFCs: that resistance to compliance will eventually mean their demise.

Notes

1. Data analysed John Christensen, then Economic Adviser to the Jersey government. As in many microstates, there are considerable problems with the reliability of official GDP figures (Hampton and Christensen, 1999).
2. An associated phenomenon, the vast Eurocurrency markets located 'offshore' initially in London have an extensive literature including the work of Einzig (1967), Strange (1971) and Little (1975).
3. The UK Overseas Territories are 13 remnants of the British Empire including many OFCs (the Cayman Islands, the BVI, the Turks and Caicos Islands etc.). However, the three British Crown Dependencies (the Isle of Man, Guernsey and Jersey) are ancient jurisdictions under the Crown, have their own parliaments, and are not within the United Kingdom.
4. Elements of the US federal government have been active against tax havens since the 1960s with dramatic IRS raids in The Bahamas in the 1970s, court action against Cayman Island banks in the 1980s and in the 1990s becoming one of the drivers against international drug money laundering. The events of 9/11, the Enron collapse and moves by Stanley Tools and others to headquarter offshore in Bermuda all appear to have renewed US interest in OFCs.
5. The KPMG Report commissioned by the Foreign Office on financial regulation in British Caribbean territories and Bermuda is a recent example (KPMG, 2000).
6. The ring-fencing of fiscal schemes for non-residents (e.g. offshore companies such as IBCs that offer effective tax rates of as low as 0.5%) from the host's domestic economy is a key tax haven characteristic identified by the OECD (1998). IBCs illustrate the disingenuous argument of many OFCs that they are low tax jurisdictions and thus should not be penalised. However, ring-fenced offshore schemes prevent residents from using IBCs which are only available to non-residents.
7. We heard concerns voiced in many OFCs that the UK government might sacrifice the British OFCs to the EU in order to retain the London Eurobond market. They feared that the UK government would rather see its OFCs reduced than lose the market share of London's financial centre.
8. Banking secrecy and confidentiality can be distinguished. The latter is the reasonable right to privacy in one's affairs, whereas the former goes beyond this. For example, in the case of an offshore bank account, if one has nothing to hide, then legitimate inquiry by the state does not breach the confidentiality expected in banker–client relationships. Bank secrecy in many OFCs prevents such legitimate inquiries. However, bank secrecy appears to be under growing threat of extinction as exemplified by Switzerland's increasing willingness to freeze assets pending court actions.

9. Certain OFCs appear on all three listings (the OECD list of ' tax havens'; FSF least well-regulated OFCs; and the FATF list of 'non co-operative' jurisdictions). OFCs appearing on all three lists are: The Bahamas, Cook Islands, Marshall Islands, Nauru, Niue, Panama, St Kitts and Nevis, St Vincent. The Cayman Islands would have appeared on all three lists, but just days before the OECD report was published agreed to roll back tax haven activities and were removed from the OECD list.

10. It can be argued that – excepting the CI and Isle of Man – the majority of Group I jurisdictions are atypical OFCs and have more features common to regional financial centres than pure 'offshore' centres such as many Caribbean OFCs. For instance whilst Singapore has an offshore function (as do London, New York and Tokyo) it is more accurately described as a regional onshore financial centre (Hampton, 1996b).

11. The inclusion or not of OFCs on the different OECD, FSF and FATF lists is fascinating, as is the way in which different forms of resistance were employed by OFC authorities in deciding whether to cooperate or not with the assessing institutions.

12. See http://visar.csustan.edu/aaba/aaba.htm

13. For example, the Jersey parliament (the States of Jersey) consists 53 elected members: 12 Senators, 29 Deputies and 12 Constables, but elections are held at different periods, and the period in office also varies. Thus the electorate does not vote in (or out) a particular administration with any form of General Election (Mitchell and Sikka *et al.*, 2002).

14. Most OFC islands have warm climates whether Mediterranean, sub-tropical or tropical. Of the temperate island OFCs, the Channel Islands' southerly location gives milder winters and warmer, sunnier summers than mainland Britain averages. The Isle of Man is the most northerly island OFC and (perhaps coincidentally) has a smaller OFC sector relative to other sectors of its economy, is further from London, and has fewer wealthy immigrants than the CI.

15. The CI are located about 120 kilometres south of mainland Britain. The two largest islands, Jersey and Guernsey, although only about 15 kilometres apart, are separate jurisdictions with their own parliaments. The bailiwick of Guernsey includes the islands of Alderney, Herm and Sark.

16. The Jersey Limited Liability Partnership (LLP) Law was devised by two of the largest accountancy firms Price Waterhouse (now PriceWaterhouseCoopers) and Ernst & Young to protect partners' personal assets. The LLP bill was 'fast-tracked' through the Jersey parliament in 1996 and the law drafting process privately funded by the two accountancy firms leading to controversy within the OFC and in the international media (Christensen and Hampton, 1999; Mitchell and Sikka *et al.*, 2002).

17. Press release from the office of Sir Ronald Sanders, Chief Foreign Affairs Representative of Antigua and Barbuda, 5 March 2001.

12
Conclusion: Global Governance, Conflict and Resistance

Rosaleen Duffy and Feargal Cochrane

Governance has become a key term in the lexicon of most social scientists, and even scientists, and is certainly not the preserve of those interested in the changing nature of global politics. 'Governance' as a global buzzword encapsulates the emerging and expanding concern with increased levels of global control through standardisation, regulation, ordering or management. In the health sector for instance, notions of health governance have become part of the common discourse of policy-making, planning and academic research. Similarly, in the realm of environmental science and resource management, terms such as forest governance and forest management transparency regularly appear.

The diffusion of power away from the hegemonic structures of state power is one of the most salient features of the post-Westphalian global order. This newly emerging form of global politics indicates that nation-states are no longer the sole entities which order the international system, but are instead intermediaries between the global and the local. While there may be disagreements about the power of the state as a source of governance within the global order, few would contest that at the beginning of the twenty-first century, notions of political, economic, social and cultural governance, are no longer contained within linear geographical boundaries, but are subject instead to a multiplicity of sites of governance and resistance.

The analysis presented by each of the contributors to this collection, clearly demonstrates that global governance is not easily defined, but rather, has numerous definitions and exists in multiple locations and at a variety of scales. In addition, regulation or governance is often presented as a politically neutral or technical project, but it is clear from the contributions here that this is far from being the case. Instead, notions of governance are clustered around a set of core ideas (liberal democracy, a healthy civil society, transnational economic or environmental management, and ultimately, the very notion of state integrity as being integral to peace and stability) that legitimate and promote a broadly liberal or neo-liberal agenda.

However, it might be expected that any reordering of the global system may generate or encounter resistances to it. As such, multiple forms and scales of resistance to global governance constituted the second core conceptual focus of this book. Rather like global governance, resistance cannot be defined simply. Within this collection resistance is defined in a deliberately broad manner. It is tempting to think of resistance as visible, public and vocal or even violent protest. However, it can also be characterised as subversion, obstruction, foot-dragging, as appearance to comply, getting by or getting around regulations. The intention of this book has been to illustrate all of these complex responses to governance and by doing so, to demonstrate the interplay between the global and the local and the synthesis of the two within a wide variety of regional contexts.

Much of the global governance literature deals with resistances to governance as problems that need to be dealt with and fixed. Thus, governance is equated with the notionally positive values of order, stability, prosperity and even, peace. The absence of governance is accordingly problematised as engendering opposite and negatively charged values such as disorder, instability, poverty and violence.

This characterisation of global governance and resistance as binary opposites is problematic. Consequently, this book views governance and resistance as inextricably inter-linked forces which, through their synthesis, form a single entity or process. Furthermore, global governance and resistance are not separate processes that stand in contravention to each other, but instead have a rather more complex and symbiotic relationship. As Dillon's Chapter 2 neatly puts it, where there is no power there is no resistance, but without resistance there is clearly no power. So multiple forms, levels and sites of global governance are inherently inter-linked with the resistances they encounter. The forms and scales of global governance and resistance are not singular processes that are easily defined, they are instead, multiple, overlapping, inter-twined and complex. As the various conceptualisations and configurations of global governance and resistance by authors within this volume also illustrates, notions of the forms, levels, sites and resistances to global governance, and where the balance of power lies in their interplay, is itself complex and contested.

Governance and resistance

One of the key questions addressed by the book is this. How powerful are the structures of global governance? Given the breadth of this collection's empirical focus, together with the range of conceptual approaches favoured by its authors, excessive generalisations on the nature and limits of global governance would be foolhardy. Finding a one-size-fits-all conceptualisation for the vast array of forms, levels and scales of governance and resistance would be impossible, and would misrepresent the range and diversity of perspectives within this volume. It is clear that for some contributors (Clapham, Cochrane, Dillon, Duffy, Large, Miall, Selby) governance is a pluralised and highly diverse regime of power, where sites of power are multiple, de-centralised and of a networked nature. For others however (Hampton and Christensen, Sum and Wilkin) global governance is a concentrated and co-ordinated neo-liberal project, where power lies clearly in the hands of the governors rather than those on the receiving end of it. Hampton and Christensen provide an analysis of the power of global governance through the threat of global sanctions against small economies who fail to comply with global offshore regulations. The power of such threats is indicated in the ways that numerous small island economies have tried to address their vulnerability to new international regulations by diversifying their economies.

Alongside the powers of global governance, a number of chapters problematise the concept and practices of global governance as being more haphazard. Looking at global governance in the form of conflict prevention initiatives, some of the contributors to this volume (Large, Miall) are sympathetic to the idea of global governance as 'global liberal governance' or even as 'good governance' and certainly a preferable alternative to the failing states of sub-Saharan Africa or the divided societies of the Balkans. Notwithstanding unintended and unfortunate policy outcomes, these authors (unlike Wilkin) do not regard global governance as being malign in its conception and basic architecture. In this view, where states have been divided by ethnic conflict, have collapsed or failed internally, there is a role for global governance, in the shape of international agencies, to intervene to encourage (if not impose) norms and mechanisms that might prevent conflict from re-emerging or escalating further. As Miall puts it, 'in principle, therefore, global governance should offer a way to improve the management of international and intrastate conflicts, and address their root causes' (Miall, Chapter 4).

Nevertheless, by detailing the wide gap between policy design and implementation, Miall and Large converge with other chapters in this collection (Clapham, Cochrane, Dillon, Duffy, Selby) in illustrating the clear boundaries of global governance through an analysis of the failures of such conflict prevention or state building initiatives. They demonstrate that while the global project might be to contribute to the development and impact of civil society within a divided community, conserve endangered species in Africa through international conventions, promote structures of governance within collapsed or fragile states in the developing world, including the Palestinian Authority, the outcomes of such policies can often be unintended, counter productive and equally violent.

In this view, the power to govern is dependent to a significant extent on the degree of consensus that can be reached at the local level to new norms of governance, on the nature of the interest groups and the interplay of agencies at the local and global levels. One example of this is the clear tension between external and internal agencies that often produces a neutralising effect on the implementation of international norms such as the ban on the ivory trade or the attempts to control software piracy. Networks of official complicity and corruption together with local vested interests, offset the capability of international agencies to impose regulations and norms from the outside. Duffy in Chapter 9 demonstrates that the trade in illegal ivory is fluid and manages to work around the imposed norms, adapting quickly to avoid external regulation. The successes and failures associated with implementing the global ivory trade ban clearly indicate the potential capacities of global governance. However, the failures of implementation also require us to rethink governance through an examination of the limits placed on its capacities by local level practices.

The operation of political power can be seen as a complex, organic and flexible amalgam between governors and governed, the two themselves being periodically fluid and interchangeable. Hampton and Christensen in Chapter 11 illustrate that in relation to attempts to regulate off-shore finance, national governments can play both roles. While in recent years the UK government has been anxious to tighten the regulatory framework surrounding off-shore tax havens to curtail money laundering and the financing of 'terrorist' activity, it is not itself beyond being an agent of resistance to global governance. Thus, proposals from the European Union in the late 1990s linked to tax harmonisation across the EU were vigorously resisted by the UK government. Other European governments have similarly played the role of resistors against transnational attempts to regulate off-shore finance. Switzerland, for instance, does not recognise tax evasion as a crime and refuses to compromise secrecy provisions in its banking sector for either fraud or 'terrorist' related investigations by tax or police authorities. Regulation of off-shore finance indicates that notions of governance and resistance are fluid rather than solid, and that the power relationship between the global and the local is mobile rather than static. Whilst governments and international agencies might wield considerable and formidable short-term power over political and legal norms on issues such as off-shore finance, post-war reconstruction, or the ivory trade, these powers are offset by the limits of their implementation. The chapters in this collection demonstrate that whilst laws may be made and conventions passed at the international level, these are often subverted in practice by the activities of global criminal networks combined with corrupt local agents and interest groups. As Selby in Chapter 7 remarks with respect to the Palestinian community, this can simply be characterised by 'sumoud', that is, by the development of coping mechanisms that enable ordinary people to get by. Several of the chapters in this collection (Clapham, Cochrane, Dillon, Duffy, Large and Selby) illustrate the point that local responses to global governance ensure that the global is never wholly dominant and never completely enforced. Whilst in some instances global actors may be the most powerful agencies, this never amounts to omnipotence due to the friction between global and local forces.

Apart from these difficulties with enforcement, global governance itself can be regarded as flexible and adaptive in a number of senses. It is clear from many of the chapters that the structures of global governance are responsive and adaptive to local level challenges in numerous ways. At one level, the institutions of global governance can be regarded as adaptive, in the sense that they respond to criticisms of rules and regulations and change them accordingly. Duffy illustrates that in the case of the Convention on the International Trade in Endangered Species (CITES), the very public and vocal resistance from Southern African states was eventually successful in instigating a change in the regime. However, there is an alternative way of thinking about the responsiveness of global governance to such challenges. Looking at governance and resistance as essentially a coherent whole, governance structures are responsive in the sense that there have been attempts to co-opt resistance actors into power structures, and thereby neutralise the challenge from them. As Sum argues, global governance may be regarded as a form of passive revolution that neutralises the capacity of disruptive forces by building civil society, market forces and liberal states. This flexible adaptation of challenges is also indicated by Wilkin's analysis of the response to the Anti-Globalisation Movement (AGM) in Chapter 5. The ways that the media have sought to define the movement as a violent disorganised rabble demonstrates for Wilkin that it provided a substantive challenge to the global governance agenda. Yet, the AGM itself is limited by the power of the institutions it seeks to challenge. So in that sense the structures of global governance are responsive, but not in a way that resistors would necessarily approve of or welcome. Instead of responding by changing to take account of the interests of resistant actors, global governance is flexible and adaptive in the sense that its response is to neutralise through institutionalisation, regulation, channelling and absorption.

The chapters in this book illustrate that the concepts and practices of global governance privilege certain actors, ideas, values and interest groups over others. One way of conceptualising global governance is to define it as a coherent hegemonic project, where the global agencies intend to enforce their project onto the recipient communities, in the belief that such a project is for the global good. However, such a belief in neo-liberalism as the way forward lacks any sensitivity to debates about the inherent power relationship involved in imposing a neo-liberal economic and political project. As Sum argues in her chapter, a neo-Gramscian approach leads us to an analysis of global governance as an attempt to legitimate and consolidate the dominant, neo-liberal norms of globalisation. In this view, global governance is a neo-liberal political and economic project whose aims are consistent, coherent and potentially, if not actually, harmful. It involves the creation of a 'global architecture' which actively encourages and attempts to enforce political and economic liberalisation, an agenda dominated by the few (the governors) at the expense of the many (the governed). Selby's Chapter 7 argues that the West Bank and Gaza Strip have been major recipients of international aid as well as being the site of an attempt to establish structures in accordance with global principles of good governance. Similarly, as Large illustrates, conflict resolution in the Balkans in reality meant the creation of a pluralistic liberal democracy based on a market economy. While global governance for some, is centred on a particular idea of universalist norms of human rights and democracy, the question here is about how these norms are implemented, who implements them and what impact does that have on the region concerned and the individuals who live there? In the examples given in this volume of global governance as an agent of conflict prevention or post-conflict peace-building, the implementation of universal ideas, agendas and practices of such post war reconstruction are highly politicised and have been interpreted and implemented by those who have the power to do so.

In addition, global governance is based on a particular definition of the relationship between statehood and global order: that states are the necessary building blocks from which stability is created from global anarchy. The chapters by Clapham Large and Miall, demonstrate the centrality of the notion of statehood to the global governance agenda. In the case of the Balkans, such a commitment to statehood as the only entity able to create global order was reflected in the invention of a new statelet, Eastern Slavonia. At the same time that this statelet was created, it was also heavily embedded in global networks, so much so that the UN had the right to dismiss officials who obstructed the project and impose laws when it was deemed necessary to do so. This highlights an inherent paradox. On the one hand, global governance contributes to the extension and deepening of the post-Westphalian global order, intervening to prevent conflict within states, reconstruct or reconstitute them altogether, as in the case of Eastern Slavonia, or supercede state sovereignty/economic integrity, in the interests of global order/prosperity. On the other hand, global governance is still reliant (to a degree) on states and state-centric political and economic structures. For example, representatives of states act as participants in international organisations, states sign global agreements, and global governance inspired schemes in post-conflict societies specifically focus on rebuilding the state as the essential building block of global and local order. Miall notes that conflict resolution as a centrepiece of legitimate and sound global governance is necessary, and that conflict prevention initiatives are increasingly becoming a feature of international interventions with limited backing from major states and the NGO community.

Large's Chapter 6 also presents a paradox in problematising global governance as 'good governance'. In the case of Eastern Slavonia at least, the international intervention has created new winners and losers, new injustices, new criminal networks and is itself guilty of replacing delegitimised or worn out political, social and economic structures with new ones that are also illegitimate in the sense of being imposed, unaccountable and undemocratic.

As many of the chapters in this volume illustrate, global governance does encounter challenges and resistances at multiple levels, from the global to the local. Any attempt to create universally applicable ideas of conservation, democracy, conflict resolution, statehood and so on, encounters real and effective challenges at the local level. The responses to global governance are a key part of any analysis of it and its capacities, since these resistances stress and strain the form of global order preferred by global governance institutions and actors. Consequently, an important focus in this book concerns how resistance impacts on, or is inter-linked with, governance itself and vice versa. The diverse, multi-centric regime of power represented by global governance, has generated multiple forms of resistance by a diverse set of actors. As Large suggests, the vertical structures of power in global governance are met with horizontal methods of resistance and coping at the local level. So in the face of global level structures, people may resort to historical and time honoured practices of kinship, bartering and other forms of informal trade. Global governance has also encountered practices which stretch back into the past and are only now redefined as resistance to global governance because they offend global liberal norms.

If governance and resistance are inter-linked, it is clearly important to look at where resistance is encountered. The chapter by Miall notes that global governance can be resisted from above and from below. An examination of conflict prevention in Macedonia and Kosovo, demonstrated that the major states were ready to abandon initiatives when they clashed with their own priorities. It would therefore appear that the commitment to universalist notions of conflict prevention has been partial and highly conditional in practice. Once again this highlights the essential paradox within global governance, namely that its project – as defined by groupings such as the Commission on Global Governance in publications such as *Our Global Neighborhood* and as underwritten by international institutions – may still be reliant on states, which the post-Westphalian world order at the very least complicates, and at most undermines.

As many of the chapters in this volume demonstrate, critical engagement with the resistances to global governance, illustrates the limitations on global agencies imposing projects of governance at the local level. When these projects are applied, or more accurately, when attempts are made to apply them, they inevitably meet resistance on the ground from parties who are either politically or economically opposed to them. As Dillon states, the issue is not so much *why* resistance as *how* resistance (Dillon, Chapter 2). Resistance operates at a number of levels or scales, at the individual, local, national, regional and even global levels. These various scales of resistance need not be mutually exclusive, rather, local level resistance can inter-link with global level resistance, or be simultaneously global and local. Indeed, it has been argued here by

Dillon, that power and resistance are always found together, that they are essentially symbiotic, so that resistance indicates that power is at work, and power is limited by that resistance. Looked at from this perspective, it is not useful to think only of governance without also looking at the responses to it at multiple levels and scales.

It is not the intention here to suggest that the local always stands in contravention to the global, or that local level actors and agencies always resist global governance initiatives. As the contributions to this volume illustrate, the relationship between the global and the local is varied, multi-faceted and complex. Rather than viewing the global and local levels as disaggregated or segregated, the picture here is of the two being closely associated, intertwined and possibly even interdependent. In Large's view, 'intermestic' manipulation indicates the ways that global and local level agendas may well intersect and coexist. For a number of the contributors it is clear that governance is not a singular concept that is effectively delivered and implemented by a small group of powerful actors onto a large group of weak and dependent recipients. While this might characterise one aspect of global governance, many of the chapters within this collection indicate a more complex relationship, where governors and governed inhabit a more integrated space and where the power to govern is mobile, flexible and fluid. As Cochrane demonstrates, while funding agencies within Northern Ireland might attempt to impose external norms on peace/conflict resolution NGOs within civil society, these are often subverted at the local level. Cochrane, along with several other contributors (Dillon, Duffy, and Selby) argues that governance is a fluid, non-linear phenomenon, not restricted to the powerful few imposing rules and regulations on to the powerless many. The chapters that detail the promotion of civil society in Northern Ireland (Cochrane), governance and resistance in Palestine (Selby), and attempts to promote and enforce international environmental norms (Duffy), illustrate that governance is a two-way street and cannot simply be imposed from the top down. These chapters suggest that even the relatively powerless can have the capacity to slow down externally driven projects of governance. The disempowered, those who are silent and muted, can place some brakes on global governance through their sheer evasiveness and disinterest in a structure of dominance that they feel excluded from.

Several of the chapters in this collection indicate that the ways in which individuals and interest groups attempt to utilise the potential benefits of global governance for their own localised purposes is also a clear form of resistance. The proliferation of NGOs at the local and global level that have become established to tap into funding opportunities has a clear rationale: local priorities can therefore be bolstered by global governance, but not in ways that the funders had initially envisaged. In this sense funders and recipients of aid enter in to a complex relationship, where each may well understand the mutual subversion that is taking place and the rules of the game that is being played. The act of resistance here is not to subvert global governance *per se*, but rather to satisfy localised or individual priorities. Thus for resistance, read pragmatism.

The way that resistance is manifested in practice is also important. Global governance is fragile and limited in the sense that in some regions of the world, notably sub-Saharan Africa, messy, insecure under-developed and ill-governed states may present a threat to any project that aims to create global order. This is not necessarily because the weak states of sub-Saharan Africa actively choose to resist global governance, but rather that they represent an area where global governance cannot be implemented through the state because the state lacks the power to do so. Cochrane's study of conflict resolution activity in Northern Ireland indicates that civil society is far from adhering to the idealised model frequently articulated at the global level, where public participation and associationalism will augment social capital, instill civic values and reduce the conflict-proneness of divided societies. Cochrane illustrates the disjuncture between global intentions and local practices and how a commitment to the ideal of civil society can have very different and often unintended outcomes in deeply divided societies, where joining together can increase, intensify and sustain local conflicts, rather than transcend or resolve them.

Resistance can also be regarded as being both visible and invisible. The most visible and public forms of resistance are organisations like the Anti-Globalisation Movement, which provides a very public challenge to global governance. However, there may also be resistances centred on lobbying within the structures of global governance, either by states, NGOs, private business or other forms of transnational organisations. Duffy's analysis of Zimbabwe's public lobbying at CITES, demonstrates the way in which resistant actors can remain within governance structures rather than standing outside them. The methods of resistance here vary from very public forms of lobbying, to less visible forms of subversion, from adaptation to simply ignoring global level controls. Duffy cites the continuance of ivory poaching by criminal networks in sub-Saharan Africa as an invisible act of subversion and resistance to the global governance project. Duffy's chapter, together with others in this volume, illustrates that the black economy continues to thrive, and continues to effectively resist any kind of market controls at the global, regional, national or local levels.

The practical forms of resistance are also partly determined by who is resisting and why. The contributions from Duffy, Large, Selby and Sum, all clearly indicate that the relatively powerless in any society use very different forms of everyday resistance to global governance. The cat and mouse strategies of software pirates and the 'sumoud', or 'getting by' amongst Palestinians, demonstrates that people may try to resist in small, but cumulatively effective, ways. The notion of 'weapons of the weak' (Scott, 1985) illustrates that everyday forms of resistance can place limitations on global governance through foot dragging, dissimulation, and false compliance. The simulation activity analysed by Selby, demonstrates that actors may covertly resist global governance through appearing to comply, while confrontation is bolder and more visible. Such strategies place real and effective limitations on global governance, because individuals have to get by and concentrate on survival. None of this is intended to romanticise local level resistance as the David to the Goliath of global governance.

Instead, the intention of the chapters in this book is to provide an analysis across a range of regional and conceptual contexts, of the every day ways that individuals resist global regulation. By doing so, the book has drawn out the complex interplay between global and local actors and the synthesis of these forces.

All of the contributors to this volume, in their different ways, convey a similar message, namely that global governance is not a consistently understood phenomenon with coherent objectives. It is contested, variable, fluid and understood in different ways by different agencies, individuals and interest groups. Equally, its impact at the local level is dependent to a large extent upon its interaction with local forces. The message here and the lesson to be drawn from this book, is that global governance and resistances to it are a network of complex, multi-faceted forces with undetermined and unforeseen outcomes. Global governance has its limits and those limits are dependent upon the interplay between governing agencies and those at the local level. Governance cannot be unilaterally imposed from the global onto the local level (at least over the long term) without encountering significant levels of resistance that will impede the successful implementation of international norms and regulations.

Bibliography

Abbott, J. (2000) 'Treasure Island or Desert Island? Offshore Finance and Development in Labuan.' *Development Policy Review*, 18 (2): 157–75.

Abed, G. (1988) *The Palestinian Economy* (London: Routledge).

Achieng, J. (2001) 'Anti Globalisation NGOs Threatened by War on Terror,' *The Daily Mail and Guardian* (Dakar), 29 October, http://www.mg.co.za/mg/za/archive/2001oct/features/29oct-ngos.html

Agamben, G. (1998) *Homo Sacer. Sovereign Power and Bare Life* (Stanford: Stanford University Press).

Alberts, D. and T.J. Czerwinski (1994) *Complexity, Global Politics and National Security* (Washington DC: National Defense University).

Alberts, David S., John J. Gartska and Frederick P. Stein (1999) Network Centric Warfare, 2nd edn, Command and Control Research Programme DOD (Washington).

Alden, C. (2001) *Mozambique and the Construction of the New African State: From Negotiations to Nation Building* (Basingstoke: Palgrave).

Anderson, C.L., L. Locker, and R. Nugent (2002) 'Microcredit, Social Capital and Common Pool Resources,' *World Development*, 30 (1): 95–105.

Applebaum, A. (2001). 'Who elected the anti-capitalist convergence?' *Slate Magazine*, 23 April, http://slate.msn.com/default.aspx?id=104829

Armstrong, H., R. de Kervenoael, R. Read and X. Li (1998) 'A Comparison of the Economic Performances of Different Microstates, and between Microstates and Larger Countries,' *World Development*, 26: 639–56.

Arquilla, J. and D. Ronfeldt (1993) *Cyberwar is Coming: RAND Report* (New York: Taylor and Francis).

Arquilla, J. and D. Ronfeldt (1996) 'Information, Power and Grand Strategy: In Athena's Camp,' in *The Information Revolution and National Security: Dimensions and Directions*, S. Schwartzstein (ed.) (Washington, DC: The Centre for Strategic and International Studies).

Arquilla, J. and D. Ronfeldt (eds) (1997) *In Athena's Camp: Preparing for Conflict in the Information Age* (Washington: RAND).

Arquilla J. and D. Ronfeldt (2000) *Swarming and the Future of Conflict* (California: RAND).

Arquilla, J. and D. Ronfeldt (2001) *Networks and Netwars. The Future of Terror, Crime and Militancy* (RAND: National Defense Research Institute).

Arrighi, G., T. Hopkins and I. Wallerstein (1989) *Anti-systemic Movements* (London: Verso).

Arrighi, G. and B. Silver (1999) *Chaos and Governance in the Modern World System* (Minneapolis: Minnesota Press).

Atkinson, M. (2000) 'Poverty row author quits World Bank,' *The Guardian* newspaper, 15 June, http://www.guardianunlimited.co.uk/Archive/Article/0,4273,4029590,00.html

Azar, E.E. (1990) *The Management of Protracted Social Conflict: Theory and Cases.* (Aldershot: Dartmouth).

Baldacchino, G. (1993) 'Bursting the Bubble: The Pseudo-Development Strategies of Microstates,' *Development and Change*, 24 (1): 29–51.

Barbier, E., J.C. Burgess, T.M. Swanson and D.W. Pearce (1990) *Elephants, Economics and Ivory* (London: Earthscan).

Barry, A. (2001) *Political Machines. Governing a Technological Society* (London: Athlone).

Bayart, J.F. (1993) *The State In Africa: The Politics of the Belly* (London and New York: Longman).

Bell, D. (1973) *The Coming of Post-Industrial Society: A Venture in Social Forecasting* (New York: Basic Books).

Bennett, R. and M. Peel, (2002) 'Sanctions threat to 'opaque' tax haven: pressure on Jersey,' *The Financial Times*, 19 February.

Benvenisti, M. (1984) *The West Bank Data Project: A Survey of Israel's Policies* (Washington DC: American Enterprise Institute).

Bergman, R. (1999a) 'Israel deposited NIS 1.5b in Arafat's personal account,' *Ha'aretz*, 8 October.

Bergman, R. (1999b) 'How much PA corruption is too much?' *Ha'aretz*, 19 October.

Berman, P. (2001) 'The passion of Joschka Fisher,' in *The New Republic*, 27 August, http://www.thenewrepublic.com/082701/berman082701_print.html

Bertram, E. (1995) 'Reinventing Governments: The Promise and Perils of United Nations Peacebuilding,' *Journal of Conflict Resolution*, 39 (3).

Bircham, E. and J. Charlton (eds) (2000) *Anti-Capitalism: A Guide to the Movement* (London: Bookmarks).

Biswas, A. (2000) 'Editorial: Comments on the World Commission on Water for the 21st Century,' *Water International*, 25 (2): 280–3.

Blair, T. (1998) *Leading the Way: A New Vision for Local Government* (London: IPPR).

Blum, J. M. Levi, R. Naylor and P. Williams (1998) *Banking Secrecy and Financial Havens* (New York: United Nations).

Bonner, R. (1993) *At the Hand of Man: Peril and Hope for Africa's Wildlife* (London: Simon and Schuster).

Bratton, M., P. M. Lewis and E. Gyimah-Boadi (2001) 'Constituencies for Reform in Ghana,' *Journal of Modern African Studies*, 39 (2).

Briguglio, L. (1995) 'Small Island States and their Economic Vulnerabilities,' *World Development*, 23: 1615–32.

Brooks, G. (2002) 'Back to Life (in Sarajevo),' *Guardian Review*, 5 February, 6–7.

Brynen, R. (1995) 'The Neopatrimonial Dimension of Palestinian Politics,' *Journal of Palestine Studies*, 25 (1): 23–36.

Brynen, R. (1996) 'International Aid to the West Bank and Gaza: A Primer,' *Journal of Palestine Studies*, 25 (2): 46–53.

Brynen, R. (2000) *A Very Political Economy: Peacebuilding and Foreign Aid in the West Bank and Gaza* (Washington, DC: US Institute of Peace).

Bullion, A. (1995) *India, Sri Lanka and Tamil Crisis 1976–1994: An International Perspective* (London: Pinter).

Burchell, G., C. Gordon and P. Miller (eds) (1991) *The Foucault Effect: Studies in Governmentality* (Hemel Hempstead: Harvester Wheatsheaf).

Business Software Alliance (2000) *Global Software Piracy Study*, http://www. bas.org/intnat/piracystudy.htm, accessed 30 October 2001.

Burgess, J. and K. Collins (1998) *Building Consensus: Jersey's Local Agenda 21* (London: University College London).

Buzan, B. and R. Little (1999) 'Beyond Westphalia? Capitalism after the "Fall",' *Review of International Studies*, 25 (Special Issue): 89–104.

Callinicos, A. (1991) *The Revenge of History* (Cambridge: Polity Press).

Camilleri, J., K. Malhotra and M. Tehranian (2000), *Reimagining the Future: Towards Democratic Governance: A Report of the Global Governance Reform Project* (Bundoora, VIC: La Trobe University).

Care For The Wild (1992) *The Elephant Harvest? An Ethical Approach* (West Sussex: CFTW).

Carnegie Commission on Preventing Violent Conflict (1997) *Preventing Violent Conflict* (Washington DC: Carnegie Corporation of New York).

Castells, M. (1996) *The Rise of the Network Society* (London: Oxford University Press).

Castells, M. (1997) *The Rise of the Network Society* (Volume 1 of *The Information Age: Economy, Society and Culture*) (Massachussets and Oxford: Blackwell).

Castells, M. (2000a) *End of Millennium* (New York: Blackwell).

Castells, M. (2000b) *The Rise of the Network Society* (Oxford: Blackwell).

Cebrowski, A.K. and J.J. Gartska, (1998) *Network-Centric Warfare: Its Origin and Future* (US Naval Institute Proceedings).

Chabal, P. and J.P. Daloz (1999) *Africa Works: Disorder as a Political Instrument* (Oxford: James Currey).

Chandler, D. (1999) 'The Limits of Peacebuilding: International Regulation and Civil Society Development in Bosnia,' in *International Peacekeeping* 6(1).

Charles, C. (1995) *The GIIC Asia Regional Meeting and International Conference for National Information Infrastructure for Social and Economic Development in Asia*, (Washington, DC: Centre for Strategic and International Studies and the Global Information Infrastructure Commission).

Chomsky, N. (1993) 'The Israel–Arafat agreement,' *Z Magazine*, October.

Chomsky, N. (1999) *Fateful Triangle: The United States, Israel and the Palestinians*, 2nd edn (London: Pluto).

Chow, D. (2000) 'Counterfeiting in the People's Republic of China', *Washington University Law Quarterly*, 78: 1–54.

Christensen, J. and M.P. Hampton (1999) 'A Legislature for Hire: The Capture of the State Jersey's Offshore Finance Centre,' in M.P. Hampton and J.P. Abbott, (eds) *Offshore Finance Centres and Tax Havens: The Rise of Global Capital* (Basingstoke: Macmillan).

Christensen, J. and M.P. Hampton (2000) 'The Economics of Offshore: Who Wins, Who Loses?' *The Financial Regulator*, 4 (4): 24–6.

Civicus World 'Civil Society and Good Governance', *Civicus World*, March/April 1999. htp//www.civicus.org

Clapham, C. (1996) *Africa in the International System* (Cambridge: Cambridge University Press).

Clapham, C. (1998) 'Rwanda: The Perils of Peacemaking,' *Journal of Peace Research*, 35: 2.

Clapham, C. (1999) 'Sovereignty and the Third World State,' *Political Studies*, 47: 3.

Clarke, M. (1986) *Regulating the City – Competition, Scandal and Reform* (Milton Keynes: Open University Press).

Cobb, S.C. (1998) 'Global Finance and the Growth of Offshore Financial Centers: the Manx Experience,' *Geoforum*, 29 (1): 7–21.

Cochrane, F. (2001) 'Unsung Heroes? The Role of Peace and Conflict Resolution Organisations in the Northern Ireland Conflict,' in McGarry, J. (ed.), *Northern Ireland and the Divided World* (Oxford: Oxford University Press), 137–56.

Cochrane, F. and S. Dunn (2002) *People Power? The Role of the Voluntary and Community Sector in the Northern Ireland Conflict* (Cork: Cork University Press).

Cockburn A. and J. St. Clair (2000) *Five Days that Shook the World* (London: Verso).

Cohen, R. and S.M. Rai (2000) *Global Social Movements* (London: The Athlone Press).

Cohen, Y. (1997) 'Software Pirates Pile Up Profits in Afflicted Asia,' *The Christian Science Monitor*, 29 December, http://www.csmonitor.com/durable/1997/12/29/intl1.html

Coleman, J. (1990) *Foundations of Social Theory* (Cambridge: Harvard University Press).

Coletta, N.J., M. Kostner and I. Wiederhofer (1996) *Case Studies in War-to-Peace Transition: The Demobilization and Reintegration of Ex-combatants in Ethiopia, Namibia, and Uganda* (Washington DC: World Bank).

Collier, P. (2000) 'Economic Causes of Civil Conflict and Their Implications for Policy' (Washington DC: World Bank).

Collier, P. and A. Hoeffler (1999) 'Justice-Seeking and Loot-Seeking in Civil War' (Washington DC: World Bank).

Commission on Global Governance (1995) *Our Global Neighbourhood: The Report of the Commission on Global Governance* (Oxford: Oxford University Press).

Commonwealth Secretariat (1997) *A Future for Small States: Overcoming Vulnerability* (London: Commonwealth Secretariat).

Comor, E. (ed.) (1996) *The Global Political Economy of Communication* (London: Macmillan).

Comor, E. (1997) 'The United States and the Global Information Infrastructure,' *Prometheus*, 15 (3): 357–67.

Corbridge, S., N. Thrift, and R. Martin (eds) (1994) *Money, Power and Space* (Oxford: Blackwell).

Corporate Watch (2000) 'If Capitalism is Pants, What are You Wearing Under Your Trousers?', Issue 10, Spring, http://www.corporatewatch.org.uk/magazine/issue10/cw10f1.html

Council on Foreign Relations (1999) *Strengthening Palestinian Public Institutions* (New York: Council on Foreign Relations).

Cousens, E. and C. Kumar (eds) (2001) *Peacebuilding as Politics* (Boulder: Lynne Rienner), 114–15.

Cox, R. (1981) 'Social Forces, States and World Orders: Beyond International Relations Theory', *Millennium*, 12 (2): 126–55.

Cox, R. (1983) 'Gramsci, Hegemony and International Relations: An Essay in Method,' *Millennium*, 12 (2): 162–75.

Cox, R. (1987) *Production, Power, and the World Order* (New York: Columbia University Press).

Cox, R. (1998) 'Production, the State and Change in World Order,' in E.O. Czempial and J. Rosenau (eds) *Global Changes and Theoretical Challenges* (Massachusetts: Lexington Books).

Cresswell, T. (2001) 'The Production of Mobilities,' *New Formations*, 43: 11–25.

Cruickshank, B. (1999) *The Will to Empower* (Cornell: Cornell University Press).

Cumming, D.H.M. and I. Bond (1991) *Animal Production in Southern Africa: Peasant Practice and Opportunities for Peasant Farmers in Arid Lands.* WWF MAPS Project paper No. 22 (Harare: WWF).

Cumming, D.H.M., R.F. Du Toit and S.N. Stuart (1990) *African Elephants and Rhinos: Status Survey and Action Plan* (Gland, Switzerland: IUCN/SSC African Elephant Specialist Group).

Cunliffe, J. (2000) 'Now I Went and Did It,' http://mail.python.org/pipermail/edu-sig/2000-October/000664.html

Cupitt, R., R. Whitlock and L. Williams (1997) 'The Immortality of International Governmental Organisations,' in P.F. Diehl, *The Politics of Global Governance: International Organizations in an Interdependent World* (London/Boulder: Lynne Rienner), 7–24.

Currey, D. and H. Moore (1994) *Living Proof: African Elephants: The Success of the CITES Appendix I Ban* (London: EIA).

Davies, J. and T.R. Gurr (eds) (1998) *Preventive Measures: Building Risk Assessment and Crisis Early Warning Systems* (Lanham: Rowman and Littlefield).

De Certeau M. (1984) *The Practice of Everyday Life* (Berkeley: University of California Press).

Deacon, B. and P. Stubbs (1998) 'International Actors and Social Policy Development in Bosnia-Herzegovina: Globalism and the "New Feudalism",' *Journal of European Social Policy*, 8 (2) (London: Sage Publications).

Deacon, B. with M. Hulse and P. Stubbs (1997) *Global Society Policy* (London: Sage).

Dean, M. (1991) *The Constitution of Poverty. Toward a Genealogy of Liberal Governance* (London: Routledge).

Dean, M. (1999) *Governmentality: Power and Rule in Modern Society* (London: Sage).

Dean, Mitchell (2002) 'Powers of Life and Death Beyond Governmentality,' *Journal for Cultural Research*, 6 (1–2), January: 119–38.

Della Porta, D. and M. Diani (1999) *Social Movements: An Introduction* (Oxford: Blackwell).

Della Porta, D., H. Kriesi and D. Rucht (eds) (1999) *Social Movements in a Globalising World* (London: Macmillan).

Denny, C. (2000a) 'Russia and Israel head money laundering List' *The Guardian*, 23 June.

Denny, C. (2000b) 'Poor countries face $50 billion bill for tax havens,' *The Guardian*, 24 June.

Dicken, P. (1998) *Global Shift: Transforming the World Economy* (London: Paul Chapman).

Diehl, P. (ed.) (2001) *The Politics of Global Governance: International Organizations in a Changing World* (Boulder, CO: Lynne Rienner).

Dillon, M. (2002) 'Network Society, Network-Centric Warfare and the State of Emergency,' *Theory, Culture and Society*, 19 (4), August.

Dillon, M. (2003) 'Culture, Governance and Global Biopolitics,' in F. Debrix and C. Weber (eds) *Rituals of Mediation* (Minneapolis: Minnesota University Press).

Dillon, M. and J. Reid (2001) 'Global Liberal Governance: Biopolitics, Security and War,' *Millennium Journal of International Studies*, 30 (1).

Divjak, B. (2001) 'The International Community is Not Immune to the Corruption Plague Either,' *Transparency International Bosnia and Herzegovina* Report No. 2 (English Translation: Banja Luka).

DNPWLM (1991) *Protected Species of Animals and Plants in Zimbabwe* (Harare: DNPWLM).

DNPWLM (1992) *Research Plan: DNPWLM, Zimbabwe* (Harare: Branch of Aquatic Ecology and Branch of Terrestrial Ecology, Research Division, DNPWLM).

Dillon, M. and J. Valentine (eds) (2002) 'Culture and Governance', Special Double Issue, *Journal of Cultural Research*, 6 (1–2), January.

Doyle, M.W. (1986) 'Liberalism and World Politics,' *American Political Science Review*, 80, December: 1151–69.

Drahos, P. (1995) 'Global Property Rights in Information: The Story of TRIPS at the GATT', *Prometheus*, 13 (1): 6–19.

Dublin, H.T. (1994) 'Status and trends of the African elephant (*Loxodonta Africana*)'. Paper presented at *The African Elephant in the Context of CITES*. Conference held in Kasane, Botswana 19–23 September 1994 (UK Dept. Of Environment) Part B.

Dublin, H.T. and H. Jachmann (1991) 'The impact of the ivory ban on illegal hunting of elephants in six range states in Africa,' WWF International Research Report. WWF Project no. 4578 (Gland, Switzerland: WWF).

Dublin, H.T., T. Milliken and R.F.W. Barnes (1995) *Four Years After the CITES Ban: Illegal Killing of Elephants, Ivory Trade and Stockpiles* (Gland, Switzerland: IUCN/SSC African Elephant Specialist Group).

Duffield, M. (2001) *Global Governance and the New Wars: The Merger of Development and Security* (London: Zed Books).

Duffy, R. (1999) 'The Role and Limitations of State Coercion: Anti-Poaching Policies in Zimbabwe,' *Journal of Contemporary African Studies*, 17: 97–121.

Edwards, A. (The Edwards Report) (1998) Review of financial regulation in the Crown dependencies: A Report (London: Home Office).

EIA (1992) *Under Fire: Elephants in the Front Line* (London: EIA).

EIA (1994) *CITES: Enforcement Not Extinction* (London: EIA).

Einzig, P. (1967) *The Eurodollar System* (Basingstoke: Macmillan).

Eisenstadt, S.N. (1973) *Traditional Patrimonialism and Modern Neo-Patrimonialism* (London: Sage).

Ellis, S. (1989) 'Tuning in to Pavement Radio,' *African Affairs*, 88: 321–30.

Ellis, S. (1999) *The Mask of Anarchy* (London: Hurst).

Elmusa, S. (1997) *Water Conflict: Economics, Politics, Law and the Palestinian–Israeli Water Resources* (Washington DC: Institute for Palestine Studies).

Englbrecht, W. (2001) 'Bosnia and Herzegovina – No Future Without Reconciliation,' *Forced Migration Review*, 11 October, Oxford Refugee Studies Programme, http://www.fmreview.org/1index.htm

Falk, R. (1995) *On Humane Governance: Towards a New Global Politics* (Cambridge: Polity Press).

Featherstone, M. and S. Lash (1995) 'Globalization, Modernity and the Spatialisation of Social Theory: An Introduction,' in M. Featherstone, S. Lash and R. Robertson (eds) *Global Modernities* (London: Sage).

Festa, P. (2001) 'Government Push Open-Source Software,' http://technews. netscape.com/news/0–1003–200–6996393.html?tag5bplst

Financial Action Task Force (FATF) (2000a) *Report on Non-Cooperative Countries and Territories*. February (Paris: FATF).

Financial Action Task Force (FATF) (2000b) *Review to Identify Non-Cooperative Countries or Territories: Increasing the Worldwide Effectiveness of Anti-Money Laundering Measures*. June (Paris: FATF).

Financial Action Task Force (FATF) (2000c) 'Progress Report on Non-Cooperative Countries and Territories.' News Release, 5 October. Published on FATF website http://www.oecd.org/fatf/

Financial Stability Forum (FSF) (2000a) *Report of the Working Group on Offshore Financial Centres.* April (Paris: FSF).

Financial Stability Forum (FSF) (2000b) 'Financial Stability Forum Releases Grouping of Offshore Financial Centres (OFCs) to Assist in Setting Priorities for Assessment.' 25 May. FSF Press Releases, Internet version: http://www.fsforum.org/Press/Home.html

Finkelstein, L. (1995) 'What is Global Governance?' *Global Governance,* 1 (3): 367–72.

Fleck, F. (2000) 'Fight Against Crime Top Priority.' Banking in Switzerland supplement, *The Financial Times,* 14 November.

Foucault, M. (1977) *Discipline and Punish: The Birth of the Prison* (Harmondsworth: Penguin).

Foucault, M. (1978) *The History of Sexuality, Vol. 1: An Introduction* (Harmondsworth: Penguin).

Foucault, M. (1979) 'Governmentality,' *I & C,* No. 4, 5–21.

Foucault, M. (1980) *Power/Knowledge: Selected Interviews and Other Writings 1972–1977* (Brighton: Harvester).

Freedom House annual. *The Comparative Survey of Freedom* (Washington DC: Freedom House).

Friedland, L.A. 'Electronic Democracy and the New Citizenship,' *Media, Culture, Society,* 18: 185–212.

Frisch, H. (1998) *Countdown to Statehood: Palestinian State Formation in the West Bank and Gaza* (Albany: SUNY Press).

Fukuyama, F. (1989) 'The End of History?' *The National Interest,* 16: 3–16.

Fukuyama, F. (1992) *The End of History and the Last Man* (New York: Avon).

Gallagher, R. (The Gallagher Report) (1990) *Survey of Offshore Finance Sectors in the Caribbean Dependent Territories* (London: Foreign and Commonwealth Office).

George, S. and F. Sabelli (1994) *Faith and Credit: The World Bank's Secular Empire* (Boulder: Westview).

Giddens, A. (1994) *Beyond Left and Right* (Cambridge: Polity Press).

Gilham, P.F. and G.T. Marx (2000) 'Complexity and Irony in Policing and Protesting: The World Trade Organisation at Seattle,' *Social Justice,* 27 (2): 212–36.

Gill, S. (1990) *American Hegemony and the Trilateral Commission* (Cambridge: Cambridge University Press).

Gill, S. (ed.) (1993) *Gramsci, Historical Materialism and International Relations* (Cambridge: Cambridge University Press).

Gill, S. (1995) 'The Global Panoptican,' *Alternatives,* 20: 1–49.

Gill, S. and D. Law (1988) *The Global Political Economy* (New York: Harvester, Wheatsheaf).

Gills, B. (ed.) (2000) *Globalization and the Politics of Resistance* (London: Macmillan).

Gilpin, R. (2001) *Global Political Economy* (Princeton: Princeton University Press).

Gilpin, R. (2002) 'A Realist Perspective on International Governance,' in D. Held and A. McGrew (eds) *Governing Globalization: Power, Authority and Global Governance* (Cambridge: Polity Press), 237–48.

Gleditsch, Nils Petter, Håvard Strand, Mikael Eriksson, Margareta Sollenberg and Peter Wallensteen (2002) 'Armed Conflict 1946–99: A New Dataset', *Journal of Peace Research,* 39 (5): 615–37.

Global Action at http://flag.blackened.net/global/

Globalise Resistance at http://www.resist.org.uk/

Global Witness (2002) 'Coltan,' at http://www.globalwitness.org/indexhome. html

Global Witness (2003) 'Conflict Diamonds', at http://www.globalwitness.org/campaigns/diamonds/index.html

Gordon, R.A. (The Gordon Report) (1981) *Tax Havens and their Use by US Taxpayers – An Overview* (Washington DC: IRS).

Gore, A. (1994) 'Remarks prepared for delivery by Vice-President Al Gore,' International Telecommunication Union, 21 March, http://www.goelzer.net/telecom/al-gore.html

Gore, A. (1995) 'Gore's speech to the G-7 Ministerial Conference,' Brussels, Belgium, 25 February, http://web.simmons.edu/lcehn/nit/NIT'94/94 Appendices-core3-385.html

Gorostiaga, X. (1984) *The Role of International Finance Centres in Underdeveloped Countries* (New York: St Martin's Press).

Gowan, P. (1999) *The Global Gamble: Washington's Faustian Bid for World Dominance* (London: Verso).

Groom, A. and D. Powell (1994) 'From World Politics to Global Governance: A Theme in Need of a Focus,' in J. Groom and M. Light (eds) *Contemporary International Relations: A Guide to Theory* (London: Pinter), 81–90.

Groom, B. (2000) 'Offshore financial havens caught up in tax debate,' *The Financial Times*, 20 March.

Guerin, D. (1970) *Anarchism* (New York: Monthly Review Press).

Gunder, F.A. (1967) *Capitalism and Underdevelopment in Latin America* (Harmondsworth: Penguin).

Gurr, M. and D. Khosla (2002) *Peace and Conflict 2001: A Global Survey of Armed Conflicts, Self-Determination Movements and Democracy* (Maryland: Centre for International Development and Conflict Management).

Gurr, T.R. (2000) *People Versus States: Minorities at Risk in the New Century* (Washington: United States of Peace).

Gutman, R. (2001) 'Bank job in a battle zone,' *Newsweek*, 30 April.

Haas, P. (1992) 'Knowledge, Power and International Policy Coordination,' *International Organization*, 46 (1): 1–35.

Habermas, J. (1987) *The Theory of Communicative Action. Vol. II, Lifeworld and System: A Critique of Functionalist Reason* (Cambridge: Polity).

Haddad, T. (2002) 'The Age of No Illusion,' *Between the Lines*, 2 (17).

Halbert, D. (1999) *Intellectual Property in the Information Age: The Politics of Expanding Ownership Rights* (Westport, CT: Quorum Books).

Hamel, P. *et al.* (2001) *Globalisation and Social Movements* (London: Palgrave).

Hamilton, M. (1997) 'The TRIPs Agreement: Imperialistic, Outdated, and Over-protective,' in A. Moore, (ed.) *Intellectual Property: Moral, Legal and International Dilemmas* (Lanham: Rowman and Littlefield), 243–63.

Hampton, M.P. (1994) 'Treasure Islands or Fool's Gold? Can and Should Small Island Economies Copy Jersey?' *World Development*, 22 (2): 237–50.

Hampton, M.P. (1996a) 'Creating Spaces. The Political Economy of Island Offshore Finance Centres: The Case of Jersey,' *Geographische Zeitschrift*, 84 (2): 103–13.

Hampton, M.P. (1996b) *The Offshore Interface: Tax Havens in the Global Economy.* (Basingstoke: Macmillan).

Hampton, M.P. and J. Christensen (1999) 'Treasure Island Revisited. Jersey's Offshore Finance Centre Crisis: Implications for Other Small Island Economies,' *Environment and Planning A*, 31 (9): 1619–37.

Hardt, M. and A. Negri (2000) *Empire* (Cambridge, MA: Harvard University Press).

Hart, J.A. and S. Kim (2002) 'Explaining the Resurgence of U.S. Competitiveness: The Rise of Wintelism,' *Information Society*, 18 (1): 1–12.

Hass, A. (2000) 'Chairman Arafat straightens out his financial accounts,' *Ha'aretz* 13 January.

Heeks, R. (1997) 'Small Enterprise Development and the "Dutch Disease" in a Small Economy: The Case of Brunei.' Paper read at the Development Studies Association Annual Conference, University of East Anglia, Norwich, 11–13 September.

Hegre, H., T. Ellingsen, S. Gates and N.P. Gleditsch (2001) 'Towards a Democratic Civil Peace? Democracy, Political Change and Civil War 1816–1992,' *American Political Science Review*, 95 (1): March: 33–48.

Heidegger, M. (1977) *Basic Writings* (San Francisco: Harper).

Held, D. (1995) *Democracy and Global Order: From the Modern State to Cosmopolitan Government* (Cambridge: Polity).

Held, D. and A. McGrew (2002) *Governing Globalization: Power, Authority and Global Governance* (Cambridge: Polity Press).

Henwood, D. (1999) 'Left Business Observer @ WTO,' Friday, December 3, http://www.panix.com/~dhenwood/SeattleFriday.html

Henwood, D. (1999) 'What is Globalisation Anyway?' http://www.angelfire.com/pr/red/anti_corporate/what_is_globalization_anyway.htm

Herbst, J. (2000) *States and Power in Africa: Comparative Lessons in Authority and Control* (Princeton, NJ: Princeton University Press).

Hewson, M. and T.J. Sinclair (eds) (1999) *Approaches To Global Governance Theory* (New York: State University of New York Press).

Hewson, M. and T.J. Sinclair (1999) 'The Emergence of Global Governance Theory,' in M. Hewson and T.J. Sinclair (eds) *Approaches To Global Governance Theory* (New York: State University of New York Press), 3–22.

Hindess, B., P. Hirst and G. Thompson (1996) *Globalisation in Question. The International Economy and the Possibilities of Governance* (Cambridge: Polity Press).

Hines, J.R. and E.M. Rice (1994) 'Fiscal Paradise: Foreign Tax Havens and American Business,' *The Quarterly Journal of Economics*, February: 149–182.

Hitchens, C. (2001) *Letters to a Young Contrarian* (Oxford: Perseus Press).

Hitchens, C. Interview with *The Stranger*, 17–23 January 2002, http://www.thestranger.com/current/logo.html

Hovey, G. (2001), 'The Rehabilitation of Homes and Return of Minorities to Republika Srpska,' Ikenberry, G.J. (ed.) *After Victory* (Princeton: Princeton University Press).

Hudson, A. (1998) 'Reshaping the Regulatory Landscape: Border Skirmishes Around the Bahamas and Cayman Offshore Financial Centres,' *Review of International Political Economy*, 5 (3): 534–64.

James, C. (2002) 'The Enron Collapse: Caribbean Tax Haven Offers Assistance,' *The Financial Times*, 13 February.

International Crisis Group (2001) 'Bosnia: Reshaping the International Machinery,' *Balkans Report* No. 121 (Sarajevo/Brussels: ICG).

International Crisis Group (2001) 'Bosnia's Precarious Economy: Still Not Open for Business,' *Balkans Report* No. 115 (Sarajevo/Brussels: ICG).

Ivory Trade Review Group (1989) *The Ivory Trade and the Future of the African Elephant*, Vol. I (Summary and Conclusions). Report prepared for the 7th CITES, Conference of the Parties, Lausanne October 1989 (ITRG: Oxford).

Jackson, R. (1990) *Quasi-States: Sovereignty, International Relations, and the Third World* (Cambridge: Cambridge University Press).

Jaggers, K. and T.R. Gurr (1995) 'Tracking Democracy's Third Wave with the Polity III Data,' *Journal of Peace Research*, 32 November: 483–8.

Jersey Tourism (2000) *A Tourism Strategy for Jersey*, October (Jersey: States Printers).

Jessop, B. (1998) 'The Rise of Governance and the Risks of Failure: The Case of Economic Development,' *International Social Science Journal*, no. 155: 29–46.

Jessop, B. (2002) *The Future of the Capitalist State* (Cambridge: Polity Press).

Jessop, B. and N.-L. Sum (2000) 'Pre-Disciplinary and Post-Disciplinary Perspectives on New Political Economy,' *New Political Economy*, 6 (1): 89–101.

Johns, R.A. (1983) *Tax Havens and Offshore Finance – A Study in Transnational Economic Development* (London: Pinter).

Johns, R.A. and C. Le Marchant (1993) *Finance Centres: British Isle Offshore Development since 1979* (London: Pinter).

Kaldor, M. (1999) *New and Old Wars: Organized Violence in a Global Era* (Cambridge: Polity).

Kaufman, D., A. Kraay and P. Loido-Lobaton (1999) *Aggregating Governance Indicators* (Washington: World Bank. World Bank Policy Research Working Paper, No. 2196).

Kebo, A. (2001) 'Bosnia: Calls for End to Days of the Consuls?' *Balkan Crisis Report* No. 283 (Sarajevo: Institute for War and Peace Reporting), September 2001.

Kegley, C.W. (1994) *Controversies in IR Theory* (New York: St Martin's Press).

Kelso, P. (2000) 'Land of Milk and Honey,' *The Guardian*, 1 September.

Kemeny, J. and C. Llewellyn-Wilson (1998) 'Both Rationed and Subsidised: Jersey's Command Economy in Housing,' *Journal of Housing Studies*, 13 (2): 259–73.

Keohane, R. (1984) *After Hegemony: Cooperation and Discord in the International Political Economy* (Princeton: Princeton University Press).

Keohane, R. and J. Nye (1977) *Power and Interdependence: World Politics in Transition* (Boston: Little, Brown).

Khrychikov, S. and H. Miall (2002) 'Conflict Prevention in Estonia: The Role of the Electoral System,' *Security Dialogue*, 33 (2): 193–208.

Klein, N. (2000) *No Logo* (London: Flamingo).

Kochen, N. (1991) 'Cleaning up by Cleaning Up,' *Euromoney*, April: 73–7.

Korton, D. (1996) *When Corporations Ruled the World* (London: Earthscan).

Kovac, J. and G. Katana (2001) 'Bosnia Hardliners Regroup: Nationalists across Bosnia have Exploited Western Preoccupation with Afghanistan to Reinforce their Hard-line Positions', *Balkan Crisis Report* No. 292 (Sarajevo: Institute for War and Peace Reporting) October 2001. http://www.iwpr.net/index

KPMG (2000) *Review of Financial Regulation in the Caribbean Overseas Territories and Bermuda*. Cm 4855 (London: Foreign and Commonwealth Office).

Krugman, P. 'In Praise of Cheap Labour,' *Slate Magazine*, 21 March, 1997. http://slate.msn.com/default.aspx?id=1918

Large, J. (1999) 'Kafka Meets Machiavelli: Post War, Post-Transition Eastern Slavonia,' *Development in Practice*, 9 (5).

Large, J., L. Subilia and A. Zwi (1998) *Health as a Bridge for Peace Evaluation Study: Post War Health Sector Transition in Eastern Slavonia (1995–1998)* Report for the UK Dept of International Development and the World Health Organisation (London and Geneva).

Larry, R. (1993) *Rethinking Critical Theory: Emancipation in the Age of Global Social Movements* (London: Sage).

Latham, R. (1999) 'Politics in a Floating World: Toward a Critique of Global Governance,' in M. Hewson and T. Sinclair (eds) *Approaches to Global Governance Theory* (Albany: State University of New York Press), 23–53.

Legard, D. (2001) 'IDC: Linux in Asia's Fastest-Growing Server OS', http://www.Linuxworld.com.au/news.php3?nid=484&tid=2

Le Marchant, C. (1999) 'Financial Regulation and Supervision Offshore: Guernsey, A Case Study,' in M.P. Hampton and J.P. Abbott (eds) *Offshore Finance Centres and Tax Havens: The Rise of Global Capital* (Basingstoke: Macmillan).

Linklater, A. (1998) *The Transformation of Political Community: Ethical Foundations of the Post-Westphalian Era* (Oxford: Polity Press).

Litfin, K. (1994) *Ozone Discourses: Science and politics in Global Environmental Co-Operation* (New York: Columbia University Press).

Little, J. (1975) *Eurodollars: The Money Market Gypsies* (New York: Harper and Row).

Lonergan, S. and D. Brooks (1994) *Watershed: The Role of Fresh Water in the Israeli–Palestinian Conflict* (Ottawa: IDRC).

Los Angeles Times (1977) 'IRS told to Stop Work on Bahamas Tax Cases as US Halts Project Haven.' 24 August.

Lovelock, P. (1997) 'The Asian NII Experience,' http://www.isoc.org/inet97/proceedings/E3/E3_2.htm

Lowndes, V. and D. Wilson (2001) 'Social Capital and Local Governance: Exploring the Institutional Design Variable,' *Political Studies*, 49.

Luard, E. (1990) *The Globalisation of Politics: The Changed Focus of Political Action in the Modern World* (Basingstoke: Macmillan Press).

Lund, M. (1995) 'Underrating Preventive Diplomacy,' *Foreign Affairs*, July/August: 160–3.

Lund, M. (1996) *Preventing Violent Conflicts* (Washington DC: United States Institute of Peace Press).

Lund, M. (2002) 'Operationalizing Lessons from Recent Experience in Conflict Prevention,' in Hampson, F. and D. Malone (eds) *From Reaction to Prevention: Opportunities for the UN System in the New Millennium* (Boulder, CT: Lynne Rienner).

Lund, M. and G. Rasamoelina (eds) (2000) *The Impact of Conflict Prevention Policy: Cases, Measures, Assessments* (Germany: Nomos Verlagsgesellschaft).

Lyons, T. (2003) 'Transforming the Structures of War: Post-Conflict Elections and the Reconstruction of Collapsed States,' in R.J. Rotberg (ed.) *Fixing Failed States: Preventing Mayhem in a Troubled World* (Princeton, NJ: Princeton University Press).

Lyotard, J-F. (1979) *The Postmodern Condition. A Report on Knowledge* (Manchester: Manchester University Press).

MacArthur, J. *NAFTA, (2000) Washington and the Subversion of American Democracy* (New York: Hill and Wang).

MacEwan, A. (1999) *Neoliberalism or Democracy?* (London: Zed Books).

Macintyre, D. (2001) 'As an Old Peace Protestor I Have no Time for Anarchists', *The Independent* Newspaper, 24 July, http://www.independent.co.uk/story.jsp?story=84987

Maloney, W., G. Smith, and G. Stoker (2000) 'Social Capital and Urban Governance: Adding a More Conceptualised "Top-Down" Perspective,' *Political Studies*, 48, September.

Mann, M. (1988) 'The Autonomous Power of the State: Its Origins, Mechanisms and Results,' in *States, War and Capitalism: Studies in Political Sociology* (Oxford: Basil Blackwell), 1–32.

Mann, M. (1993) *The Sources of Social Power, Vol. II: The Rise of Classes and Nation–States, 1760–1914* (Cambridge: Cambridge University Press).

Marshall, D.D. (1996) 'Tax Havens in the Commonwealth Caribbean: A Merchant Capital-Global Finance Connection,' *Global Society*, 10 (3): 255–77.

Martin, J. (2000) 'The Third Sector' *Fortnight* magazine, 389, November: 16.

Maurer, B. (1995) 'Orderly Families for the New Economic Order: Belonging and Citizenship in the British Virgin Islands,' *Identities: Global Studies in Culture and Power*, 2 (1–2): 149–71.

McCarthy, I. (1979) 'Offshore Banking Centers: Benefits and Costs,' *Finance and Development*, 16 (4): 45–8.

McGrew, A.G. (1992) 'Conceptualising Global Politics,' in A.G. McGrew and P.G. Lewis, *Global Politics* (Cambridge: Polity Press), 1–28.

McGrew, A.G. (2002) 'Liberal Internationalism: Between Realism and Cosmopolitanism', in Held, D. and A.G. McGrew (eds) *Governing Globalization: Power, Authority and Global Governance* (Cambridge: Polity Press), 267–89.

McGrew, A.G. and P.G. Lewis (1992) *Global Politics* (Cambridge: Polity Press).

Melucci, A. (1996) *Challenging Codes: Collective Action in an Age of Information* (Cambridge: Cambridge University Press).

Messner, D. (1997) *Network Society* (London: Frank Cass).

Meyer, M. and E. Prugl (eds) (1999) *Gender Politics in Global Governance* (London: Rowman and Littlefield).

Miall, H. (1992) *The Peacemakers: Peaceful Settlement of Disputes Since 1945* (London: Macmillan).

Miall, H. (1997) 'The OSCE Role in Albania: A Success for Conflict Prevention?' *Helsinki Monitor*, 8 (4): 74–85.

Miall, H. (2000) 'Preventing Potential Conflicts: Assessing the Impact of "Light" and "Deep" Conflict Prevention in Central and Eastern Europe and the Balkans,' in Lund, M. and G. Rasamoelina (eds) *The Impact of Conflict Prevention Policy: Cases, Measures, Assessments* (Germany: Nomos Verlagsgesellschaft).

Miall, H., O. Ramsbotham and T. Woodhouse (1999) *Contemporary Conflict Resolution* (Cambridge: Polity Press).

Milliken, T. (1994) 'Current Trade in, Demand for and Stockpiles of Ivory in Range and Consumer States.' Paper presented at *The African Elephant in the Context of CITES*.

Conference held in Kasane, Botswana 19–23 September 1994 (UK Dept. Of Environment)

Mills, C.W. (1959) *The Sociological Imagination* (London: Oxford University Press).

Mitchell, A. and P. Sikka (1999) 'Jersey: Auditors' Liabilities versus Peoples' Rights,' *The Political Quarterly*, 70 (1): 3–15.

Mitchell, A., P. Sikka, J. Christensen, P. Morris and S. Filling (2002) *No Accounting for Tax Havens* (Basildon: Essex: Association for Accountancy and Business Affairs).

Mittelman, J. (2000) *The Globalization Syndrome: Transformation and Resistance* (Princeton: Princeton University Press).

Mobilisation for Global Justice at http://www.a16.org/

Multilateral Working Group on Water Resources (1996) *Declaration on Principles for Cooperation on Water-Related Matters and New and Additional Water Resources* (Oslo, 13 February).

Murphy, C. (1994) *International Organization and Industrial Change: Global Governance Since 1850* (Cambridge: Polity).

Murphy, C. (2000) 'Global Governance: Poorly Done and Poorly Understood,' *International Affairs*, 76 (4): 789–803.

NACLA (1997) 'Contesting Mexico', 30 (4), January–February.

NACLA (1994) 'Mexico Out of Balance', 27 (1), July–August.

NACLA (1991) 'The New Gospel: North American Free Trade,' 24 (6), May.

Nadelman, E.A. (1990) 'Global Prohibition Regimes: The Evolution of Norms in International Society,' *International Organisation*, 44: 479–526.

Nel, E., T. Binns and N. Motteux (2001) 'Community-based Development, Non-Governmental Organizations and Social Capital in Post-Apartheid South Africa,' *Geografiska Annaler B Human Geography*, 83 (1): 3–13.

Neumann, R.P. (2000) 'Primitive Ideas: Protected Area Buffer Zones and the Politics of Land in Africa,' in Vigdis Broch-Due and R.A. Schroeder (eds) *Producing Nature and Poverty in Africa* (Uppsala: Nordiska Afrikainstitutet), 220–42.

Noronha, F. (2001) '*Linux*: Open Source Software for South Asia,' http://www.sasianet.org/Linux.html

Northern Ireland Council for Voluntary Action (NICVA) *The State of the Sector* (Belfast, 1997).

Norton-Taylor, R. (2002) 'Ashdown to Supervise Bosnia Peace Process' in *The Guardian*, 23 February.

O'Brien, R., A. Goetz, J. Scholte and M. Williams (2000) *Contesting Global Governance: Multilateral Economic Institutions and Global Social Movements* (Cambridge: Cambridge University Press).

OECD (1987) *International Tax Avoidance and Evasion – Four Related Studies* (Paris: OECD).

OECD (1998) *Harmful Tax Competition: An Emerging Global Issue* (Paris: OECD).

OECD (2000) *Towards Global Tax Co-operation: Report to the 2000 Ministerial Council Meeting and Recommendations by the Committee on Fiscal Affairs. Progress in Identifying and Eliminating Harmful Tax Practices.* June (Paris: OECD).

OECD (2001) *The OECD's Project on Harmful Tax Practices: the 2001 Progress Report.* November (Paris: OECD).

Ohlsson, L. and J. Lundqvist (2000) 'The Turn of the Screw: Social Adaptation to Water Scarcity,' in J. Lundqvist *et al.* (eds) *New Directions in Water Security* (Rome: Food and Agriculture Organisation).

Oliver, Q. (1998) *Working for 'Yes': The Story of the May 1998 Referendum in Northern Ireland* (Belfast: The 'Yes' Campaign).

Omach, P. (2000) 'The African Crisis Response Initiative: Domestic Politics and Convergence of National Interests,' *African Affairs*, 99: 394.

Oxfam (2000) Tax Havens: Releasing the Hidden Billions for Poverty Eradication. Oxfam Briefing Paper (Oxford: Oxfam GB).

Pagden, A. (1998) 'The Genesis of "Governance" and Enlightenment Conceptions of the Cosmopolitan World Order,' *International Social Science Journal*, 155: 7–16.

Palan, R. (1999) 'Offshore and the Structural Enablement of Sovereignty,' in M.P. Hampton, and J.P. Abbott (eds) *Offshore Finance Centres and Tax Havens: The Rise of Global Capital* (Basingstoke: Macmillan).

Paolini, A., A. Jarvis and C. Reus-Smit (1998) *Between Sovereignty and Global Governance: The United Nations, State and Civil Society* (Basingstoke: Macmillan).

Parapak, J. and B. Sulistyo (1995) 'Perspectives on the Indonesian Tele-communications Market,' in Charles, C. (1995) *The GIIC Asia Regional Meeting and International Conference for National Information Infrastructure for Social and Economic Development in Asia* (Washington, DC: Centre for Strategic and International Studies and the Global Information Infrastructure Commission).

Paris, R. (1997) 'Peacebuilding and the Limits of Liberal Internationalism,' in *International Security*, 22(1).

Park, Y. (1982) 'The Economics of Offshore Finance Centers,' *Columbia Journal of World Business*, Winter, 31–5.

Parker, I. (1979) *The Ivory Trade Vol. 3: Discussions and Recommendations* (Nairobi: Wildlife Services Limited).

Parsons (1951) *The Social System* (Glencoe, IL: Free Press).

Peagam, N. (1989) 'Treasure Islands,' *Euromoney* Supplement, May.

Peck, C. (1998) *Sustainable Peace: The Role of the UN and Regional Organizations in Preventing Conflict* (Lanham: Rowman and Littlefield).

Peel, M. (2002a) 'Financial supervision: Antigua settlement May Pave Way for More Deals with Blacklisted Nations,' *The Financial Times*, 21 February.

Peel, M. (2002b) 'Sunset in the Tax Haven: Offshore Financial Centres are Cleaning Up Their Act. But as the World Economy Evolves Their Existence Seems Ever More Questionable,' *The Financial Times*, 28 February.

People's Global Action web site: http://www.nadir.org/nadir/initiativ/agp/free/actions.htm

Peters, J. (1996) *Pathways to Peace: The Multilateral Arab–Israeli Peace Talks* (London: Royal Institute for International Affairs).

Picciotto, S. (1999) 'Offshore: The State as Legal Fiction,' in M.P. Hampton, and J.P. Abbott (eds) *Offshore Finance Centres and Tax Havens: The Rise of Global Capital* (Basingstoke: Macmillan).

Picciotto, S. and J. Haines (1999) 'Regulating Global Financial Markets,' *Journal of Law and Society*, 26 (3): 351–68.

Pile, S. and M. Keith (eds) (1997) *Geographies of Resistance* (London: Routledge).

Pogge, T.W. (2002) *World Poverty and Human Rights: Cosmopolitan Responsibilities and Reforms* (Cambridge: Polity Press).

Possekel, A. (1996) 'Offshore Financial Centres in the Caribbean: Potential and Pitfalls,' *Caribbean Geography*, 7 (2): 81–97.

Powell, G.C. (1971) *An Economic Survey of Jersey* (Jersey: Bigwoods).

Prenda, A. (2001) 'Bosnian Smuggling Ring Smashed,' *Balkan Crisis Report* No. 278, 7 September 2001; also reports no. 154 and 213. http://www.iwpr.net/index

Pugh, M. (2000a) 'Protectorates and Spoils of Peace: Intermestic Manipulation of Political Economy in Southeast Europe,' (Discussion Paper: Plymouth and London).

Pugh, M. (ed.) (2000b) *Regeneration of War-Torn Societies* (London: Macmillan Press).

Putnam, R.D. (2000) *Bowling Alone: The Collapse and Revival of American Community* (New York: Simon & Schuster).

Princen, T. and M. Finger (eds) (1994) *Environmental NGOs in World Politics: Linking the Local and the Global* (London: Routledge).

Putnam, R.D. (1993) *Making Democracy Work: Civic Traditions in Modern Italy* (Princeton: Princeton University Press).

Raknerud, A. and H. Hegre (1997) 'The Hazard of War: Reassessing the Evidence of the Democratic Peace,' *Journal of Peace Research*, 34 (4): 385–404.

Ramsbotham, O. and T. Woodhouse (1996) *Humanitarian Intervention in Contemporary Conflict* (Cambridge: Polity).

Ranciére, J. (1999) *Disagreement* (Minneapolis: Minnesota University Press).

Ray, L. (1993) *Rethinking Critical Theory: Emancipation in the Age of Global Social Movements* (London: Sage).

Reclaim the streets at http://www.reclaimthestreets.net/

Reinicke, W. (1989) *Global Public Policy: Governing without Government?* (Washington: Brookings Institution).

Reno, W. (1998) *Warlord Politics and African States* (Boulder CO: Lynne Rienner).

Reynal-Querol, Marta (2001) 'Ethricity, Political Systems and Civil Wars,' Paper presented for the Conference on 'Identifying Wars: Systemic Conflict Research and its Utility in Conflict Resolution and Prevention', Department of Peace and Conflict Research, Uppsala University, 8–9 June.

Roberts, S. (1994) 'Fictitious Capital, Fictitious Spaces: The Geography of Offshore Financial Flows,' in Corbridge, S., R. Martin and N. Thrift (eds) *Money, Power and Space* (Oxford: Blackwell).

Roberts, S. (1995) 'Small Place, Big Money: The Cayman Islands and the International Financial System,' *Economic Geography*, 71 (3): 237–56.

Roberts, S. (1999) 'Confidence Men: Offshore Finance and Citizenship,' in M.P. Hampton and J.P. Abbott (eds) *Offshore Finance Centres and Tax Havens: The Rise of Global Capital* (Basingstoke: Macmillan).

Robson, T. (2000) *The State and Community Action* (London: Pluto Press).

Ronson, J. (2001) *Them: Adventures with Extremists* (London: Picador Press).

Rose, N. (1999) *Powers of Freedom* (Cambridge: Cambridge University Press).

Rosenau, J.(1990) *Turbulence in World Politics: A Theory of Change and Continuity* (New York: Harvester Wheatsheaf).

Rosenau, J. (1992) 'Governance, Order, and Change in World Politics,' in Rosenau, J. and E. Czempiel (eds) *Governance without Government: Order and Change in World Politics* (Cambridge: Cambridge University Press), 1–29.

Rosenau, J. (1995) 'Governance in the Twenty First Century,' *Global Governance*, 1 (1): 13–43.

Rosenau, J. (1999) 'Toward an Ontology for Global Governance,' in M. Hewson and T. Sinclair (eds) *Approaches to Global Governance Theory* (Albany: State University of New York Press), 287–301.

Rosenau, J. and E. Czempiel (eds) (1992) *Governance without Government: Order and Change in World Politics* (Cambridge: Cambridge University Press).

Rosenberg, J. (2000) *The Follies of Globalization Theory: Polemical Essays* (London: Verso).

Rouyer, A. (2000) *Turning Water into Politics: The Water Issue in the Palestinian–Israeli Conflict* (London: Macmillan).

Roy, S. (1995) *The Gaza Strip: The Political Economy of De-Development* (Washington DC: Institute for Palestine Studies).

Roy, S. (1999) 'De-development Revisited: Palestinian Economy and Society Since Oslo,' *Journal of Palestine Studies*, 28 (3): 64–82.

Royle, S.A. (2001) *A Geography of Islands: Small Island Insularity* (London: Routledge).

Rubinstein, D. (1999) 'Protection Racket, PA-style,' *Ha'aretz* (3 November).

Rupert, M. (1995) *Producing Hegemony: The Politics of Mass Production and American Global Power* (Cambridge: Cambridge University Press).

Rupesinghe, K. (1998) *Civil Wars, Civil Peace* (London: Pluto).

Russett, B. (1993) *Grasping the Democratic Peace: Principles for a Post-Cold War World* (Princeton, NJ: Princeton University Press).

Ryan, S. (2000) *The United Nations and International Politics* (London: Macmillan).

Samara, A. (2000) 'Globalization, the Palestinian Economy and the Peace Process,' *Journal of Palestine Studies*, 29 (2): 20–34.

Sayigh, Y. (1986) 'The Palestinian Economy Under Occupation: Dependency and Pauperisation,' *Journal of Palestine Studies*, 15 (4): 46–67.

Sayigh, Y. (1997) 'Armed Struggle and State Formation,' *Journal of Palestine Studies*, 26 (4): 17–32.

Schiff, Z. and E. Ya'ari (1989) *Intifada: The Palestinian Uprising – Israel's Third Front* (New York: Simon and Schuster).

Schöpflin, G. (1994) *Politics in Eastern Europe* (London: Blackwell).

Scott, A. (ed.) (1997) *The Limits of Globalization: Cases and Arguments* (London: Routledge).

Scott, J.C. (1985) *Weapons of the Weak: Everyday Forms of Peasant Resistance* (New Haven, CT: Yale University Press).

Scott, J.C. (1990) *Domination and the Arts of Resistance: Hidden Transcripts* (New Haven, CT: Yale University Press).

Selby, J. (2003a) 'Dressing up Domination as "Co-operation": the Case of Israeli–Palestinian Water Relations,' *Review of International Studies*, 29 (1): 121–38.

Selby, J. (2003b) *Water, Power and Politics in the Middle East* (London: IB Tauris).

Sesit, M. (1996a) 'Offshore Hazard. Isle of Jersey Proves Less Than a Haven to Currency Investors,' *Wall Street Journal*, 17 September.

Sesit, M. (1996b) 'UBS Unit in Jersey Charged with Fraud,' *Wall Street Journal*, 29 October.

Shihata, I. (1991) *The World Bank in a Changing World: Selected Essays* (Dordrecht: Martinus Nijhoff).

Sikka, P. (1996) 'Jersey: A Pawn in a Regulatory Game,' *Accountancy Age*, September.

Simai, M. (1994) *The Future of Global Governance: Managing Risk and Change in the International System* (Washington DC: US Institute of Peace).

Simon, R. (1982) *Gramsci's Political Thought* (London: Lawrence and Wishart).

Singleton, R. (2000) 'Knowledge and Technology: The Bias of Wealth and Power,' in Balaam, D. and M. Veseth (eds) *Introduction to International Political Economy* (London: Prentice Hall), 208–27.

Sivaramakrishnan, K. (1999) *Modern Forests: Statemaking and Environmental Change in Colonial Eastern India* (Oxford: Oxford University Press).

Slater, C.A. 'Anti WTO Community Should Propose Trade Solutions,' *The Seattle Press*, 28 June 2000. http://www.seattlepress.com/print-8580.html

Smart, B. (1999) *Resisting McDonalidization* (London: Sage).

Smith, G. (2001) 'Guerillas in their Midst', *Business Week*, 13 March, http://www.businessweek.com/bwdaily/dnflash/mar2001/nf20010313_125.htm

Smith, R. (2000) 'No Fit State: Questionable Sovereignty, Sealand and the Dominion of Melchizedek.' Read at Islands of the World VI Conference, Skye, Scotland, 16–20 October.

Soederberg, S. (2001) 'The Emperor's New Suit: The International Financial Architecture as a Reinvention of the Washington Consensus,' *Global Governance*, October–December, 7 (4): 453–67.

Southern African Centre for Ivory Marketing (SACIM) (1994) 'The SACIM Treaty: Its Aims and Objectives.' A Position Paper Presented by Botswana, Malawi, Namibia and Zimbabwe. Paper presented at *The African Elephant in the Context of CITES* Conference held in Kasane, Botswana 19–23 September (UK Dept. Of Environment) Part B.

Starr, A. (2000) *Naming the Enemy: Anti-Corporate Movements Confront Globalisation* (London: Zed Books).

Steans, J. (2002) 'Global Governance: A Feminist Perspective,' in D. Held and A. McGrew (eds) *Governing Globalization: Power, Authority and Global Governance* (Cambridge: Polity Press), 87–108.

Steans, J. and L. Pettiford (2001) *International Relations: Perspectives and Themes* (London: Longman).

Stedman, S.J. (1995) 'Alchemy for a New World Order: Overselling "Preventive Diplomacy",' *Foreign Affairs* 74 (May/June): 14–20.

Strange, S. (1971) *Sterling and British Policy* (Oxford: Oxford University Press).

Struthers, J. (1990) 'Nigerian Oil and Exchange Rates: Indicators of 'Dutch disease,' *Development and Change*, 21: 309–41.

Sutton, M. (1994) *Bear in Mind These Dead: An Index of Deaths from the Conflict in Northern Ireland 1969–1993* (Belfast: Blackstaff Press).

Swartze, D. (2001) 'The Intellectual Property Battle,' *Bangkok Post*, 29 October, http://www.bangkokpost.net/breakfast/a291200.html

Sweeney, J. (2000) 'Stench of Sleaze Beneath Monaco's Perfumed Glitz,' *The Observer*, 25 June.

Taylor, R. (2001) 'Northern Ireland: Consociation or Social Transformation?' in J. McGarry (ed.) (2001) *Northern Ireland and the Divided World* (Oxford: Oxford University Press).

Taylor, R.D. and D.H.M. Cumming (1993) *Elephant Management in Southern Africa*, WWF MAPS Project paper no. 40 (Harare: WWF).

The Economist (1999) Editorial, 'Clueless in Seattle,' 4 December.

The Economist (2000) 'Cheesed off,' review of *No Logo*, 29 January.

The Economist (1999) Editorial: 'The non governmental order,' 1 February.

The Economist (2000) 'The electric revolution,' 3 August.

The Economist (2000) 'Survey: globalisation and tax.' 29 January, 18pp.

The Economist (2001) 'Hitting terrorists' cash: the financial front line' 27 October.

The Financial Times (2000) 'Isle of Man to reform offshore sector,' 25 July.

The Guardian (2001) Editorial, 'Looking out for liberty', 28 July, http://www.guardian.co.uk/Archive/Article/0,4273,4229829,00.html

The Independent (2001) Editorial, 'Mr Berlusconi's response is entirely inadequate', 28 July. http://www.independent.co.uk/story.jsp?story=85730

The South Centre at http://www.southcentre.org/; Corporate Watch at http://www.corporatewatch.org/.

Thomas, C. (2001) *Global governance, development and human security* (London: Pluto).

Thomas, C. 'Global Governance, Development and Human Security: Exploring the Links', *Third World Quarterly*, 22, (2): 168–73.

Thornton, A. and D. Currey (1991) *To Save an Elephant* (London: Bantam Books).

Tickell, C. (1998) 'Security, Environment and Global Governance' (*Lancaster Papers* 1: Lancaster University, Department of Politics & International Relations).

Tilly, C. (1990) *Coercion, Capital and European States, AD 990–1990.* (Oxford: Blackwell).

Trottier, J. (1999) *Hydropolitics in the West Bank and Gaza Strip* (Jersualem: PASSIA).

Trottier, J. (2000) 'Water and the Challenge of Palestinian Institution Building,' *Journal of Palestine Studies*, 29 (2): 35–50.

Twyman, C. (1998) 'Rethinking Community Resource Management: Managing Resources or Managing People in Western Botswana?' *Third World Quarterly*, 19: 745–70.

Ungoed-Thomas, J. and Jay, M. (2000) 'Channel Islands Face Tax Haven Threat,' *The Sunday Times*, 21 May.

UNHCR (1998) *Information Notes, No1/98* (Office of the Special Envoy and Former Yugoslav Liaison Office).

UN Information Service (2000) '31 International Financial Centers Support UN in Global Anti-Money Laundering Initiative.' Issued 25 October. UNIS/NAR/702 (Vienna: United Nations Information Service).

UNTAES (1996) *Fact sheets* (United Nations Department of Public Information: DPI/1823/F6-96.13041) June.

USAID (1999) 'US Assistance to the West Bank and Gaza,' http://www.info.usaid.gove/regions/ane/newpages/one_pagers/wbg.htm

Usher, G. (1996) 'The Politics of Internal Security: The PA's New Intelligence Services,' *Journal of Palestine Studies*, 25 (2): 21–34.

Van der Pijl, K. (1984) *The Making of an Atlantic Ruling Class* (London: Verso).

Van der Pijl, K. (1998) *Transnational Classes and International Relations* (London: Routledge).

Vatter, M. (2000) *Between Form and Event: Machiavelli's Theory of Political Freedom.* (Dodrecht: Kluwer Academic Publishers).

Vayrynen, R. (1999) 'Norms, Compliance, and Enforcement in Global Governance,' in Vayrynen, R. (ed.) *Globalization and Global Governance* (Oxford: Rowman and Littlefield), 25–46.

Vengross, R. and M. Magala (2001) 'Democratic Reform, Transformation and Consolidation: Evidence from Senegal's 2000 Presidential Election,' *Journal of Modern African Studies*, 39: 1.

Verhofstad, G. (2001) 'The Paradox of Anti-Globalisation', *The Guardian* 28 September, http://www.guardian.co.uk/globalisation/story/0,7369,559887,00.html

Vigdis B.D. and R.A. Schroeder (eds) (2000) *Producing Nature and poverty in Africa* (Uppsala: Nordiska Afrikainstitutet).

Wainwright, J., S. Prudham and J. Glassman (2000) 'The Battle in Seattle,' *Environment and Planning D: Society and Space*, 18 (1): 5–15.

Wallensteen, P. (2002) *Understanding Conflict Resolution* (London: Sage).

Wallensteen, P. and M. Sollenberg (2001) 'Armed Conflict 1989–2000,' *Journal of Peace Research*, 38 (5): 629–44.

Wallerstein, I. (1974) *The Modern World System, Vol. 1* (New York: Academic Press).

Wallerstein, I. (1995) *After Liberalism* (New York: New Press).

Wallerstein, I. (2001) 'Uncertainty and Creativity,' in *The End of the World as We Know It* (Minnesota: University of Minnesota Press).

Wallerstein, I. (2001) *The End of the World as We Know It* (Minnesota: University of Minnesota Press).

Walsh, C. (2002) 'Crackdown on Havens. Gangsters' Paradise Lost: Americans are Gunning for the Offshore Havens Favored by Fraudsters and Terrorists. But the UK Doesn't Seem so Keen,' *The Observer*, 24 February.

Waltz, K. (1999) 'Globalization and Governance', *PS: Political Science and Politics*, 32.

Ward, M.D. and K.S. Gleditsch (1998) 'Democratizing for Peace,' *American Political Science Review*, 92, March: 51–62.

Waters, M. (1995) *Globalization* (London: Routledge).

Webster, T. (2000) 'Insulted Rainier Turns on France: Monaco Threatens to Declare Independence from Neighbour,' *The Guardian*, 1 November.

Weiss, T. and L. Gordenker (eds) (1996) *NGOs, the UN and Global Governance* (Boulder: Lynne Rienner).

Welch, I. and G. Chesters (2001) 'Re-Framing Social Movements', *Cardiff University School of Social Sciences working Papers* No. 19, November. http://www.cardiff.ac.uk/socsi/publications/workingpapers/wrkgpaper19.pdf

Weller, M. (2000) *Missed Opportunities of Conflict Prevention in Kosovo: A Transatlantic Evaluation* (Ebenhausen: Conflict Prevention Network/SWP).

Wight, M. (1977) *Systems of States* (Leicester: Leicester University Press).

Wijnstekers, W. (1994) 'Basic Requirements for Trade in Parts and Derivatives of CITES Listed Species.' Paper presented at *The African Elephant in the Context of CITES*. Conference held in Kasane, Botswana 19–23 September 1994 (UK Dept. Of Environment) Part B.

Wildlife Society of Zimbabwe (1993) *Zimbabwe's Great Elephant Debate*. A Report on Discussions held during the AGM of the Wildlife Society of Zimbabwe at Hwange National Park on August 13 (Harare: Wildlife Society).

Wilkin, P. (2001) *The Political Economy of Global Communication* (London: Pluto Press).

Wilkinson, R. and S. Hughes (eds) (2002) *Global Governance: Critical Perspectives* (London: Routledge).

Wilson, R. (1998) 'Placing Northern Ireland,' in *New Order? International Models of Peace and Reconciliation* (Belfast: Democratic Dialogue).

Wolf, M. (2001) 'Responding to the Anti-Globalisation Protestors,' *Financial Times*, 4 September.

Woods, N. (1999) 'Good Governance in International Organizations,' *Global Governance*, 5 (1): 39–61.

Woodward, S. (1995) *Balkan Tragedy* (Washington, DC: The Brookings Institute).

World Bank (1989) *Sub-Saharan Africa: From Crisis to Sustainable Growth* (Washington DC: World Bank).

World Bank (1992) *Governance and Development* (Washington DC: World Bank).
World Bank (1993) *Developing the Occupied Territories: An Investment in Peace, 6 vols* (Washington DC: World Bank).
World Bank (1994) *Emergency Assistance Program for the Occupied Territories* (Washington DC: World Bank).
World Bank (1994) *Governance: The World Bank's Experience* (Washington DC: World Bank).
World Commission on Environment and Development (1987) *Our Common Future* (Oxford: Oxford University Press).
World Water Council (2000) 'Report of the World Commission on Water for the 21st Century,' presented at the 2nd World Water Forum (The Hague, March 2000), reprinted in *Water International*, 25 (2): 284–302.
Wright, R. (1999) 'We're all one-worlders now,' *Slate Magazine*, 23 December, http://slate.msn.com/?id=2021
Xi, X. (1995) 'Speeding Up Information Infrastructure Development and Promoting Information Cooperation in Asia,' in Charles, C. (1995) *The GIIC Asia Regional Meeting and International Conference for National Information Infrastructure for Social and Economic Development in Asia* (Washington DC: Centre for Strategic and International Studies and the Global Information Infrastructure Commission).
Young, G. (1994) *Global Water Resource Issues* (Cambridge: Cambridge University Press).
Young, O. (ed.) (1997) *Global Governance: Drawing Insights from the Environmental Experience* (Cambridge, MA: MIT Press).
Zysman, J. and M. Borrus (1997) 'Globalization with Borders: The Rise of Wintelism as the Future of Industrial Competition,' *Industry and Innovation*, 4 (2): 141–66.

Index